Before the Flood

Before the Flood

Will Stickle

CONTENTS

Preface

There are whispers in the past—echoes of a world that existed before history, before the flood, before the stories we accept as truth were written in stone. Across civilizations, from ancient Sumer to Egypt, from the lost lands of Atlantis to the sacred scriptures of prophets, remnants of this forgotten age remain.

The texts in this collection—The Book of Enoch, The Epic of Gilgamesh, and The Emerald Tablets of Thoth—are among the most controversial and enigmatic writings known to mankind. Each one offers a different glimpse into the pre-flood world: the fall of divine beings, the quest for immortality, and the preservation of secret wisdom that was nearly lost to time.

The Forbidden Legacy of the Ancients

For centuries, scholars, theologians, and seekers of truth have debated the meaning and authenticity of these writings. Were they myths? Warnings? Encoded knowledge meant to survive the destruction of an advanced civilization? If so, who was meant to find them?

In The Book of Enoch, we see a cosmic battle between the heavens and the Earth—angels who defy their Creator, intermingling with mankind and giving rise to the Nephilim, a race of giants and beings of unnatural knowledge. Their actions provoke divine wrath, leading to the great flood meant to cleanse the corruption from the Earth.

The Epic of Gilgamesh brings us one of the oldest known written accounts of this deluge. This ancient Sumerian poem tells the story of a king who seeks the secret to eternal life and finds a man who survived the flood—a tale that predates and parallels the biblical account of Noah. If different cultures have recorded the same event, was it truly just a myth?

Then we come to The Emerald Tablets of Thoth. Unlike the first two, this text does not focus on a flood but instead on the destruction of a great civilization—one whose knowledge was hidden and safeguarded by initiates for future generations. The legendary Thoth, known also as Hermes Trismegistus, speaks of timeless wisdom, cosmic cycles, and the rise and fall of powerful empires. Could this be a veiled reference to Atlantis? Was the knowledge of the ancients lost in fire and water, only to be rediscovered by those who dared to seek it?

Truth or Myth? The Choice is Yours

Throughout history, religious institutions, ruling elites, and modern scholars have often dismissed these writings as mere legend, yet their themes and symbols continue to resonate. The flood, the fall of divine beings, the pursuit of immortality, and the preservation of secret knowledge—these are not isolated stories but recurring motifs across ancient texts worldwide.

Perhaps these texts are remnants of something deeper, something humanity was never meant to remember. Perhaps they are keys to understanding our true origins.

The answer, as always, lies within.

Will Stickle

THE EPIC OF GILGAMESH

THE EPIC OF GILGAMESH

The world's oldest epic. A hero's quest for immortality. A flood that reshaped history.

The Epic of Gilgamesh is one of the earliest and most influential literary works, originating from ancient Mesopotamia over 4,000 years ago. This epic poem follows Gilgamesh, the mighty king of Uruk, as he embarks on a perilous journey to uncover the secret of eternal life. Along the way, he confronts gods, monsters, and the limits of human destiny.

This legendary text includes:

The Friendship of Gilgamesh and Enkidu – A wild man tamed by civilization, whose bond with Gilgamesh changes the course of history. The Slaying of Humbaba and the Bull of Heaven – Acts of heroism that bring both glory and divine wrath.

The Search for Immortality – A journey to the ends of the earth in pursuit of everlasting life.

The Flood Narrative – The story of Utnapishtim, a man who survived a great flood and shares a tale that predates the biblical account of Noah.

The Tragic Realization – Gilgamesh's discovery that mortality is inescapable, yet his legacy will endure.

Rediscovered in the 19th century on Sumerian and Akkadian clay tablets, The Epic of Gilgamesh remains one of the most profound reflections on the human experience, loss, and the pursuit of meaning. Does this ancient tale contain hidden truths about the great flood and the origins of civilization?

This edition preserves the full text, allowing you to uncover the mysteries of the oldest recorded story in human history.

PROLOGUE

GILGAMESH KING IN URUK
I WILL proclaim to the world the deeds of Gilgamesh. This was the man to whom all things were known; this was the king who knew the countries of the world. He was wise, he saw mysteries and knew secret things, he brought us a tale of the days before the flood. He went on a long journey, was weary, worn-out with labour, returning he rested, he engraved on a stone the whole story.

When the gods created Gilgamesh they gave him a perfect body. Shamash the glorious sun endowed him with beauty, Adad the god of the storm endowed him with courage, the great gods made his beauty perfect, surpassing all others, terrifying like a great wild bull. Two thirds they made him god and one third man.

In Uruk he built walls, a great rampart, and the temple of blessed Eanna for the god of the firmament Anu, and for Ishtar the goddess of love. Look at it still today: the outer wall where the cornice runs, it shines with the brilliance of copper; and the inner wall, it has no equal. Touch the threshold, it is ancient. Approach Eanna the dwelling of Ishtar, our lady of love and war, the like of which no latter-day king, no man alive can equal. Climb upon the wall of Uruk; walk along it, I say; regard the foundation terrace and examine the masonry; is it not burnt brick and good? The seven sages laid the foundations.

1 - THE COMING OF ENKIDU

GILGAMESH went abroad in the world, but he met with none who could withstand his arms till he came to Uruk. But the men of Uruk muttered in their houses, 'Gilgamesh sounds the tocsin for his amusement, his arrogance has no bounds by day or night. No son is left with his father, for Gilgamesh takes them all, even the children; yet the king should be a shepherd to his people. His lust leaves no virgin to her lover, neither the warrior's daughter nor the wife of the noble; yet this is the shepherd of the city, wise, comely, and resolute.'

The gods heard their lament, the gods of heaven cried to the Lord of Uruk, to Anu the god of Uruk: 'A goddess made him, strong as a savage bull, none can withstand his arms. No son is left with his father, for Gilgamesh takes them all; and is this the king, the shepherd of his people? His lust leaves no virgin to her lover, neither the warrior's daughter nor the wife of the noble. When Anu had heard their lamentation the gods cried to Aruru, the goddess of creation, 'You made him, O Aruru; now create his equal; let it be as like him as his own reflection, his second self; stormy heart for stormy heart. Let them contend together and leave Uruk in quiet.'

So the goddess conceived an image in her mind, and it was of the stuff of Anu of the firmament. She dipped her hands in water and pinched off clay, she let it

fall in the wilderness, and noble Enkidu was created. There was virtue in him of the god of war, of Ninurta himself. His body was rough, he had long hair like a woman's; it waved like the hair of Nisaba, the goddess of corn. His body was covered with matted hair like Samugan's, the god of cattle. He was innocent of mankind; he knew nothing of the cultivated land.

Enkidu ate grass in the hills with the gazelle and lurked with wild beasts at the water-holes; he had joy of the water with the herds of wild game. But there was a trapper who met him one day face to face at the drinking-hole, for the wild game had entered his territory. On three days he met him face to face, and the trapper was frozen with fear. He went back to his house with the game that he had caught, and he was dumb, benumbed with terror. His face was altered like that of one who has made a long journey. With awe in his heart he spoke to his father: 'Father, there is a man, unlike any other, who comes down from the hills. He is the strongest in the world, he is like an immortal from heaven. He ranges over the hills with wild beasts and eats grass; the ranges through your land and comes down to the wells. I am afraid and dare not go near him. He fills in the pits which I dig and tears up my traps set for the game; he helps the beasts to escape and now they slip through my fingers.'

His father opened his mouth and said to the trapper, 'My son, in Uruk lives Gilgamesh; no one has ever prevailed against him, he is strong as a star from heaven. Go to Uruk, find Gilgamesh, extol the strength of this wild man. Ask him to give you a harlot, a wanton from the temple of love; return with her, and let her woman's power overpower this man. When next he comes down to drink at the wells she will be there, stripped naked; and when he sees her beckoning he will embrace her, and then the wild beasts will reject him.'

So the trapper set out on his journey to Uruk and addressed himself to Gilgamesh saying, 'A man unlike any other is roaming now in the pastures; he is as strong as a star from heaven and I am afraid to approach him. He helps the wild game to escape; he fills in my pits and pulls up my traps.' Gilgamesh said, 'Trapper, go back, take with you a harlot, a child of pleasure. At the drinking hole she will strip, and when, he sees her beckoning he will embrace her and the game of the wilderness will surely reject him.'

Now the trapper returned, taking the harlot with him. After a three days' journey they came to the drinking hole, and there they sat down; the harlot and the trapper sat facing one another and waited for the game to come. For the first day and for the second day the two sat waiting, but on the third day the herds came; they came down to drink and Enkidu was with them. The small wild creatures of the plains were glad of the water, and Enkidu with them, who ate grass with the gazelle and was born in the hills; and she saw him, the savage man, come from far-off in the hills. The trapper spoke to her: 'There he is. Now, woman, make your breasts bare, have no shame, do not delay but welcome his love. Let him see you naked, let him possess your body. When he comes near uncover yourself and lie with him; teach him, the savage man, your woman's art, for when he murmurs love to you the wild beasts that shared his life in the hills will reject him.'

She was not ashamed to take him, she made herself naked and welcomed his eagerness; as he lay on her murmuring love she taught him the woman's art. For six days and seven nights they lay together, for Enkidu had forgotten his home in the hills; but when he was satisfied he went back to the wild beasts. Then, when the gazelle saw him, they bolted away; when the wild creatures saw him they fled. Enkidu would have followed, but his body was bound as though with a cord, his knees gave way when he started to run, his swiftness was gone. And now the wild creatures had all fled away; Enkidu was grown weak, for wisdom was in him, and the thoughts of a man were in his heart. So he returned and sat down at the woman's feet, and listened intently to what she said. 'You are wise, Enkidu, and now you have become like a god. Why do you want to run wild with the beasts in the hills? Come with me. I will take you to strong-walled Uruk, to the blessed temple of Ishtar and of Anu, of love and of heaven there Gilgamesh lives, who is very strong, and like a wild bull he lords it over men.'

When she had spoken Enkidu was pleased; he longed for a comrade, for one who would understand his heart. 'Come, woman, and take me to that holy temple, to the house of Anu and of Ishtar, and to the place where Gilgamesh lords it over the people. I will challenge him boldly, I will cry out aloud in Uruk, "I am the strongest here, I have come to change the old order, I am he who was born in the hills, I am he who is strongest of all."

She said, 'Let us go, and let him see your face. I know very well where Gilgamesh is in great Uruk. O Enkidu, there all the people are dressed in their gorgeous robes, every day is holiday, the young men and the girls are wonderful to see. How sweet they smell! All the great ones are roused from their beds. O Enkidu, you who love life, I will show you Gilgamesh, a man of many moods; you shall look at him well in his radiant manhood. His body is perfect in strength and maturity; he never rests by night or day. He is stronger than you, so leave your boasting. Shamash the glorious sun has given favours to Gilgamesh, and Anu of the heavens, and Enlil, and Ea the wise has given him deep understanding. I tell you, even before you have left the wilderness, Gilgamesh will know in his dreams that you are coming.'

Now Gilgamesh got up to tell his dream to his mother Ninsun, one of the wise gods. 'Mother, last night I had a dream. I was full of joy, the young heroes were round me and I walked through the night under the stars of the firmament, and one, a meteor of the stuff of Anu, fell down from heaven. I tried to lift it but it proved too heavy. All the people of Uruk came round to see it, the common people jostled and the nobles thronged to kiss its feet; and to me its attraction was like the love of woman. They helped me, I braced my forehead and I raised it with thongs and brought it to you, and you yourself pronounced it my brother.'

Then Ninsun, who is well-beloved and wise, said to Gilgamesh, 'This star of heaven which descended like a meteor from the sky, which you tried to lift, but found too heavy, when you tried to move it, it would not budge, and so you brought it to my feet; I made it for you, a goad and spur, and you were drawn as though to a woman. This is the strong comrade, the one who brings help to his friend in his need. He is the strongest of wild creatures, the stuff of Anu; born in the grasslands and the wild hills reared him; when you see him you will be glad; you will love him as a woman and he will never forsake you. This is the meaning of the dream.'

Gilgamesh said, 'Mother, I dreamed a second dream. In the streets of strong-walled Uruk there lay an axe; the shape of it was strange and the people thronged round. I saw it and was glad. I bent down, deeply drawn towards it; I loved it like a woman and wore it at my side.' Ninsun answered, 'That axe, which you saw, which drew you so powerfully like love of a woman, that is the comrade whom I give you, and he will come in his strength like one of the hosts of heaven. He is the brave companion who rescues his friend in necessity.' Gilgamesh

said to his mother, 'A friend, a counsellor has come to me from Enlil, and now I shall befriend and counsel him.' So Gilgamesh told his dreams, and the harlot retold them to Enkidu.

And now she said to Enkidu, 'When I look at you, you have become like a god. Why do you yearn to run wild again with the beasts in the hills? Get up from the ground, the bed of a shepherd.' He listened to her words with care. It was good advice that she gave. She divided her clothing in two and with the one half she clothed him and with the other herself, and holding his hand she led him like a child to the sheepfolds, into the shepherds' tents. There all the shepherds crowded round to see him, they put down bread in front of him, but Enkidu could only suck the milk of wild animals. He fumbled and gaped, at a loss what to do or how he should eat the bread and drink the strong wine. Then the woman said, 'Enkidu, eat bread, it is the staff of life; drink the wine, it is the custom of the land.' So he ate till he was full and drank strong wine, seven goblets. He became merry, his heart exulted and his face shone. He rubbed down the matted hair of his body and anointed himself with oil. Enkidu had become a man; but when he had put on man's clothing he appeared like a bridegroom. He took arms to hunt the lion so that the shepherds could rest at night. He caught wolves and lions and the herdsmen lay down in peace; for Enkidu was their watchman, that strong man who had no rival.

He was merry living with the shepherds, till one day lifting his eyes he saw a man approaching. He said to the harlot, 'Woman, fetch that man here. Why has he come? I wish to know his name.' She went and called the man saying, 'Sir, where are you going on this weary journey?' The man answered, saying to Enkidu, 'Gilgamesh has gone into the marriage-house and shut out the people. He does strange things in Uruk, the city of great streets. At the roll of the drum work begins for the men, and work for the women. Gilgamesh the king is about to celebrate marriage with the Queen of Love, and he still demands to be first with the bride, the king to be first and the husband to follow, for that was ordained by the gods from his birth, from the time the umbilical cord was cut. But now the drums roll for the choice of the bride and the city groans.' At these words Enkidu turned white in the face. 'I will go to the place where Gilgamesh lords it over the people, I will challenge him boldly, and I will cry aloud in Uruk, "I have come to change the old order, for I am the strongest here."

Now Enkidu strode in front and the woman followed behind. He entered Uruk, that great market, and all the folk thronged round him where he stood in the street in strong-walled Uruk. The people jostled; speaking of him they said, 'He is the spit of Gilgamesh.' 'He is shorter.' 'He is bigger of bone.' 'This is the one who was reared on the milk of wild beasts. His is the greatest strength.' The men rejoiced: 'Now Gilgamesh has met his match. This great- one, this hero whose beauty is like a god, he is a match even for Gilgamesh.'

In Uruk the bridal bed was made, fit for the goddess of love. The bride waited for the bridegroom, but in the night Gilgamesh got up and came to the house. Then Enkidu stepped out, he stood in the street and blocked the way. Mighty Gilgamesh came on and Enkidu met him at the gate. He put out his foot and prevented Gilgamesh from entering the house, so they grappled, holding each other like bulls. They broke the doorposts and the walls shook, they snorted like bulls locked together. They shattered the doorposts and the walls shook. Gilgamesh bent his knee with his foot planted on the ground and with a turn Enkidu was thrown. Then immediately his fury died. When Enkidu was thrown he said to Gilgamesh,

'There is not another like you in the world. Ninsun, who is as strong as a wild ox in the byre, she was the mother who bore you, and now you are raised above all men, and Enlil has given you the kingship, for your strength surpasses the strength of men.' So Enkidu and Gilgamesh embraced and their friendship was sealed.

2 THE FOREST JOURNEY

ENLIL of the mountain, the father of the gods, had decreed the destiny of Gilgamesh. So Gilgamesh dreamed and Enkidu said, 'The meaning of the dream is this. The father of the gods has given you kingship, such is your destiny, everlasting life is not your destiny. Because of this do not be sad at heart, do not be grieved or oppressed. He has given you power to bind and to loose, to be the darkness and the light of mankind. He has given you unexampled supremacy over the people, victory in battle from which no fugitive returns, in forays and assaults from which there is no going back. But do not abuse this power, deal justly with your servants in the palace, deal justly before Shamash.'

The eyes of Enkidu were full of tears and his heart was sick. He sighed bitterly and Gilgamesh met his eye and said,' My friend, why do you sigh so bitterly? But Enkidu opened his mouth and said, 'I am weak, my arms have lost their strength, the cry of sorrow sticks in my throat, I am oppressed by idleness.' It was then that the lord Gilgamesh turned his thoughts to the Country of the Living; on the Land of Cedars the lord Gilgamesh reflected. He said to his servant Enkidu, 'I have not established my name stamped on bricks as my destiny decreed; therefore I will go to the country where the cedar is felled. I will set up my name in the place where the names of famous men are written, and where no man's name is written yet I will rise a monument to the gods. Because of the evil that is in the land, we will go to the

forest and destroy the evil; for in the forest lives Humbaba whose name is "Hugeness", a ferocious giant. But Enkidu sighed bitterly and said,

'When I went with the wild beasts ranging through the wilderness I discovered the forest; its length is ten thousand leagues in every direction. Enlil has appointed Humbaba to guard it and armed him in sevenfold terrors, terrible to all flesh is Humbaba. When he roars it is like the torrent of the storm, his breath is like fire, and his jaws are death itself. He guards the cedars so well that when the wild heifer stirs in the forest, though she is sixty leagues distant, he hears her. What man would willingly walk into that country and explore its depths? I tell you, weakness overpowers whoever goes near it; it is not an equal struggle when one fights with Humbaba; he is a great warrior, a battering-ram. Gilgamesh, the watchman of the forest never sleeps.

Gilgamesh replied: 'Where is the man who can clamber to heaven? Only the gods live for ever with glorious Shamash, but as for us men, our days are numbered, our occupations are a breath of wind. How is this, already you are afraid! I will go first although I am your lord, and you may safely call out, "Forward, there is nothing to fear!" Then if I fall I leave behind me a name that endures; men will say of me, "Gilgamesh has fallen in fight with ferocious Humbaba." Long after the child has been bony in my house, they will say it, and remember.' Enkidu spoke again to Gilgamesh, 'O my lord, if you will enter that country, go first to the hero Shamash, tell the Sun God, for the land is his. The country where the cedar is cut belongs to Shamash.'

Gilgamesh took up a kid, white without spot, and a brown one with it; he held them against his breast, and he carried them into the presence of the sun. He took in his hand his silver sceptre and he said to glorious Shamash, 'I am going to that country, O Shamash, I am going; my hands supplicate, so let it be well with my soul and bring me back to the quay of Uruk. Grant, I beseech, your protection, and let the omen be good.' Glorious Shamash answered, 'Gilgamesh, you are strong, but what is the Country of the Living to you?

'O Shamash, hear me, hear me, Shamash, let my voice be heard. Here in the city man dies oppressed at heart, man perishes with despair in his heart. I have looked over the wall and I see the bodies floating on the river, and that will be my lot also. Indeed I know it is so, for whoever is tallest among men cannot reach the heavens, and the greatest cannot encompass the earth. Therefore I would enter that country; because I have not established my name stamped on brick as my destiny decreed, I will go to the country where the cedar is cut. I will set up my name where the names of famous men are written; and where no man's name is written I will raise a monument to the gods.' The tears, ran down his face and he said, 'Alas, it is a long journey that I must take to the Land of Humbaba. If this enterprise is not to be accomplished, why did you move me, Shamash, with the restless desire to perform it? How can I succeed if you will not succour me? If I die in that country I will die without rancour, but if I return I will make a glorious offering of gifts and of praise to Shamash.'

So Shamash accepted the sacrifice of his tears; like the compassionate man he showed him mercy. He appointed strong allies for Gilgamesh, sons of one mother, and stationed them in the mountain caves. The great winds he appointed; the north wind, the whirlwind, the stone and the icy wind, the tempest and the scorching wind. Like vipers, like dragons, like a scorching fire, like a serpent that freezes the heart, a destroying flood and the lightning's fork, such were they and Gilgamesh rejoiced.

He went to the forge and said, 'I will give orders to the armourers; they shall cast us our weapons while we watch them.' So they gave orders to the armourers and the craftsmen sat down in conference. They went into the groves of the plain and cut willow and box-wood; they cast for them axes of nine score pounds, and great swords they cast with blades of six score pounds each one, with pommels and hilts of thirty pounds. They cast for Gilgamesh the axe 'Might of Heroes' and the bow of Anshan; and Gilgamesh was armed and Enkidu; and the weight of the arms they carried was thirty score pounds.

The people collected and the counsellors in the streets and in the market-place of Uruk; they came through the gate of seven bolts and Gilgamesh spoke to them in the market-place: 'I, Gilgamesh, go to see that creature of whom such things are spoken, the rumour of whose name fills the world. I will conquer him in his cedar wood and show the strength of the sons of Uruk, all the world shall know of it. I am committed to this enterprise: to climb the mountain, to cut down the cedar, and leave behind me an enduring name.' The counsellors of Uruk, the great market, answered him, 'Gilgamesh, you are young, your courage carries you too far, you cannot know what this enterprise means which you plan. We have heard that Humbaba is not like men who die, his weapons are such that none can stand against them; the forest stretches for ten thousand leagues in every direction; who would willingly go down to explore its depths? As for Humbaba, when he roars it is like the torrent of the storm, his breath is like fire and his jaws are death itself. Why do you crave to do this thing, Gilgamesh? It is no equal struggle when one fights with Humbaba, that battering-ram.

When he heard these words of the counsellors Gilgamesh looked at his friend and laughed, 'How shall I answer them; shall I say I am afraid of Humbaba, I will sit at home all the rest of my days?' Then Gilgamesh opened his mouth again and said to Enkidu, 'My friend, let us go to the Great Palace, to Egalmah, and stand before Ninsun the queen. Ninsun is wise with deep knowledge, she will give us counsel for the road we must go.' They took each other by the hand as they went to Egalmah, and they went to Ninsun the great queen. Gilgamesh approached, he entered the palace and spoke to Ninsun. 'Ninsun, will you listen to me; I have a long journey to go, to the Land of Humbaba, I must travel an unknown road and fight a strange battle. From the day I go until I return, till I reach the cedar forest and destroy the evil which Shamash abhors, pray for me to Shamash.'

Ninsun went into her room, she put on a dress becoming to her body, she put on jewels to make her breast beautiful, she placed a tiara on her head and her skirts swept the ground. Then she went up to the altar of the Sun, standing upon the roof of the palace; she burnt incense and lifted her arms to Shamash as the smoke ascended: 'O Shamash, why did you give this restless heart to Gilgamesh, my son; why did you give it? You have moved him and now he sets out on a long journey to the Land of Humbaba, to travel an unknown road and fight a strange battle. Therefore from the day that he goes till the day he returns, until he reaches the cedar forest, until he kills Humbaba and destroys the evil thing which you, Shamash, abhor, do not forget him; but let the dawn, Aya, your dear bride, remind you always, and when day is done give him to the watchman of the night to keep him from harm.' Then Ninsun the mother of Gilgamesh extinguished the incense, and she called to Enkidu with this exhortation: 'Strong Enkidu, you are not the child of my body, but I will receive you as my adopted son; you are my other child like the foundlings they bring to the temple. Serve Gilgamesh as a foundling serves the temple and the priestess who reared him. In the presence of my women, any votaries and hierophants, I declare it.' Then she placed the amulet for a pledge round his neck, and she said to him, 'I entrust my son to you; bring him back to me safely.' And now they brought to them the weapons, they put in their hands the great swords in their golden scabbards, and the bow and the quiver. Gilgamesh took the axe, he slung the quiver from his shoulder, and the bow of Anshan, and buckled the sword to his belt; and so they were armed and ready for the journey. Now all the people came and pressed on them and said, 'When will you return to the city? The counsellors blessed Gilgamesh and warned him, 'Do not trust too much in your own strength, be watchful, restrain your blows at first. The one who goes in front protects his companion; the good guide who knows the way guards his friend. Let Enkidu lead the way, he knows the road to the forest, he has seen Humbaba and is experienced in battles; let him press first into the passes, let him be watchful and look to himself. Let Enkidu protect his friend, and guard his companion, and bring him safe through the pitfalls of the road. We, the counsellors of Uruk entrust our king to you, O Enkidu; bring him back safely to us.' Again to Gilgamesh, they said, 'May Shamash give you your heart's desire, may he let you see with your eyes the thing accomplished which your lips have spoken; may he open a path for you where it is blocked, and a road for your feet to tread. May he open the mountains for your crossing, and may the night time bring you the blessings of night, and Lugulbanda, your guardian god, stand beside you for victory. May you have victory in the battle as though you fought with a child. Wash your feet in the river of Humbaba to which you are journeying; in the evening dig a well, and let there always be pure water in your water- skin. Offer cold water to Shamash and do not forget Lugulbanda.'

Then Enkidu opened his mouth and said, 'Forward, there is nothing to fear. Follow me, for I know the place where Humbaba lives and the paths where he walks. Let the counsellors go back. Here is no cause for fear.' When the counsellors heard this they sped the hero on his way. 'Go, Gilgamesh, may your guardian god protect you on the road and bring you safely back to the quay of Uruk.'

After twenty leagues they broke their fast; after another thirty leagues they stopped for the night. Fifty leagues they walked in one day; in three days they had walked as much as a journey of a month and two weeks. They crossed seven mountains before they came to the gate of the forest. Then Enkidu called out to Gilgamesh, 'Do not go down into the forest; when I opened the gate my hand lost its strength.' Gilgamesh answered him, 'Dear friend, do not speak like a coward. Have we got the better of so many dangers and travelled so far, to turn back at last? You, who are tried in wars and battles, hold close to me now and you will feel no fear of death; keep beside me and your weakness will pass, the trembling will leave your hand. Would my friend rather stay behind? No, we will, go down together into the heart of the forest. Let your courage be roused by the battle to come; forget death and follow me, a man resolute in action, but one who is not foolhardy. When two go together each will protect himself and shield his companion, and if they fall they leave an enduring name.'

Together they went down into the forest and they came to the green mountain. There they stood still; they were struck dumb; they stood still and gazed at the forest. They saw the height of the cedar; they saw the way into the forest and the track where Humbaba was used to walk.

The way was broad and the going was good. They gazed at the mountain of cedars, the dwelling-place of the gods and the throne of Ishtar. The hugeness of the cedar rose in front of the mountain, its shade was beautiful, full of comfort; mountain and glade were green with brushwood.

There Gilgamesh dug a well before the setting sun. He went up the mountain and poured out fine meal on the ground and said, 'O mountain, dwelling of the gods, bring me a favourable dream.' Then they took each other by the hand and lay down to sleep; and sleep that flows from the night lapped over them. Gilgamesh dreamed, and at midnight sleep left him, and he told his dream to his friend. 'Enkidu, what was it that woke me if you did not? My friend, I have dreamed a dream. Get up, look at the mountain precipice. The sleep that the gods sent me is broken. Ah, my friend, what a dream I have had! Terror and confusion; I seized hold of a wild bull in the wilderness. It bellowed and beat up the dust till the whole sky was dark, my arm was seized and my tongue bitten. I fell back on my knee; then someone refreshed me with water from his water-skin.'

Enkidu said, 'Dear friend, the god to whom we are travelling is no wild bull, though his form is mysterious. That wild bull which you saw is Shamash the Protector; in our moment of peril he will take our hands. The one who gave water from his water-skin, that is your own god who cares for your good name, your Lugulbanda. United with him, together we will accomplish a work the fame of which will never die.'

Gilgamesh said, 'I dreamed again. We stood in a deep gorge of the mountain, and beside it we two were like the smallest of swamp flies; and suddenly the mountain fell, it struck me and caught my feet from under me. Then came an intolerable light blazing out, and in it was one whose grace and whose beauty were greater than the beauty of this world. He pulled me out from under the mountain, he gave me water to drink and my heart was comforted, and he set my feet on the ground.'

Then Enkidu the child of the plains said, 'Let us go down from the mountain and talk this thing over together.' He said to Gilgamesh the young god, 'Your dream is good, your dream is excellent, the mountain which you saw is Humbaba. Now, surely, we will seize and kill him, and throw his body down as the mountain fell on the plain.'

The next day after twenty leagues they broke their fast, and after another thirty they stopped for the night. They dug a well before the sun had set and Gilgamesh ascended the mountain. He poured out fine meal on the ground and said, 'O mountain, dwelling of the gods, send a dream for Enkidu, make him a favourable dream.' The mountain fashioned a dream for Enkidu; it came, an ominous dream; a cold shower passed over him, it caused him to cower like the mountain barley under a storm of rain. But Gilgamesh sat with his chin on his knees till the sleep which flows over all mankind lapped over him. Then, at midnight, sleep left him; he got up and said to his friend, 'Did you call me, or why did I wake? Did you touch me, or why am I terrified? Did not some god pass by, for my limbs are numb with fear? My friend, I saw a third dream and this dream was altogether frightful. The heavens roared and the earth roared again, daylight failed and darkness fell, lightnings flashed, fire blazed out, the clouds lowered, they rained down death. Then the brightness departed, the fire went out, and all was turned to ashes fallen about us. Let us go down from the mountain and talk this over, and consider what we should do.'

When they had come down from the mountain Gilgamesh seized the axe in his hand; he felled the cedar. When Humbaba heard the noise far off he was enraged; he cried out, 'Who is this that has violated my woods and cut down my cedar?' But glorious Shamash called to them out of heaven, 'Go forward, do not be afraid.' But now Gilgamesh was overcome by weakness, for sleep had seized him suddenly, a profound sleep held him; he lay on the ground, stretched out speechless, as though in a dream. When Enkidu touched him he did not rise, when he spoke to him he did not reply. 'O Gilgamesh, Lord of the plain of Kullab, the world grows dark, the shadows have spread over it, now is the glimmer of dusk. Shamash has departed, his bright head is quenched in the bosom of his mother Ningal. O Gilgamesh, how long will you lie like this, asleep? Never let the mother who gave you birth be forced in mourning into the city square.'

At length Gilgamesh heard him; he put on his breastplate, 'The Voice of Heroes', of thirty shekels' weight; he put it on as though it had been a light garment that he carried, and it covered him altogether. He straddled the earth like a bull that snuff's the ground and his teeth were clenched. 'By the life of my mother Ninsun who gave me birth, and by the life of my father, divine Lugulbanda, let me live to be the wonder of my mother, as when she nursed me on her lap.' A second time he said to him, 'By the life of Ninsun my mother who gave me birth, and by the life of my father, divine Lugulbanda, until we have fought this man, if man he is, this god, if god he is, the way that I took to the Country of the Living will not turn back to the city.'

Then Enkidu, the faithful companion, pleaded, answering him, 'O my lord, you do not know this monster and that is the reason you are not afraid. I who know him, I am terrified. His teeth are dragon's fangs, his countenance is like a lion, his charge is the rushing of the flood, with his look he crushes alike the trees of the forest and reeds in the swamp. O my Lord, you may go on if you choose into this land, but I will go back to the city. I will tell the lady your mother all your glorious deeds till she shouts for joy; and then I will tell the death that followed till she weeps for bitterness.' But Gilgamesh said, 'Immolation and sacrifice are not yet for me, the boat of the dead shall not go down, nor the three-ply cloth be cut for my shrouding. Not yet will my people be desolate, nor the pyre be lit in my house and my dwelling burnt on the fire. Today, give me your aid and you shall have mine; what then can go amiss with us two? All living creatures born of the flesh shall sit at last in the boat of the West, and when it sinks, when the boat of Magilum sinks, they are gone; but we shall go forward and fix our eyes on this monster. If your heart is fearful throw away fear; if there is terror in it throw away terror. Take your axe in your hand and attack. He who leaves the fight unfinished is not at peace.'

Humbaba came out from his strong house of cedar. Then Enkidu called out, 'O Gilgamesh, remember now your boasts in Uruk. Forward, attack, son of Uruk, there is nothing to fear.' When he heard these words his courage rallied; he answered, 'Make haste, close in, if the watchman is there do not let him escape to the woods where he will vanish. He has put on the first of his seven splendours but not yet the other six, let us trap him before he is armed.' Like a raging wild bull he snuffed the ground; the watchman of the woods turned full of threatenings, he cried out. Humbaba came from his strong house of cedar. He nodded his head and shook it, menacing Gilgamesh; and on him he fastened his eye, the eye of death. Then Gilgamesh called to Shamash and his tears were flowing, 'O glorious Shamash, I have followed the road you commanded but now if you send no succour how shall I escape? Glorious Shamash heard his prayer and he summoned the great wind, the north wind, the whirlwind, the storm and the icy wind, the tempest and the scorching wind; they came like dragons, like a scorching fire, like a serpent that freezes the heart, a destroying flood and the lightning's fork. The eight winds rose up against Humbaba, they beat against his eyes; he was gripped, unable to go forward or back. Gilgamesh shouted, 'By the life of Ninsun my mother and divine Lugulbanda my father, in the Country of the Living, in this Land I have discovered your dwelling; my weak arms and my small weapons I have brought to this Land against you, and now I will enter your house'.

So he felled the first cedar and they cut the branches and laid them at the foot of the mountain. At the first stroke Humbaba blazed out, but still they advanced. They felled seven cedars and cut and bound the branches and laid them at the foot of the mountain, and seven times Humbaba loosed his glory on them. As the seventh blaze died out they reached his lair. He slapped his thigh in scorn. He approached like a noble wild bull roped on the mountain, a warrior whose elbows are bound together. The tears started to his eyes and he was pale, 'Gilgamesh, let me speak. I have never known a mother, no, nor a father who reared me. I was born of the mountain, he reared me, and Enlil made me the keeper of this forest. Let me go free, Gilgamesh, and I will be your servant, you shall be my lord; all the trees of the forest that I tended on the mountain shall be yours. I will cut them down and build you a palace.' He took him by the hand and led him to his house, so that the heart of Gilgamesh was moved with compassion. He swore by the heavenly life, by the earthly life, by the underworld itself: 'O Enkidu, should not the snared bird return to its nest and the captive man return to his mother's arms?' Enkidu answered, 'The strongest of men will fall to fate if he has no judgement. Namtar, the evil fate that knows no distinction between men, will devour him. If the snared bird returns to its nest, if the captive man returns to his mother's arms, then you my friend will never return to the city where the mother is waiting who gave you birth. He will bar the mountain road against you, and make the pathways impassable.'

Humbaba said, 'Enkidu, what you have spoken is evil; you, a hireling, dependent for your bread! In envy and for fear of a rival you have spoken evil words.' Enkidu said, 'Do not listen, Gilgamesh: this Humbaba must die. Kill Humbaba first and his servants after.' But Gilgamesh said, 'If we touch him the blaze and the glory of light will be put out in confusion, the glory and glamour will vanish, its rays will be quenched.' Enkidu said to Gilgamesh, 'Not so, my friend. First entrap the bird, and where shall the chicks run then? Afterwards we can search out the glory and the glamour, when the chicks run distracted through the grass.'

Gilgamesh listened to the word of his companion, he took the axe in his hand, he drew the sword from his belt, and he struck Humbaba with a thrust of the sword to the neck, and Enkidu his comrade struck the second blow. At the third blow Humbaba fell. Then there followed confusion for this was the guardian of the forest whom they had felled to the ground. For as far as two leagues the cedars shivered when Enkidu felled the watcher of the forest, he at whose voice Hermon and Lebanon used to tremble. Now the mountains were moved and all the hills, for the guardian of the forest was killed. They attacked the cedars, the seven splendours of Humbaba were extinguished. So they pressed on into the forest bearing the sword of eight talents. They uncovered the sacred dwellings of the Anunnaki and while Gilgamesh felled the first of the trees of the forest Enkidu cleared their roots as far as the banks of Euphrates. They set Humbaba before the gods, before Enlil; they kissed the ground and dropped the shroud and set the head before him. When he saw the head of Humbaba, Enlil raged at them. 'Why did you do this thing? From henceforth may the fire be on your faces, may it eat the bread that you eat, may it drink where you drink.' Then Enlil took again the blaze and the seven splendours that had been Humbaba's; he gave the first to the river, and he gave to the lion, to the stone of execration, to the mountain and to the dreaded daughter of the Queen of Hell.

O Gilgamesh, king and conqueror of the dreadful blaze; wild bull who plunders the mountain, who crosses the sea, glory to him, and from the brave the greater glory is Enki's!

5

3 ISHTAR AND GILGAMESH

GILGAMESH Washed out his long locks and cleaned his weapons; he flung back his hair from his shoulders; he threw off his stained clothes and changed them for new. He put on his royal robes and made them fast. When Gilgamesh had put on the crown, glorious Ishtar lifted her eyes, seeing the beauty of Gilgamesh. She said, 'Come to me Gilgamesh, and be my bridegroom; grant me seed of your body, let me be your bride and you shall be my husband. I will harness for you a chariot of lapis lazuli and of gold, with wheels of gold and horns of copper; and you shall have mighty demons of the storm for draft mules. When you enter our house in the fragrance of cedar-wood, threshold and throne will kiss your feet. Kings, rulers, and princes will bow down before you; they shall bring you tribute from the mountains and the plain. Your ewes shall drop twins and your goats triplets; your pack-ass shall outrun mules; your oxen shall have no rivals, and your chariot horses shall be famous far-off for their swiftness.'

Gilgamesh opened his mouth and answered glorious Ishtar, 'If I take you in marriage, what gifts can I give in return? What ointments and clothing for your body? I would gladly give you bread and all sorts of food fit for a god. I would give you wine to drink fit for a queen. I would pour out barley to stuff your granary; but as for making you my wife - that I will not. How would it go with me? Your lovers have found you like a brazier which smoulders in the cold, a backdoor which keeps out neither squall of wind nor storm, a castle which crushes the garrison, pitch that blackens the bearer, a water-skin that chafes the carrier, a stone which falls from the parapet, a battering-ram turned back from the enemy, a sandal that trips the wearer. Which of your lovers did you ever love for ever? What shepherd of yours has pleased you for all time? Listen to me while I tell the tale of your lovers. There was Tammuz, the lover of your youth, for him you decreed wailing, year after year. You loved the many coloured roller, but still you struck and broke his wing; now in the grove he sits and cries, "kappi, kappi, my wing, my wing." You have loved the lion tremendous in strength; seven pits you dug for him, and seven. You have loved the stallion magnificent in battle, and for him you decreed whip and spur and a thong, to gallop seven leagues by force and to muddy the water before he drinks; and for his mother Silili lamentations. You have loved the shepherd of the flock; he made meal-cake for you day after day, he killed kids for your sake. You struck and turned him into a wolf, now his own herd-boys chase him away, his own hounds worry his flanks. And did you not love Ishullanu, the gardener of your father's palm grove? He brought you baskets filled with dates without end; every day he loaded your table. Then you turned your eyes on him and said, "Dearest Ishullanu, come here to me, let us enjoy your manhood, come forward and take me, I am yours.' Ishullanu answered, "What are you asking from me? My mother has baked and I have eaten; why should I come to such as you for food that is tainted and rotten? For when was a screen of rushes sufficient protection from frosts?" But when you had heard his answer you struck him. He was changed to a blind mole deep in the earth, one whose desire is always beyond his reach. And if you and I should be lovers, should not I be served in the same fashion as all these others whom you loved once?'

When Ishtar heard this she fell into a bitter rage, she went up to high heaven. Her tears poured down in front of her father Anu, and Antum her mother. She said, 'My father,

Gilgamesh has heaped insults on me, he has told over all my abominable behaviour, my foul and hideous acts.' Anu opened his mouth and said, 'Are you a father of gods? Did not you quarrel with Gilgamesh the king, so now he has related your abominable behaviour, your foul and hideous acts.'

Ishtar opened her mouth and said again, 'My father, give me the Bull of Heaven to destroy Gilgamesh. Fill Gilgamesh, I say, with arrogance to his destruction; but if you refuse to give me the Bull of Heaven I will break in the doors of hell and smash the bolts; there will be confusion of people, those above with those from the lower depths. I shall bring up the dead to eat food like the living; and the hosts of dead will outnumber the living.' Anu said to great Ishtar, 'If I do what you desire there will be seven years of drought throughout Uruk when corn will be seedless husks. Have you saved grain enough for the people and grass for the cattle? Ishtar replied. 'I have saved grain for the people, grass for the cattle; for seven years of seedless husks, there is grain and there is grass enough.'

When Anu heard what Ishtar had said he gave her the Bull of Heaven to lead by the halter down to Uruk. When they reached the gates of Uruk the Bull went to the river; with his first snort cracks opened in the earth and, a hundred young men fell down to death. With his second snort cracks opened and two hundred fell down to death. With his third snort cracks opened, Enkidu doubled over but instantly recovered, he dodged aside and leapt on the Bull and seized it by the horns. The Bull of Heaven foamed in his face, it brushed him with the thick of its tail. Enkidu cried to Gilgamesh, 'my friend, we boasted that we would leave enduring names behind us. Now thrust in your sword between the nape and the horns.' So Gilgamesh followed the Bull, he seized the thick of its tail, he thrust the sword between the nape and the horns and slew the Bull. When they had killed the Bull of Heaven they cut out its heart and gave it to Shamash, and the brothers rested.

But Ishtar rose tip and mounted the great wall of Uruk; she sprang on to the tower and uttered a curse: 'Woe to Gilgamesh, for he has scorned me in killing the Bull of Heaven.' When Enkidu heard these words he tore out the Bull's right thigh and tossed it in her face saying, 'If I could lay my hands on you, it is this I should do to you, and lash the entrails to your side.' Then Ishtar called together her people, the danc-

ing and singing girls, the prostitutes of the temple, the courtesans. Over
the thigh of the Bull of Heaven she set up lamentation.

But Gilgamesh called the smiths and the armourers, all of them together. They admired the immensity of the horns. They were plated
with lapis lazuli two fingers thick. They were thirty pounds each in
weight, and their capacity in oil was six measures, which he gave to his
guardian god, Lugulbanda. But he carried the horns into the palace and
hung them on the wall. Then they washed their hands in Euphrates,
they embraced each other and went away. They drove through the
streets of Uruk where the heroes were gathered to see them, and Gilgamesh called to the singing girls, 'Who is most glorious of the heroes,
who is most eminent among men?' 'Gilgamesh is the most glorious of
heroes, Gilgamesh is most eminent among men.' And now there was
feasting, and celebrations and joy in the palace, till the heroes lay down
saying, 'Now we will rest for the night.'

When the daylight came Enkidu got up and cried to Gilgamesh, 'O
my brother, such a dream I had last night. Anu, Enlil, Ea and heavenly
Shamash took counsel together, and Anu said to Enlil, "Because they
have killed the Bull of Heaven, and because they have killed Humbaba
who guarded the Cedar Mountain one of the two must die." Then glorious Shamash answered the hero Enlil, "It was by your command they
killed the Bull of Heaven, and killed Humbaba, and must Enkidu die although innocent?" Enlil flung round in rage at glorious Shamash, "You
dare to say this, you who went about with them every day like one of
themselves!"

So Enkidu lay stretched out before Gilgamesh; his tears ran down in
streams and he said to Gilgamesh, 'O my brother, so dear as you are to
me, brother, yet they will take me from you.' Again he said, 'I must sit
down on the threshold of the dead and never again will I see my dear
brother with my eyes.'

While Enkidu lay alone in his sickness he cursed the gate as though it
was living flesh, 'You there, wood of the gate, dull and insensible, witless,
I searched for you over twenty leagues until I saw the towering cedar.

There is no wood like you in our land. Seventy-two cubits high and twenty-four wide, the pivot and the ferrule and the jambs are perfect. A master craftsman from Nippur has made you; but O, if I had known the conclusion! If I had known that this was all the good that would come of it, I would have raised the axe and split you into little pieces and set up here a gate of wattle instead. Ah, if only some future king had brought you here, or some god had fashioned you. Let him obliterate my name and write his own, and the curse fall on him instead of on Enkidu.'

With the first brightening of dawn Enkidu raised his head and wept before the Sun God, in the brilliance of the sunlight his tears streamed down. 'Sun God, I beseech you, about that vile Trapper, that Trapper of nothing because of whom I was to catch less than my comrade; let him catch least, make his game scarce, make him feeble, taking the smaller of every share, let his quarry escape from his nets.'

When he had cursed the Trapper to his heart's content he turned on the harlot. He was roused to curse her also. 'As for you, woman, with a great curse I curse you! I will promise you a destiny to all eternity. My curse shall come on you soon and sudden. You shall be without a roof for your commerce, for you shall not keep house with other girls in the tavern, but do your business in places fouled by the vomit of the drunkard. Your hire will be potter's earth, your thievings will be flung into the hovel, you will sit at the cross-roads in the dust of the potter's quarter, you will make your bed on the dunghill at night, and by day take your stand in the wall's shadow. Brambles and thorns will tear your feet, the drunk and the dry will strike your cheek and your mouth will ache. Let you be stripped of your purple dyes, for I too once in the wilderness with my wife had all the treasure I wished.'

When Shamash heard the words of Enkidu he called to him from heaven: 'Enkidu, why are you cursing the woman, the mistress who taught you to eat bread fit for gods and drink wine of kings? She who put upon you a magnificent garment, did she not give you glorious Gilgamesh for your companion, and has not Gilgamesh, your own brother, made you rest on a royal bed and recline on a couch at his left hand? He has made the princes of the earth kiss your feet, and now all the people of Uruk lament and wail over you. When you are dead he will let his hair grow long for your sake, he will wear a lion's pelt and wander through the desert.'

When Enkidu heard glorious Shamash his angry heart grew quiet, he called back the curse and said, 'Woman, I promise you another destiny. The mouth which cursed you shall bless you! Kings, princes and nobles shall adore you. On your account a man though twelve miles off will clap his hand to his thigh and his hair will twitch. For you he will undo his belt and open his treasure and you shall have your desire; lapis lazuli, gold and carnelian from the heap in the treasury. A ring for your hand and a robe shall be yours. The priest will lead you into the presence of the gods. On your account a wife, a mother of seven, was forsaken.'

As Enkidu slept alone in his sickness, in bitterness of spirit he poured out his heart to his friend. 'It was I who cut down the cedar, I who levelled the forest, I who slew Humbaba and now see what has become of me. Listen, my friend, this is the dream I dreamed last night. The heavens roared, and earth rumbled back an answer; between them stood I before an awful being, the sombre-faced man-bird; he had directed on me his purpose. His was a vampire face, his foot was a lion's foot, his hand was an eagle's talon. He fell on me and his claws were in my hair, he held me fast and I smothered; then he transformed me so that my arms became wings covered with feathers. He turned his stare towards me, and he led me away to the palace of Irkalla, the Queen of Darkness, to the house from which none who enters ever returns, down the road from which there is no coming back.

'There is the house whose people sit in darkness; dust is their food and clay their meat. They are clothed like birds with wings for covering, they see no light, they sit in darkness. I entered the house of dust and I saw the kings of the earth, their crowns put away for ever; rulers and princes, all those who once wore kingly crowns and ruled the world in the days of old. They who had stood in the place of the gods like Anu and Enlil stood now like servants to fetch baked meats in the house of dust, to carry cooked meat and cold water from the water-skin. In the house of dust which I entered were high priests and acolytes, priests of the incantation and of ecstasy; there were servers of the temple, and there was Etana, that king of Dish whom the eagle carried to heaven in the days of old. I saw also Samuqan, god of cattle, and there was Ereshki-gal the Queen of the Underworld; and Befit-Sheri squatted in front of her, she who is recorder of the gods and keeps the book of death. She held a tablet from which she read. She raised her head; she saw me and spoke:" Who has brought this one here?" Then I awoke like a man drained of blood who wanders alone in a waste of rashes; like one whom the bailiff has seized and his heart pounds with terror.'

Gilgamesh had peeled off his clothes, he listened to his words and wept quick tears, Gilgamesh listened and his tears flowed. He opened his mouth and spoke to Enkidu: 'Who is there in strong-walled Uruk who has wisdom like this? Strange things have been spoken, why does your heart speak strangely? The dream was marvellous but the terror was great; we must treasure the dream whatever the terror; for the dream has shown that misery comes at last to the healthy man, the end of life is sorrow.' And Gilgamesh lamented, 'Now I will pray to the great gods, for my friend had an ominous dream.'

This day on which Enkidu dreamed came to an end and he lay stricken with sickness. One whole day he lay on his bed and his suffering increased. He said to Gilgamesh, the friend on whose account he had left the wilderness, 'Once I ran for you, for the water of life, and I now have nothing.' A second day he lay on his bed and Gilgamesh watched over him but the sickness increased. A third day he lay on his bed, he called out to Gilgamesh, rousing him up.

Now he was weak and his eyes were blind with weeping. Ten days he lay and his suffering increased, eleven and twelve days he lay on his bed of pain. Then he called to Gilgamesh, 'My friend, the great goddess cursed me and I must die in shame. I shall not die like a man fallen in battle;

I feared to fall, but happy is the man who falls in the battle, for I must die in shame.' And Gilgamesh wept over Enkidu. With the first light of dawn he raised his voice and said to the counsellors of Uruk:

'Hear me, great ones of Uruk, I weep for Enkidu, my friend,
Bitterly moaning like a woman mourning I weep for my brother.
O Enkidu, my brother,
You were the axe at my side,
My hand's strength, the sword in my belt, The shield before me,
A glorious robe, my fairest ornament; An evil Fate has robbed me.
The wild ass and the gazelle That were father and mother,
All long-tailed creatures that nourished you Weep for you,
All the wild things of the plain and pastures; The paths that you loved in the forest of cedars Night and day murmur.
Let the great ones of strong-walled Uruk Weep for you;
Let the finger of blessing
Be stretched out in mourning; Enkidu, young brother. Hark,
There is an echo through all the country Like a mother mourning.
Weep all the paths where we walked together; And the beasts we hunted, the bear and hyena, Tiger and panther, leopard and lion,
The stag and the ibex, the bull and the doe. The river along whose banks we used to walk, Weeps for you,
Ula of Elam and dear Euphrates
Where once we drew water for the water-skins.
The mountain we climbed where we slew the Watchman, Weeps for you.
The warriors of strong-walled Uruk Where the Bull of Heaven was killed, Weep for you.
All the people of Eridu Weep for you Enkidu.
Those who brought grain for your eating
Mourn for you now;
Who rubbed oil on your back Mourn for you now;
Who poured beer for your drinking Mourn for you now.
The harlot who anointed you with fragrant ointment Laments for you

now;

The women of the palace, who brought you a wife, A chosen ring of good advice,

Lament for you now.

And the young men your brothers As though they were women

Go long-haired in mourning.

What is this sleep which holds you now?

You are lost in the dark and cannot hear me.'

He touched his heart but it did not beat, nor did he lift his eyes again. When Gilgamesh touched his heart it did not beat. So Gilgamesh laid a veil, as one veils the bride, over his friend. He began to rage like a lion, like a lioness robbed of her whelps. This way and that he paced round the bed, he tore out his hair and strewed it around. He dragged of his splendid robes and flung them down as though they were abominations.

In the first light of dawn Gilgamesh cried out, 'I made you rest on a royal bed, you reclined on a couch at my left hand, the princes of the earth kissed your feet. I will cause all the people of Uruk to weep over you and raise the dirge of the dead. The joyful people will stoop with sorrow; and when you have gone to the earth I will let my hair grow long for your sake, I will wander through the wilderness in the skin of a lion.' The next day also, in the first light, Gilgamesh lamented; seven days and seven nights he wept for Enkidu, until the worm fastened on him. Only then he gave him up to the earth, for the Anunnaki, the judges, had seized him.

Then Gilgamesh issued a proclamation through the land, he summoned them all, the coppersmiths, the goldsmiths, the stone-workers, and commanded them, 'Make a statue of my friend.' The statue was fashioned with a great weight of lapis lazuli for the breast and of gold for the body. A table of hard-wood was set out, and on it a bowl of carnelian filled with honey, and a bowl of lapis lazuli filled with butter. These he exposed and offered to the Sun; and weeping he went away.

4 THE SEARCH FOR
EVERLASTING LIFE

BITTERLY Gilgamesh wept for his friend Enkidu; he wandered over the wilderness as a hunter, he roamed over the plains; in his bitterness he cried, 'How can I rest, how can I be at peace? Despair is in my heart. What my brother is now, that shall I be when I am dead. Because I am afraid of death I will go as best I can to find Utnapishtim whom they call the Faraway, for he has entered the assembly of the gods.' So Gilgamesh travelled over the wilderness, he wandered over the grasslands, a long journey, in search of Utnapishtim, whom the gods took after the deluge; and they set him to live in the land of Dilmun, in the garden of the sun; and to him alone of men they gave everlasting life.

At night when he came to the mountain passes Gilgamesh prayed: 'In these mountain passes long ago I saw lions, I was afraid and I lifted my eyes to the moon; I prayed and my prayers went up to the gods, so now, O moon god Sin, protect me.' When he had prayed he lay down to sleep, until he was woken from out of a dream. He saw the lions round him glorying in life; then he took his axe in his hand, he drew his sword from his belt, and he fell upon them like an arrow from the string, and struck and destroyed and scattered them.

So at length Gilgamesh came to Mashu, the great mountains about which he had heard many things, which guard the rising and the setting sun. Its twin peaks are as high as the wall of heaven and its paps reach down to the underworld. At its gate the Scorpions stand guard, half man and half dragon; their glory is terrifying, their stare strikes death into men, their shimmering halo sweeps the mountains that guard the rising sun. When Gilgamesh saw them he shielded his eyes for the length of a moment only; then he took courage and approached. When they saw him so undismayed the Man-Scorpion called to his mate, 'This one who comes to us now is flesh of the gods.' The mate of the Man-Scorpion answered, 'Two thirds is god but one third is man.'

Then he called to the man Gilgamesh, he called to the child of the gods: ' Why have you come so great a journey; for what have you travelled so far, crossing the dangerous waters; tell me the reason for your coming?' Gilgamesh answered, 'For Enkidu; I loved him dearly, together we endured all kinds of hardships; on his account I have come, for the common lot of man has taken him. I have wept for him day and night, I would not give up his body for burial, I thought my friend would come back because of my weeping. Since he went, my life is nothing; that is why I have travelled here in search of Utnapishtim my father; for men say he has entered the assembly of the gods, and has found everlasting life. I have a desire to question him, concerning the living and the dead.' The Man-Scorpion opened his mouth and said, speaking to Gilgamesh, 'No man born of woman has done what you have asked, no mortal man has gone into the mountain; the length of it is twelve leagues of darkness; in it there is no light, but the heart is oppressed with darkness. From the rising of the sun to the setting of the sun there is no light.' Gilgamesh said, 'Although I should go in sorrow and in pain, with sighing and with weeping, still I must go. Open the gate of the mountain.' And the Man- Scorpion said, 'Go, Gilgamesh, I permit you to pass through the mountain of Mashu and through the high ranges; may your feet carry you safely home. The gate of the mountain is open.'

When Gilgamesh heard this he did as the Man-Scorpion had said, he followed the sun's road to his rising, through the mountain. When he had gone one league the darkness became thick around him, for there was no light, he could see nothing ahead and nothing behind him. After two leagues the darkness was thick and there was no light, he could see nothing ahead and nothing behind him. After three leagues the darkness was thick, and there was no light, he could see nothing ahead and nothing behind him. After four leagues the darkness was thick and there was no light, he could see nothing ahead and nothing behind him. At the end of five leagues the darkness was thick and there was no light, he could see nothing ahead and nothing behind him. At the end of six leagues the darkness was thick and there was no light, he could see nothing ahead and nothing behind him. When he had gone seven leagues the darkness was thick and there was no light, he could see nothing ahead and nothing behind him. When he had gene eight leagues Gilgamesh gave a great cry, for the darkness was thick and he could see nothing ahead and nothing behind him. After nine leagues he felt the north- wind on his face, but the darkness was thick and there was no light, he could see nothing ahead and nothing behind him. After ten leagues the end was near. After eleven leagues the dawn light appeared. At the end of twelve leagues the sun streamed out.

There was the garden of the gods; all round him stood bushes bearing gems. Seeing it he went down at once, for there was fruit of carnelian with the vine hanging from it, beautiful to look at; lapis lazuli leaves hung thick with fruit, sweet to see. For thorns and thistles there were haematite and rare stones, agate, and pearls from out of the sea. While Gilgamesh walked in the garden by the edge of the sea Shamash saw him, and he saw that he was dressed in the skins of animals and ate their flesh. He was distressed, and he spoke and said, 'No mortal man has gone this way before, nor will, as long as the winds drive over the sea.' And to Gilgamesh he said, 'You will never find the life for which you are searching.' Gilgamesh said to glorious Shamash, 'Now that I have toiled and strayed so far over the wilderness, am I to sleep, and let the earth cover my head for ever? Let my eyes see the sun until they are dazzled with looking. Although I am no better than a dead man, still let me see the light of the sun.'

Beside the sea she lives, the woman of the vine, the maker, of wine; Siduri sits in the garden at the edge of the sea, with the golden bowl and the golden vats that the gods gave her. She is covered with a veil; and where she sits she sees Gilgamesh coming towards her, wearing skins, the flesh of the gods in his body, but despair in his heart, and his face like the face of one who has made a long journey. She looked, and as she scanned the distance she said in her own heart, 'Surely this is some felon; where is he going now? And she barred her gate against him with the cross-bar and shot home the bolt. But Gilgamesh, hearing the sound of the bolt, threw up his head and lodged his foot in the gate; he called to her, 'Young woman, maker of wine, why do you bolt your door; what did you see that made you bar your gate? I will break in your door and burst in your gate, for I am Gilgamesh who seized and killed the Bull of Heaven, I killed the watchman of the cedar forest, I overthrew Humbaba who lived in the forest, and I killed the lions in the passes of the mountain.'

Then Siduri said to him, 'If you are that Gilgamesh who seized and killed the Bull of Heaven, who killed the watchman of the cedar forest, who overthrew Humbaba that lived in the forest, and killed the lions in the passes of the mountain, why are your cheeks so starved and why is your face so drawn? Why is despair in your heart and your face like the face of one who has made a long journey? Yes, why is your face burned from heat and cold, and why do you come here wandering over the pastures in search of the wind?

Gilgamesh answered her, 'And why should not my cheeks be starved and my face drawn? Despair is in my heart and my face is the face of one who has made a long journey, it was burned with heat and with cold. Why should I not wander over the pastures in search of the wind? My friend, my younger brother, he who hunted the wild ass of the wilderness and the panther of the plains, nay friend, my younger brother who seized and killed the Bull of Heaven and overthrew Humbaba in the cedar forest, my friend who was very dear to me and who endured dangers beside me, Enkidu my brother, whom I laved, the end of mortality has overtaken him. I wept for him seven days and nights till the worm fastened on him. Because of my brother I am afraid of death, because of my brother I stray through the wilderness and cannot rest. But now, young woman, maker of wine, since I have seen your face do not let me see the face of death which I dread so much.'

She answered, 'Gilgamesh, where are you hurrying to? You will never find that life for which you are looking. When the gods created man they allotted to him death, but life they retained in their own keeping. As for you, Gilgamesh, fill your belly with good things; day and night, night and day, dance and be merry, feast and rejoice. Let your clothes be fresh, bathe yourself in water, cherish the little child that holds your hand, and make your wife happy in your embrace; for this too is the lot of man.'

But Gilgamesh said to Siduri, the young woman, 'How can I be silent, how can I rest, when Enkidu whom I love is dust, and I too shall die and be laid in the earth. You live by the sea- shore and look into the heart of it; young woman, tell me now, which is the way to Utnapish-tim, the son of Ubara-Tutu? What directions are there for the passage; give me, oh, give me directions. I will cross the Ocean if it is possible; if it is not I will wander still farther in the wilderness.' The wine-maker said to him, 'Gilgamesh, there is no crossing the Ocean; whoever has come, since the days of old, has not been able to pass that sea. The Sun in his glory crosses the Ocean, but who beside Shamash has ever crossed it? The place and the passage are difficult, and the waters of death are deep which flow between. Gilgamesh, how will you cross the Ocean? When you come to the waters of death what will you do? But Gilgamesh, down in the woods you will find Urshanabi, the ferryman of Utnapish-tim; with him are the holy things, the things of stone. He is fashioning the serpent prow of the boat. Look at him well, and if it is possible, per-haps you will cross the waters with him; but if it is not possible, then you must go back.'

When Gilgamesh heard this he was seized with anger. He took his axe in his hand, and his dagger from his belt. He crept forward and he fell on them like a javelin. Then he went into the forest and sat down. Urshanabi saw the dagger flash and heard the axe, and he beat his head, for Gilgamesh had shattered the tackle of the boat in his rage. Urshanabi said to him, 'Tell me, what is your name? I am Urshanabi, the ferryman of Utnapishtim the Faraway.'' He replied to him, 'Gilgamesh is my name, I am from Uruk, from the house of Anu.' Then Urshanabi said to him, 'Why are your cheeks so starved and your face drawn? Why is despair in your heart and your face like the face of one who has made a long journey; yes, why is your face burned with heat and with cold, and why do you come here wandering over the pastures in search of the wind?

Gilgamesh said to him, 'Why should not my cheeks be starved and my face drawn? Despair is in my heart, and my face is the face of one who has made a long journey. I was burned with heat and with cold. Why should I not wander over the pastures? My friend, my younger brother who seized and killed the Bull of Heaven, and overthrew Humbaba in the cedar forest, my friend who was very dear to me, and who endured dangers beside me, Enkidu my brother whom I loved, the end of mortality has overtaken him. I wept for him seven days and nights till the worm fastened on him. Because of my brother I am afraid of death, because of my brother I stray through the wilderness. His fate lies heavy upon me. How can I be silent, how can I rest? He is dust and I too shall die and be laid in the earth for ever. I am afraid of death, therefore, Urshanabi, tell me which is the road to Utnapishtim? If it is possible I will cross the waters of death; if not I will wander still farther through the wilderness.'

Urshanabi said to him, 'Gilgamesh, your own hands have prevented you from crossing the Ocean; when you destroyed the tackle of the boat you destroyed its safety.' Then the two of them talked it over and Gilgamesh said, 'Why are you so angry with me, Urshanabi, for you yourself cross the sea by day and night, at all seasons you cross it' 'Gilgamesh, those things you destroyed, their property is to carry me over the water, to prevent the waters of death from touching me. It was for this reason that I preserved them, but you have destroyed them, and the urnu snakes with them. But now, go into the forest, Gilgamesh; with your axe cut poles, one hundred and twenty, cut them sixty cubits long, paint them with bitumen, set on them ferrules and bring them back.'

When Gilgamesh heard this he went into the forest, he cut poles one hundred and twenty; he cut them sixty cubits long, he painted them with bitumen, he set on them ferrules, and he brought them to Urshanabi. Then they boarded the boat, Gilgamesh and Urshanabi together, launching it out on the waves of Ocean. For three days they ran on as it were a journey of a month and fifteen days, and at last Urshanabi brought the boat to the waters of death. Then Urshanabi said to Gilgamesh, 'Press on, take a pole and thrust it in, but do not let your hands touch the waters. Gilgamesh, take a second pole, take a third, take a fourth pole. Now, Gilgamesh, take a fifth, take a sixth and seventh pole. Gilgamesh, take an eighth, and ninth, a tenth pole. Gilgamesh, take an eleventh, take a twelfth pole.' After one hundred and twenty thrusts Gilgamesh had used the last pole. Then he stripped himself, he held up his arms for a mast and his covering for a sail. So Urshanabi the ferryman brought Gilgamesh to Utnapishtim, whom they call the Faraway, who lives in Dihnun at the place of the sun's transit, eastward of the mountain. To him alone of men the gods had given everlasting life.

Now Utnapishtim, where he lay at ease, looked into the distance and he said in his heart, musing to himself, 'Why does the boat sail here without tackle and mast; why are the sacred stones destroyed, and why does the master not sail the boat? That man who comes is none of mine; where I look I see a man whose body is covered with skins of beasts. Who is this who walks up the shore behind Urshanabi, for surely he is no man of mine? So Utnapishtim looked at him and said, 'What is your name, you who come here wearing the skins of beasts, with your cheeks starved and your face drawn? Where are you hurrying to now? For what reason have you made this great journey, crossing the seas whose passage is difficult? Tell me the reason for your coming.'

He replied, 'Gilgamesh is my name. I am from Uruk, from the house of Anu.' Then Utnapishtim said to him, 'If you are Gilgamesh, why are your cheeks so starved and your face drawn? Why is despair in your heart and your face like the face of one who has made a long journey? Yes, why is your face burned with heat and cold; and why do you come here, wandering over the wilderness in search of the wind?

Gilgamesh said to him, 'Why should not my cheeks be starved and my face drawn? Despair is in my heart and my face is the face of one who has made a long journey. It was burned with heat and with cold. Why should I not wander over the pastures? My friend, my younger brother who seized and killed the Bull of Heaven and overthrew Humbaba in the cedar forest, my friend who was very dear to me and endured dangers beside me, Enkidu, my brother whom I loved, the end of mortality has overtaken him. I wept for him seven days and nights till the worm fastened on him. Because of my brother I am afraid of death; because of my brother I stray through the wilderness. His fate lies heavy upon me. How can I be silent, how can I rest? He is dust and I shall die also and be laid in the earth for ever.' Again Gilgamesh said, speaking to Utnapishtim, 'It is to see Utnapishtim whom we call the Faraway that I have come this journey. For this I have wandered over the world, I have crossed many difficult ranges, I have crossed the seas, I have wearied myself with travelling; my joints are aching, and I have lost acquaintance with sleep which is sweet. My clothes were worn out before I came to the house of Siduri. I have killed the bear and hyena, the lion and panther, the tiger, the stag and the ibex, all sorts of wild game and the small creatures of the pastures. I ate their flesh and I wore their skins; and that was how I came to the gate of the young woman, the maker of wine, who barred her gate of pitch and bitumen against me. But from her I had news of the journey; so then I came to Urshanabi the ferryman, and with him I crossed over the waters of death. Oh, father Utnapishtim, you who have entered the assembly of the gods, I wish to question you concerning the living and the dead, how shall I find the life for which I am searching?

Utnapishtim said, 'There is no permanence. Do we build a house to stand for ever, do we seal a contract to hold for all time? Do brothers divide an inheritance to keep for ever, does the flood-time of rivers endure? It is only the nymph of the dragon-fly who sheds her larva and sees the sun in his glory. From the days of old there is no permanence. The sleeping and the dead, how alike they are, they are like a painted death. What is there between the master and the servant when both have fulfilled their doom? When the Anunnaki, the judges, come together, and Mammetun the mother of destinies, together they decree the fates of men. Life and death they allot but the day of death they do not disclose.'

Then Gilgamesh said to Utnapishtim the Faraway, 'I look at you now, Utnapishtim, and your appearance is no different from mine; there is nothing strange in your features. I thought I should find you like a hero prepared for battle, but you here taking your ease on your back. Tell me truly, how was it that you came to enter the company of the gods and to possess everlasting life?' Utnapishtim said to Gilgamesh, 'I will reveal to you a mystery, I will tell you a secret of the gods.'

5 THE STORY OF THE FLOOD

'You know the city Shurrupak, it stands on the banks of Euphrates? That city grew old and the gods that were in it were old. There was Anu, lord of the firmament, their father, and warrior Enlil their counsellor, Ninurta the helper, and Ennugi watcher over canals; and with them also was Ea. In those days the world teemed, the people multiplied, the world bellowed like a wild bull, and the great god was aroused by the clamour. Enlil heard the clamour and he said to the gods in council, "The uproar of mankind is intolerable and sleep is no longer possible by reason of the babel." So the gods agreed to exterminate mankind. Enlil did this, but Ea because of his oath warned me in a dream. He whispered their words to my house of reeds, "Reed-house, reed-house! Wall, O wall, hearken reed-house, wall reflect; O man of Shurrupak, son of Ubara-Tutu; tear down your house and build a boat, abandon possessions and look for life, despise worldly goods and save your soul alive. Tear down your house, I say, and build a boat. These are the measurements of the barque as you shall build her: let hex beam equal her length, let her deck be roofed like the vault that covers the abyss; then take up into the boat the seed of all living creatures."

'When I had understood I said to my lord, "Behold, what you have commanded I will honour and perform, but how shall I answer the people, the city, the elders?" Then Ea opened his mouth and said to me, his servant, "Tell them this: I have learnt that Enlil is wrathful against me, I dare no longer walk in his land nor live in his city; I will go down to the Gulf to dwell with Ea my lord. But on you he will rain down abundance, rare fish and shy wild-fowl, a rich harvest-tide. In the evening the rider of the storm will bring you wheat in torrents."

'In the first light of dawn all my household gathered round me, the children brought pitch and the men whatever was necessary. On the fifth day I laid
the keel and the ribs, then I made fast the planking. The ground-space was one acre, each side of the deck measured one hundred and twenty cubits, making a square. I built six decks below, seven in all, I divided them into nine sections with bulkheads between. I drove in wedges where needed, I saw to the punt poles, and laid in supplies. The carriers brought oil in baskets, I poured pitch into the furnace and asphalt and oil; more oil was consumed in caulking, and more again the master of the boat took into his stores. I slaughtered bullocks for the people and every day I killed sheep. I gave the shipwrights wine to drink as though it were river water, raw wine and red wine and oil and white wine. There was feasting then as
-there is at the time of the New Year's festival; I myself anointed my head. On the seventh day the boat was complete.

'Then was the launching full of difficulty; there was shifting of ballast above and below till two thirds was submerged. I loaded into her all that 1 had of gold and of living things, my family, my kin, the beast of the field both wild and tame, and all the craftsmen. I sent them on board, for the time that Shamash had ordained was already fulfilled when he said, "in the evening, when the rider of the storm sends down the destroying rain, enter the boat and batten her down." The time was fulfilled, the evening came, the rider of the storm sent down the rain. I looked out at the weather and it was terrible, so I too boarded the boat and battened her down. All was now complete, the battening and the caulking; so I handed the tiller to Puzur- Amurri the steersman, with the navigation and the care of the whole boat.

'With the first light of dawn a black cloud came from the horizon; it thundered within where Adad, lord of the storm was riding. In front over hill and plain Shullat and Hanish, heralds of the storm, led on.

Then the gods of the abyss rose up; Nergal pulled out the dams of the nether waters, Ninurta the war-lord threw down the dykes, and the seven judges of hell, the Annunaki, raised their torches, lighting the land with their livid flame. A stupor of despair went up to heaven when the god of the storm turned daylight to darkness, when he smashed the land like a cup. One whole day the tempest raged, gathering fury as it went, it poured over the people like the tides of battle; a imam could not see his brother nor the people be seen from heaven. Even the gods were terrified at the flood, they fled to the highest heaven, the firmament of Ann; they crouched against the walls, cowering like curs. Then Ishtar the sweet-voiced Queen of Heaven cried out like a woman in travail: "Alas the days of old are turned to dust because I commanded evil; why did I command thus evil in the council of all the gods? I commanded wars to destroy the people, but are they not my people, for I brought them forth? Now like the spawn of fish they float in the ocean." The great gods of heaven and of hell wept, they covered their mouths.

'For six days and six nights the winds blew, torrent and tempest and flood overwhelmed the world, tempest and flood raged together like warring hosts. When the seventh day dawned the storm from the south subsided, the sea grew calm, the flood was stilled; I looked at the face of the world and there was silence, all mankind was turned to clay. The surface of the sea stretched as flat as a roof-top; I opened a hatch and the light fell on my face. Then I bowed low, I sat down and I wept, the tears streamed down my face, for on every side was the waste of water. I looked for land in vain, but fourteen leagues distant there appeared a mountain, and there the boat grounded; on the mountain of Nisir the boat held fast, she held fast and did not budge. One day she held, and a second day on the mountain of Nisir she held fast and did not budge. A third day, and a fourth day she held fast on the mountain and did not budge; a fifth day and a sixth day she held fast on the mountain. When the seventh day dawned I loosed a dove and let her go. She flew away, but finding no resting-place she returned. Then I loosed a swallow, and she flew away but finding no resting-place she returned. I loosed a raven, she saw that the waters had retreated, she ate, she flew around, she cawed, and she did not come back. Then I threw everything open to the four winds, I made a sacrifice and poured out a libation on the mountain top. Seven and again seven cauldrons I set up on their stands, I heaped up wood and cane and cedar and myrtle. When the gods smelled the sweet savour, they gathered like flies over the sacrifice. Then, at last, Ishtar also came, she lifted her necklace with the jewels of heaven that once Anu had made to please her. "O you gods here present, by the lapis lazuli round my neck I shall remember these days as I remember the jewels of my throat; these last days I shall not forget. Let all the gods gather round the sacrifice, except Enlil. He shall not approach this offering, for without reflection he brought the flood; he consigned my people to destruction."

'When Enlil had come, when he saw the boat, he was wrath and swelled with anger at the gods, the host of heaven, "Has any of these mortals escaped? Not one was to have survived the destruction." Then the god of the wells and canals Ninurta opened his mouth and said to the warrior Enlil, "Who is there of the gods that can devise without Ea? It is Ea alone who knows all things." Then Ea opened his mouth and spoke to warrior Enlil, "Wisest of gods, hero Enlil, how could you so senselessly bring down the flood?

Lay upon the sinner his sin,
Lay upon the transgressor his transgression, Punish him a little when he breaks loose,
Do not drive him too hard or he perishes, Would that a lion had ravaged mankind Rather than the flood,
Would that a wolf had ravaged mankind Rather than the flood,
Would that famine had wasted the world Rather than the flood,
Would that pestilence had wasted mankind Rather than the flood.

It was not I that revealed the secret of the gods; the wise man learned it in a dream. Now take your counsel what shall be done with him."

'Then Enlil went up into the boat, he took me by the hand and my wife and made us enter the boat and kneel down on either side, he standing between us. He touched our foreheads to bless us saying, "In time past Utnapishtim was a mortal man; henceforth he and his wife shall live in the distance at the mouth of the rivers." Thus it was that the gods took me and placed me here to live in the distance, at the mouth of the rivers.'

6 THE RETURN

UTNAPISHTIM said, 'As for you, Gilgamesh, who will assemble the gods for your sake, so that you may find that life for which you are searching? But if you wish, come and put into the test; only prevail against sleep for six days and seven nights.' But while Gilgamesh sat there resting on his haunches, a mist of sleep like soft wool teased from the fleece drifted over him, and Utnapishtim said to his wife, 'Look at him now, the strong man who would have everlasting life, even now the mists of sleep are drifting over him.' His wife replied, 'Touch the man to wake him, so that he may return to his own land in peace, going back through the gate by which he came.' Utnapishtim said to his wife, 'All men are deceivers, even you he will attempt to deceive; therefore bake loaves of bread, each day one loaf, and put it beside his head; and make a mark on the wall to number the days he has slept.'

So she baked loaves of bread, each day one loaf, and put it beside his head, and she marked on the wall the days that he slept; and there came a day when the first loaf was hard, the second loaf was like leather, the third was soggy, the crust of the fourth had mould, the fifth was mildewed, the sixth was fresh, and the seventh was still on the embers. Then Utnapishtim touched him and he woke. Gilgamesh said to Utnapishtim the Faraway, 'I hardly slept when you touched and roused me.' But Utnapishtim said, 'Count these loaves and learn how many days you slept, for your first is hard, your second like leather, your third is soggy, the crust of your fourth has mould, your fifth is mildewed, your sixth is fresh and your seventh was still over the glowing embers

when I touched and woke you.' Gilgamesh said, 'What shall I do, O Utnapishtim, where shall I go? Already the thief in the night has hold of
my limbs, death inhabits my room; wherever my foot rests, there I find
death.'

Then Utnapishtim spoke to Urshanabi the ferryman: 'Woe to you
Urshanabi, now and for ever more you have become hateful to this har-
bourage; it is not for you, nor for you are the crossings of this sea. Go
now, banished from the shore. But this man before whom you walked,
bringing him here, whose body is covered with foulness and the grace
of whose limbs has been spoiled by wild skins, take him to the washing-
place. There he shall wash his long hair clean as snow in the water, he
shall throw off his skins and let the sea carry them away, and the beauty
of his body shall be shown, the fillet on his forehead shall be renewed,
and he shall be given clothes to cover his nakedness. Till he reaches his
own city and his journey is accomplished, these clothes will show no
sign of age, they will wear like a new garment.' So Urshanabi took Gilgamesh and led him to the washing-place, he washed his long hair as
clean as snow in the water, he threw off his skins, which the sea carried away, and showed the beauty of his body. He renewed the fillet on
his forehead, and to cover his nakedness gave him clothes which would
show no sign of age, but would war like a new garment till he reached
his own city, and his journey was accomplished.

Then Gilgamesh and Urshanabi launched the boat on to the water
and boarded it, and they made ready to sail away; but the wife of Utnapishtim the Faraway said to him, 'Gilgamesh came here wearied out,
he is worn out; what will you give him to carry him back to his own
country? So Utnapishtim spoke, and Gilgamesh took a pole and
brought the boat in to the bank. 'Gilgamesh, you came here a man wearied out, you have worn yourself out; what shall I give you to carry you
back to your own country? Gilgamesh, I shall reveal a secret thing, it is
a mystery of the gods that I am telling you. There is a plant that grows
under the water, it has a prickle like a thorn, like a rose; it will wound

your hands, but if you succeed in taking it, then your hands will hold that which restores his lost youth to a man.

When Gilgamesh heard this he opened the sluices so that a sweet water current might carry him out to the deepest channel; he tied heavy stones to his feet and they dragged him down to the water-bed. There he saw the plant growing; although it pricked him he took it in his hands; then he cut the heavy stones from his feet, and the sea carried him and threw him on to the shore. Gilgamesh said to Urshanabi the ferryman, `Come here, and see this marvellous plant. By its virtue a man may win back all his former strength. I will take it to Uruk of the strong walls; there I will give it to the old men to eat. Its name shall be "The Old Men Are Young Again"; and at last I shall eat it myself and have back all my lost youth.' So Gilgamesh returned by the gate through which he had come, Gilgamesh and Urshanabi went together. They travelled their twenty leagues and then they broke their fast; after thirty leagues they stopped for the night.

Gilgamesh saw a well of cool water and he went down and bathed; but deep in the pool there was lying a serpent, and the serpent sensed the sweetness of the flower. It rose out of the water and snatched it away, and immediately it sloughed its skin and returned to the well. Then Gilgamesh sat down and wept, the tears ran down his face, and he took the hand of Urshanabi; 'O Urshanabi, was it for this that I toiled with my hands, is it for this I have wrung out my heart's blood? For myself I have gained nothing; not I, but the beast of the earth has joy of it now. Already the stream has carried it twenty leagues back to the channels where I found it. I found a sign and now I have lost it. Let us leave the boat on the bank and go.'

After twenty leagues they broke their fast, after thirty leagues they stopped for the night; in three days they had walked as much as a journey of a month and fifteen days. When the journey was accomplished they arrived at Uruk, the strong-walled city. Gilgamesh spoke to him, to Urshanabi the ferryman, 'Urshanabi, climb up on to the wall of Uruk, inspect its foundation terrace, and examine well the brickwork; see if it is not of burnt bricks; and did not the seven wise men lay these foundations? One third of the whole is city, one third is garden, and one third is field, with the precinct of the goddess Ishtar. These parts and the precinct are all Uruk.'

This too was the work of Gilgamesh, the king, who knew the countries of the world. He was wise; he saw mysteries and knew secret things, he brought us a tale of the days before the flood. He went a long journey, was weary, worn out with labour, and returning engraved on a stone the whole story.

9

7 THE DEATH OF GILGAMESH

THE destiny was fulfilled which the father of the gods, Enlil of the mountain, had decreed for Gilgamesh: 'In nether-earth the darkness will show him a light of mankind, all that are known, none will leave a monument for generations to come to compare with his. The heroes, the wise men, like the new moon have their waxing and waning. Men will say, "Who has ever ruled with might and with power like him?" As in the dark month, the month of shadows, so without him there is no light. O Gilgamesh, this was the meaning of your dream. You were given the kingship, such was your destiny, everlasting life was not your destiny. Because of this do not be sad at heart, do not be grieved or oppressed; he has given you power to bind and to loose, to be the darkness and the light of mankind. He has given unexampled supremacy over the people, victory in battle from which no fugitive returns, in forays and assaults from which there is no going back. But do not abuse this power, deal justly with your servants in the palace, deal justly before the face of the Sun.'

The king has laid himself down and will not rise again, The Lord of Kullab will not rise again;
He overcame evil, he will not come again;
Though he was strong of arm he will not rise again;
He had wisdom and a comely face, he will not come again; He is gone into the mountain, he will not come again;
On the bed of fate he lies, he will not rise again,
Front the couch of many colours he will not come again.

The people of the city, great and small, are not silent; they lift up, the lament, all men of flesh and blood lift up the lament. Fate has spoken; like a hooked fish he lies stretched on the bed, like a gazelle that is caught in a noose. Inhuman Namtar is heavy upon him, Namtar that has neither hand nor foot, that drinks no water and eats no meat.

For Gilgamesh, son of Ninsun, they weighed out their offerings; his dear wife, his son, his concubine, his musicians, his jester, and all his household; his servants, his stewards, all who lived in the palace weighed out their offerings for Gilgamesh the son of Ninsun, the heart of Uruk. They weighed out their offerings to Ereshkigal, the Queen of Death, and to all the gods of the dead. To Namtar, who is fate, they weighed out the offering. Bread for Ned the Keeper of the Gate, bread for Ningizzida the god of the serpent, the lord of the Tree of Life; for Dumuzi also, the young shepherd, for Enki and Ninki, for Endukugga and Nindukugga, for Enmul and Nimnul, all the ancestral gods, forbears of Enlil. A feast for Shulpae the god of feasting. For Samuqan, god of the herds, for die mother Ninhursag, and the gods of creation in the place of creation, for the host of heaven, priest and priestess weighed out the offering of the dead.

Gilgamesh, the son of Ninsun, lies in the tomb. At the place of offerings he weighed the bread- offering, at the place of libation he poured out the wine. In those days the lord Gilgamesh departed, the son of Ninsun, the king, peerless, without an equal among men, who did not neglect Enlil his master. O Gilgamesh, lord of Kullab, great is thy praise.

10

GLOSSARY OF NAMES

A SHORT description of the gods and of other persons and places mentioned in the Epic will be found in this Glossary. The gods were credited at different times with a variety of attributes and characteristics, sometimes contradictory; only such as are relevant to the material of the Gilgamesh Epic are given here. The small number of gods and other characters who play a more important part in the story are described in the introduction; in their case a page reference to this description is given at the end of the Glossary note. Cross-references to other entries in the Glossary are indicated by means of italics.

ADAD: Storm-, rain-, and weather-god.

ANUNNAKI: Usually gods of the underworld, judges of the dead and offspring of Anu.

ANSHAN: A district of Elam in south-west Persia; probably the source of supplies of wood for making bows. Gilgamesh has a 'bow of Anshan'.

ANTUM: Wife of Anu.

ANU: Sumerian An; father of gods, and god of the firmament, the 'great above'. In the Sumerian cosmogony there was, first of all, the primeval sea, from which was born the cosmic mountain consisting of heaven, 'An', and earth, 'Ki'; they were separated by Enlil, then An carried off the heavens, and Enlil the earth. Ann later retreated more and more into the background; he had an important temple in Uruk.

APSU: The Abyss; the primeval waters under the earth; in the later mythology of the Enuma Elish, more particularly the sweet water which mingled with the bitter waters of the sea and with a third watery element, perhaps cloud, from which the first gods were engendered. The waters of Apsu were thought of as held immobile underground by the 'spell' of Ea in a death- like sleep.

ARURU: A goddess of creation, she created Enkidu from clay in the image of Anu. AYA: The dawn, the bride of the Sun God Shamash. BELIT-SHERI: Scribe and recorder of the underworld gods.

BULL of HEAVEN: A personification of drought created by Anu for Ishtar.

DILMUN: The Sumerian paradise, perhaps the Persian Gulf; sometimes described as 'the place where the sun rises' and 'the Land of the Living'; the scene of a Sumerian creation myth and the place where the deified Sumerian hero of the flood, Ziusudra, was taken by the gods to live for ever. See p. 39.

DUMUZI: The Sumerian form of Tammuz; a god of vegetation and fertility, and so of the underworld, also called 'the Shepherd and lord of the sheepfolds'. As the companion of Ningizzida 'to all eternity' he stands at the gate of heaven. In the Sumerian 'Descent of Inanna'

he is the husband of the goddess Inanna, the Sumerian counterpart of Ishtar. According to the Sumerian King-List Gilgamesh was descended from 'Dumuzi a shepherd'.

EA: Sumerian Enki; god of the sweet waters, also of wisdom, a patron of arts and one of the creators of mankind, towards whom he is usually well-disposed. The chief god of Eridu, where he had a temple, he lived 'in the deep'; his ancestry is uncertain, but he was probably a child of Anu.

EANNA: The temple precinct in Uruk sacred to Anu and Ishtar.

EGALMAH: The 'Great Palace' in Uruk, the home of the goddess Ninsun, the mother of Gilgamesh.

ENDUSUGGA: With Nindukugga, Sumerian gods living in the underworld; parents of Enlil.

ENKIDU: Moulded by Aruru, goddess of creation, out of clay is the image and 'of the essence of Anu', the sky-god, and of Ninurta the war-god. The companion of Gilgamesh, he is wild or natural reran; he was later considered a patron or god of anima b and may have been the hero of another cycle. See P. 30.

ENLIL: God of earth, wind, and the universal air, ultimately spirit; the executive of Anu. In the Sumerian cosmogony he was born of the union of An heaven, and Ki earth. These he separated, and he then carried off earth as his portion. In later times he supplanted Anu as chief god. He was the patron of the city of Nippur. See p. 24.

ENMUL: See Endukugga.

ENNUGI: God of irrigation and inspector of Canals.

ENUMA ELLISH: The Semitic creation epic which describes the creation of the gods, the defeat of the powers of chaos by the young god Marduk, and the creation of man from the blood of Kingu, the defeated champion of chaos. The title is taken from the first words of the epic 'When on high'.

ERESHKIGAL: The Queen of the underworld, a counterpart of Persephone; probably once a sky-goddess. In the Sumerian cosmogony she was carried off to the underworld after the separation of heaven and earth. See p. 27.

ETANA: Legendary king of Kish who reigned after the flood; in the epic which bears his name he was carried to heaven on the back of an eagle.

GILGAMESH: The hero of the Epic; son of the goddess Ninsun and of a priest of Kullab, fifth king of Uruk after the flood, famous as a great builder and as a judge of the dead. A cycle of epic poems has collected round his name.

HANISH: A divine herald of storm and bad weather.

HUMBABA: Also Huwawa; a guardian of the cedar forest who opposes Gilgamesh and is killed by him and Enkidu. A nature divinity, perhaps an Anatolian, Elamite, or Syrian god. See p. 32.

IGIGI: Collective name for the great gods of heaven.

IRKALLA: Another name for Ereshkigal; the Queen of the underworld.

ISHTAR: Sumerian Inanna; the goddess of love and fertility, also goddess of war, called the Queen of Heaven. She is the daughter of Anu and patroness of Uruk, where she has a temple. See p. 25.

ISHULLANA: The: gardener of Anu, once loved by Ishtar whom he rejected; he was turned by her into a mole or frog.

KI: The earth. KULLAS: Part of Uruk.

LUGULEANDA: Third king of the post-diluvian dynasty of Uruk, a god and shepherd, and hero of a cycle of Sumerian poems; protector of Gilgamesh.

MAGAN: A land to the west of Mesopotamia, sometimes Egypt or Arabia, and sometimes the land of the dead, the underworld.

MAGILUM: Uncertain meaning, perhaps 'the boat of the dead'.

MAMMETUM: Ancestral goddess responsible for destinies.

MAN-SCORPION: Guardian, with a similar female monster, of the mountain into which the sun descends at nightfall. Shown on sealings and ivory inlays as a figure with the upper part of the body human and the lower part ending in a scorpion's mil. According to the Enuma Elish created by the primeval waters in order to fight the gods.

MASHU: The word means 'twins' in the Akkadian language. A mountain with twin peaks into which the sun descends at nightfall and from which it returns at dawn. Sometimes thought of as Lebanon and Anti-Lebanon.

NAMTAR: Fate, destiny in its evil aspect; pictured as a demon of the underworld, also a messenger and chief minister of Ereshkigal; a bringer of disease and pestilence.

NEDU: See Ned.

NERGAL: Underworld god, sometimes the husband of Ereshkigal, he is the subject of an Akkadian poem which describes his translation from heaven to the underworld; plague-god.

NETI: The Sumerian form of Nedu, the chief gatekeeper in the underworld. NINDUKUGGA: With Endukugga, parental gods living in the underworld.

NINGAL: Wife of the Moon God and mother of the Sun.

NINGIESU: An earlier form of Ninurta; god of irrigation and fertility, he had a field near Lagash where all sorts of plants flourished; he was the child of a she-goat.

NINGIZZIDA: Also Gizzida; a fertility god, addressed as 'Lord of the Tree of Life'; sometimes he is a serpent with human head, but later he was a god of healing and magic; the companion of Tammuz, with whom he stood at the gate of heaven.

NINHURSAG: Sumerian mother-goddess; one of the four principal Sumerian gods with An, Enlil, and Enki; sometimes the wife of Enki, she created all vegetation. The name means 'the Mother'; she is also called 'Nintu', lady of birth, and IG, the earth.

NINKI: The 'mother' of Enlil, probably a form of Ninhursag.

NINLIL: Goddess of heaven, earth, and air and in one aspect of the underworld; wife of Enlil and mother of the Moon; worshipped with Enlil in Nippur.

NINSUM The mother of Gilgamesh, a minor goddess whose house was in Uruk; she was noted for wisdom, and was the wife of Lugulbaada.

NINURTA: The later forth of Ningirsu; a warrior and god of war, a herald, the south wind, and god of wells and irrigation. According to one poem he once dammed up the bitter waters of the underworld and conquered various monsters.

NISABA: Goddess of grain.

NISIR: Probably means 'Mountain of Salvation'; sometimes identified with the Pir Oman Gudrun range south. of the lower Zab, or with the Biblical Ararat north of Lake Van.

PUZUR-AMURRI: The steersman of Utnapishtim during the flood. SAMUQAN: God of cattle;

SEVEN SAGES: Wise men who brought civilization to the seven oldest cities of Mesopotamia.

SHAMASH: Sumerian Utu; the sun; for the Sumerians he was principally the judge and law-giver with some fertility attributes. For the Semites he was also a victorious warrior, the god of wisdom, the son of Sin, and 'greater than his father'. He was the husband and brother of Ishtar. He is represented with the saw with which he cuts decisions. In the poems 'Shamash' may mean the god, or simply the sun.

SHULLAT: A divine herald of storm and of bad weather. SHUL-PAE: A god who presided over feasts and feasting.

SHURRUPAX: Modem Fara, eighteen miles north-west of Uruk; one of the oldest cities of Mesopotamia, and one of the five named by the Sumerians as having existed before the flood. The home of the hero of the flood story.

SIDURI: The divine wine-maker and brewer; she lives on the shore of the sea (perhaps the Mediterranean), in the garden of the sun. Her name in the Hurrian language means 'young woman' and she may be a form of Ishtar.

SILILI: The mother of the stallion; a divine mare?

SIN: Sumerian Nama, the moon. The chief Sumerian astral deity, the father of Utu-Shamash, the sun, and of Ishtar. His parents were Enlil and Ninlil. His chief temple was in Ur.

TAMMUZ: Sumerian Dumuzi; the dying god of vegetation, bewailed by Ishtar, the subject of laments and litanies. In an Akkadian poem Ishtar descends to the underworld in search of her young husband Tammuz; but in the Sumerian poem on which this is based it is Inanna herself who is responsible for sending Dumuzi to the underworld because of his pride and as a hostage for her own safe return.

UBARA-TUTU: A king of Shurrupak and father of Utnapishtim. The only king of Kish named in the prediluvian Ring-List, apart from Utnapishtim.

URSHANABI: Old Babylonian Sursunabu; the boatman of Utnapishtim who ferries daily across the waters of death which divide the garden of the sun from the paradise where Utnapishtim lives for ever (the Sumerian Dilmun). By accepting Gilgamesh as a passenger he forfeits this right, and accompanies Gilgamesh back to Uruk instead.

URUK: Biblical Erech, modem Warka, in southern Babylonia between Fara (Shutrupak) and Ur. Shown by excavation to have been an important city from very early times, with great temples to the gods Anu and Ishtar. Traditionally the enemy of the city of Kish, and after the flood the seat of a dynasty of kings, among whom Gilgamesh was the fifth and most famous.

UTNAPISHTIM: Old Babylonian Utanapishtim, Sumerian Ziusudra; in the Sumerian poems he is a wise king and priest of Shurrupak; in the Akkadian sources he is a wise citizen of Shurrupak. He is the son of Ubara Tutu, and his name is usually translated, 'He Who Saw Life'. He is the protege of the god Ea, by whose connivance he Survives the flood, with his family and with 'the seed of all living creatures'; afterwards he is taken by the gods to live for ever at 'the mouth of the rivers' and given the epithet 'Faraway'; or according to the Sumerians he lives in Dihnun where the sun rises.

THE COMPLETE BOOK
OF ENOCH

THE COMPLETE BOOK OF ENOCH.

Banned from the biblical canon and hidden for centuries, The Book of Enoch is one of the most mysterious and controversial ancient texts ever discovered. Traditionally attributed to Enoch, the great-grandfather of Noah, this apocalyptic scripture expands on the Genesis narrative, revealing a pre-flood world of angels, giants, and divine judgment.

This extraordinary text provides:

The Story of the Watchers – Fallen angels who descended to Earth, took human wives, and corrupted mankind with forbidden knowledge.

The Rise of the Nephilim – The hybrid offspring of angels and humans, described as giants with great power.

The Prophecy of the Great Flood – The coming destruction of a world tainted by sin and divine retribution.

Visions of Heaven and Hell – Enoch's journey through celestial realms, encountering divine secrets hidden from humanity.

The Final Judgment – The fate of the righteous and the wicked in the eyes of the Almighty.

Suppressed by religious authorities and rediscovered in the Dead Sea Scrolls, The Book of Enoch challenges conventional theology and offers a profound glimpse into the supernatural forces at play in ancient history. Was Enoch truly taken up to heaven without dying, as the Bible suggests? Were these events recorded to warn future generations?

This edition presents the complete text, allowing you to explore its mysteries for yourself. Read it, and decide what secrets have been hidden from you.

11

Book 1: The Watchers

Chapter 1
The Words of the Blessing of Enoch

1   The words of the blessing of Enoch, wherewith he blessed the elect and righteous, who will be living in the days of tribulation, when all the wicked and godless are to be removed.

2   And Enoch, a righteous man whose eyes were opened by God took up his parable and said, "I saw the vision of the Holy One in the heavens, which the angels showed me, and from them I heard everything, and from them I understood as I saw, but not for this generation, but for a remote one which is for to come."

3   Concerning the elect I said, and took up my parable concerning them: "The Holy Great One will come forth from His dwelling,

4   And the eternal God will tread upon the earth, even on Mount Sinai and will appear in the strength of His might from the heaven of heavens.

5   And all shall be smitten with fear and the Watchers shall quake, and great fear and trembling shall seize them unto the ends of the earth.

6   And the high mountains shall be shaken and the high hills shall be made low, and shall melt like wax before the flame.

7   And the earth shall be wholly rent in sunder and all that is upon the earth shall perish, and there shall be a judgement upon all.

8   But with the righteous He will make peace. And will protect the elect,
And mercy shall be upon them. And they shall all belong to God, And

they shall be prospered, And they shall all be blessed.
And He will help them all,
And light shall appear unto them,

And He will make peace with them.

9 And behold! He cometh with ten thousands of His holy ones
to execute judgement upon all, And to destroy all the ungodly: And to
convict all flesh Of all the works of their ungodliness which they have
ungodly committed, And of all the hard things which ungodly sinners
have spoken against Him."

Chapter 2 The Creation

1 Observe ye everything that takes place in the heaven, how they do
not change their orbits, and the luminaries which are in the heaven, how
they all rise and set in order each in its season, and transgress not against
their appointed order.

2 Behold ye the earth, and give heed to the things which take place
upon it from first to last, how steadfast they are, how none of the things
upon earth change, but all the works of God appear to you. Behold the
summer and the winter, how the whole earth is filled with water, and
clouds and dew and rain lie upon it.

3 Observe and see how in the winter all the trees seem as though
they had withered and shed all their leaves, except fourteen trees, which
do not lose their foliage but retain the old foliage from two to three years
till the new comes.

4 And again, observe ye the days of summer how the sun is above
the earth over against it. And you seek shade and shelter by reason of the
heat of the sun, and the earth also burns with growing heat, and so you
cannot tread on the earth, or on a rock by reason of its heat.

5 Observe ye how the trees cover themselves with green leaves
and bear fruit: wherefore give ye heed and know with regard to all His
works, and recognize how He that liveth for ever hath made them so.

6   And all His works go on thus from year to year for ever, and all the tasks which they accomplish for Him, and their tasks change not, but according as God hath ordained so is it done.

7   And behold how the sea and the rivers in like manner accomplish and change not their tasks from His commandments.

8   But ye have not been steadfast, nor done the commandments of the Lord, But ye have turned away and spoken proud and hard words With your impure mouths against His greatness. Oh, ye hard–hearted, ye shall find no peace.

9   Therefore shall ye execrate your days, and the years of your life shall perish, and the years of your destruction shall be multiplied in eternal abomination, and ye shall find no mercy.

10   In those days ye shall make your names an eternal abomination unto all the righteous, and by you shall all who curse, curse. All the sinners and godless shall imprecate by you. And for you, the godless there shall be a curse."

11   And all the righteous shall rejoice, and there shall be forgiveness of sins, and every mercy and peace and forbearance.

12   There shall be salvation unto them, a goodly light.

13   And for all of you sinners there shall be no salvation but on you all shall abide the curse of the beast.

14   But for the elect there shall be light and joy and peace, and they shall inherit the earth.

15   And then there shall be bestowed upon the elect wisdom, and they shall all live and never again sin either through ungodliness or through pride: But they who are wise shall be humble.

16   And they shall not again transgress, nor shall they sin all the days of their life, nor shall they die of anger or wrath but they shall complete the number of the days of their life.

17   And their lives shall be increased in peace, and the years of their joy shall be multiplied in eternal gladness and peace all the days of their life.

Chapter 3 Fallen Angels

1   And it came to pass when the children of men had multiplied that in those days were born unto them beautiful and comely daughters.

2   And the angels, the children of the heaven, saw and lusted after them, and said to one another: "Come, let us choose us wives from among the children of men and beget us children."

3   And Semjaza, who was their leader, said unto them: "I fear ye will not indeed agree to do this deed, and I alone shall have to pay the penalty of a great sin."

4   And they all answered him and said: "Let us all swear an oath, and all bind ourselves by mutual imprecations not to abandon this plan but to do this thing."

5   Then sware they all together and bound themselves by mutual imprecations upon it. And they were in all two hundred; who descended in the days of Jared on the summit of Mount Hermon, and they called it Mount Hermon, because they had sworn and bound themselves by mutual imprecations upon it.

6   And these are the names of their leaders: Samlazaz, their leader, Araklba, Rameel, Kokablel, Tamlel, Ramlel, Danel, Ezeqeel, Baraqijal, Asael, Armaros, Batarel, Ananel, Zaqlel, Samsapeel, Satarel, Turel, Jomjael, Sariel. These are their chiefs of tens.

7   And all the others together with them took unto themselves wives, and each chose for himself one, and they began to go in unto them and to defile themselves with them.

8   And they taught them charms and enchantments, and the cutting of roots, and made them acquainted with plants.

9   And they became pregnant, and they bare great giants, whose height was three thousand ells: Who consumed all the acquisitions of men. And when men could no longer sustain them, the giants turned against them and devoured mankind.

10   And they began to sin against birds, and beasts, and reptiles, and

fish, and to devour one another's flesh, and drink the blood. Then the earth laid accusation against the lawless ones.

11   And Azazel taught men to make swords, and knives, and shields, and breastplates, and made known to them the metals of the earth and the art of working them, and bracelets, and ornaments, and the use of antimony, and the beautifying of the eyelids, and all kinds of costly stones, and all colouring tinctures.

12   And there arose much godlessness, and they committed fornication, and they were led astray, and became corrupt in all their ways.

13   Semjaza taught enchantments and root–cuttings, Armaros the resolving of enchantments, Baraqijal taught astrology, Kokabel the constellations, Ezeqeel the knowledge of the clouds, Araqiel the signs of the earth, Shamsiel the signs of the sun, and Sariel the course of the moon.

14   And as men perished, they cried, and their cry went up to heaven.

Chapter 4 Intercession of Angels

1   And then Michael, Uriel, Raphael, and Gabriel looked down from heaven and saw much blood being shed upon the earth, and all lawlessness being wrought upon the earth.

2   And they said one to another, "The earth made without inhabitant cries the voice of their cryingst up to the gates of heaven."

3   And now to you, the holy ones of heaven, the souls of men make their suit, saying, "Bring our cause before the Most High."

4   And they said to the Lord of the ages, "Lord of lords, God of gods, King of kings, and God of the ages, the throne of Thy glory standeth unto all the generations of the ages, and Thy name holy and glorious and blessed unto all the ages! Thou hast made all things, and power over all things hast Thou, and all things are naked and open in Thy sight, and Thou seest all things, and nothing can hide itself from Thee.

5   Thou seest what Azazel hath done, who hath taught all unrighteousness on earth and revealed the eternal secrets which were in heaven,

which men were striving to learn; and Samlazaz, to whom Thou hast given authority to bear rule over his associates.

6   And they have gone to the daughters of men upon the earth, and have slept with the women, and have defiled themselves, and revealed to them all kinds of sins. And the women have borne giants, and the whole earth has thereby been filled with blood and unrighteousness.

7   And now, behold, the souls of those who have died are crying out making their suit to the gates of heaven, and their lamentations have ascended and cannot cease because of the lawless deeds which are wrought on the earth.

8   And Thou knowest all things before they come to pass, and Thou seest these things and Thou dost suffer them, and Thou dost not say to us what we are to do

to them in regard to these."

9   Then said the Most High, the Holy and Great One spake, and sent Uriel to the son of Lamech and said to him, "Go to Noah and tell him in my name 'Hide thyself!' and reveal to him the end that is approaching, that the whole earth will be destroyed, and a deluge is about to come upon the whole earth, and will destroy all that is on it. And now instruct him that he may escape and his seed may be preserved for all the generations of the world."

10   And again the Lord said to Raphael, "Bind Azazel hand and foot, and cast him into the darkness: and make an opening in the desert, which is in Dudael, and cast him therein. And place upon him rough and jagged rocks, and cover him with darkness, and let him abide there for ever, and cover his face that he may not see light. And on the day of the great judgement he shall be cast into the fire.

11   And heal the earth which the angels have corrupted, and proclaim the healing of the earth, that they may heal the plague, and that all the children of men may not perish through all the secret things that the Watchers have disclosed and have taught their sons. And the whole

earth has been corrupted through the works that were taught by Azazel, to him ascribe all sin."

12   And to Gabriel said the Lord, "Proceed against the bastards and the reprobates, and against the children of fornication and destroy the children of the Watchers from amongst men. Send them one against the other that they may destroy each other in battle, for length of days shall they not have. And no request that they make of thee shall be granted unto their fathers on their behalf; for they hope to live an eternal life, and that each one of them will live five hundred years."

13   And the Lord said unto Michael, "Go, bind Samlazaz and his associates who have united themselves with women so as to have defiled themselves with them in all their uncleanness. And when their sons have slain one another, and they have seen the destruction of their beloved ones, bind them fast for seventy generations in the valleys of the earth, till the day of their judgement and of their consummation, till the judgement that is for ever and ever is consummated. In those days they shall be led off to the abyss of fire and to the torment and the prison in which they shall be confined for ever.

14   And whosoever shall be condemned and destroyed will from thenceforth be bound together with them to the end of all generations. and destroy all the spirits of the reprobate and the children of the Watchers because they have wronged mankind.

15   Destroy all wrong from the face of the earth and let every evil work come to an end, and let the plant of righteousness and truth appear, and it shall prove a blessing; the works of righteousness and truth shall be planted in truth and joy for evermore.

16   And then shall all the righteous escape and shall live till they beget thousands of children, and all the days of their youth and their old age shall they complete in peace.

17   And then shall the whole earth be tilled in righteousness, and shall all be planted with trees and be full of blessing.

18   And all desirable trees shall be planted on it, and they shall plant vines on it and the vine which they plant thereon shall yield wine in abundance, and as for all the seed which is sown thereon each measure shall bear a thousand, and each measure of olives shall yield ten presses of oil.

19   And cleanse thou the earth from all oppression, and from all unrighteousness, and from all sin, and from all godlessness, and all the uncleanness that is wrought upon the earth destroy from off the earth.

20   And all the children of men shall become righteous, and all nations shall offer adoration and shall praise Me, and all shall worship Me. And the earth shall be cleansed from all defilement, and from all sin, and from all punishment, and from all torment, and I will never again send upon it from generation to generation and for ever.

21   And in those days I will open the store chambers of blessing which are in the heaven, so as to send them down upon the earth over the work and labour of the children of men. And truth and peace shall be associated together throughout all the days of the world and throughout all the generations of men."

22   Before these things Enoch was hidden, and no one of the children of men knew where he was hidden, and where he abode, and what had become of him.

And his activities had to do with the Watchers, and his days were with the holy ones.

23   And I Enoch was blessing the Lord of Majesty and the King of the ages, and lo! the Watchers called me, Enoch the scribe, and said to me: "Enoch, thou scribe of righteousness, go, declare to the Watchers of the heaven who have left the high heaven, the holy eternal place, and have defiled themselves with women, and have done as the children of earth do, and have taken unto themselves wives.

24   Say to them: 'Ye have wrought great destruction on the earth and ye shall have no peace nor forgiveness of sin.'

25   And inasmuch as they delight themselves in their children the murder of their beloved ones shall they see, and over the destruction of their children shall they lament, and shall make supplication unto eternity, but mercy and peace shall ye not attain."

26   And Enoch went and said: "Azazel, thou shalt have no peace, a severe sentence has gone forth against thee to put thee in bonds and thou shalt not have toleration nor request granted to thee, because of the unrighteousness which thou hast taught, and because of all the works of godlessness and unrighteousness and sin which thou hast shown to men."

27   Then I went and spoke to them all together, and they were all afraid, and fear and trembling seized them. And they besought me to draw up a petition for them that they might find forgiveness, and to read their petition in the presence of the Lord of heaven.

28   For from thenceforward they could not speak with Him nor lift up their eyes to heaven for shame of their sins for which they had been condemned.

29   Then I wrote out their petition, and the prayer in regard to their spirits and their deeds individually and in regard to their requests that they should have forgiveness and length.

30   And I went off and sat down at the waters of Dan, in the land of Dan, to the south of the west of Hermon, I read their petition till I fell asleep.

31   And behold a dream came to me, and visions fell down upon me, and I saw

visions of chastisement, and a voice came bidding me to tell it to the sons of heaven, and reprimand them.

32   And when I awaked, I came unto them, and they were all sitting gathered together, weeping in Abelsjail, which is between Lebanon and Seneser, with their faces covered.

33   And I recounted before them all the visions which I had seen in sleep, and I began to speak the words of righteousness, and to repri-

mand the heavenly Watchers.

Chapter 5
Book of the Words of Righteousness

1 The book of the words of righteousness, and of the reprimand of the eternal Watchers in accordance with the command of the Holy Great One in that vision I saw in my sleep.

2 What I will now say with a tongue of flesh and with the breath of my mouth, which the Great One has given to men to converse therewith and understand with the heart.

3 As He has created and given to man the power of understanding the word of wisdom, so hath He created me also and given me the power of reprimanding the Watchers, the children of heaven.

4 "I wrote out your petition, and in my vision it appeared thus, that your petition will not be granted unto you throughout all the days of eternity, and that judgement has been finally passed upon you.

5 Your petition will not be granted unto you. And from henceforth you shall not ascend into heaven unto all eternity, and in bonds of the earth the decree has gone forth to bind you for all the days of the world.

6 And previously you shall have seen the destruction of your beloved sons and ye shall have no pleasure in them, but they shall fall before you by the sword.

7 And your petition on their behalf shall not be granted, nor yet on your own even though you weep and pray and speak all the words contained in the writing which I have written.

8 And the vision was shown to me thus: Behold, in the vision clouds invited me and a mist summoned me, and the course of the stars and the lightnings sped and hastened me, and the winds in the vision caused me to fly and lifted me upward, and bore me into heaven.

9 And I went in till I drew nigh to a wall which is built of crystals and

surrounded by tongues of fire: and it began to affright me.

10   And I went into the tongues of fire and drew nigh to a large house which was built of crystals and the walls of the house were like a tesselated floor made of crystals, and its groundwork was of crystal.

11   Its ceiling was like the path of the stars and the lightnings, and between them were fiery cherubim, and their heaven was water.

12   A flaming fire surrounded the walls, and its portals blazed with fire.

13   And I entered into that house, and it was hot as fire and cold as ice. There were no delights of life therein; fear covered me, and trembling got hold upon me.

14   And as I quaked and trembled, I fell upon my face and I beheld a vision, and lo! there was a second house, greater than the former, and the entire portal stood open before me, and it was built of flames of fire.

15   And in every respect it so excelled in splendor and magnificence and extent that I cannot describe to you its splendor and its extent.

16   And its floor was of fire, and above it were lightnings and the path of the stars, and its ceiling also was flaming fire. And I looked and saw therein a lofty throne, its appearance was as crystal, and the wheels thereof as the shining sun, and there was the vision of cherubim.

17   And from underneath the throne came streams of flaming fire so that I could not look thereon.

18   And the Great Glory sat thereon, and His raiment shone more brightly than the sun and was whiter than any snow.

19   None of the angels could enter and could behold His face by reason of the magnificence and glory and no flesh could behold Him.

20   The flaming fire was round about Him, and a great fire stood before Him, and none around could draw nigh Him; ten thousand times ten thousand were before Him, yet He needed no counselor.

21   And the most holy ones who were nigh to Him did not leave by night nor depart from Him. And until then I had been prostrate on my face, trembling and the Lord called me with His own mouth, and said to me: "Come hither, Enoch, and hear my word."

22   And one of the holy ones came to me and waked me, and He made me rise up and approach the door, and I bowed my face downwards.

23   And He answered and said to me, and I heard His voice: "Fear not, Enoch, thou righteous man and scribe of righteousness. Approach hither and hear my voice.

24   And go, say to the Watchers of heaven, who have sent thee to intercede for them: 'You should intercede for men, and not men for you. Wherefore have ye left the high, holy, and eternal heaven, and lain with women, and defiled yourselves with the daughters of men and taken to yourselves wives, and done like the children of earth, and begotten giants as your sons.

25   And though ye were holy, spiritual, living the eternal life, you have defiled yourselves with the blood of women, and have begotten with the blood of flesh, and, as the children of men, have lusted after flesh and blood as those also do who die and perish.

26   Therefore have I given them wives also that they might impregnate them, and beget children by them, that thus nothing might be wanting to them on earth.

27   But you were formerly spiritual, living the eternal life, and immortal for all generations of the world. And therefore I have not appointed wives for you; for as for the spiritual ones of the heaven, in heaven is their dwelling.

28   And now, the giants, who are produced from the spirits and flesh, shall be called evil spirits upon the earth, and on the earth shall be their dwelling.

29   Evil spirits have proceeded from their bodies; because they are born from men and from the Watchers is their beginning and primal origin; they shall be evil spirits on earth, and evil spirits shall they be called.

30   And the spirits of the giants afflict, oppress, destroy, attack, do battle, and

work destruction on the earth, and cause trouble. They take no food, but nevertheless hunger and thirst, and cause offences.

31   And these spirits shall rise up against the children of men and against the women, because they have proceeded from them.

32   From the days of the slaughter and destruction and death of the giants, from the souls of whose flesh the spirits, having gone forth, shall destroy without incurring judgement, thus shall they destroy until the day of the consummation, the great judgement in which the age shall be consummated, over the Watchers and the godless, yea, shall be wholly consummated.

33   And now as to the Watchers who have sent thee to intercede for them, who had been aforetime in heaven, say to them: "You have been in heaven, but all the mysteries had not yet been revealed to you, and you knew worthless ones, and these in the hardness of your hearts you have made known to the women, and through these mysteries women and men work much evil on earth."

34   Say to them therefore: "You have no peace."

Chapter 6 Taken by Angels

1   Angels took and brought me to a place in which those who were there were like flaming fire, and when they wished, they appeared as men.

2   And they brought me to the place of darkness, and to a mountain the point of whose summit reached to heaven.

3   And I saw the places of the luminaries and the treasuries of the stars and of the thunder and in the uttermost depths, where were a fiery bow and arrows and their quiver, and a fiery sword and all the lightnings.

4   And they took me to the living waters, and to the fire of the west, which receives every setting of the sun.

5   And I came to a river of fire in which the fire flows like water and discharges itself into the great sea towards the west.

6 I saw the great rivers and came to the great river and to the great darkness, and went to the place where no flesh walks. I saw the mountains of the darkness of winter and the place whence all the waters of the deep flow.

7 I saw the mouths of all the rivers of the earth and the mouth of the deep.

8 I saw the treasuries of all the winds, I saw how He had furnished with them the whole creation and the firm foundations of the earth.

9 And I saw the corner–stone of the earth, I saw the four winds which bear the firmament of the heaven.

10 And I saw how the winds stretch out the vaults of heaven, and have their station between heaven and earth: these are the pillars of the heaven.

11 I saw the winds of heaven which turn and bring the circumference of the sun and all the stars to their setting.

12 I saw the winds on the earth carrying the clouds: I saw the paths of the angels.

13 I saw at the end of the earth the firmament of the heaven above and I proceeded and saw a place which burns day and night, where there are seven mountains of magnificent stones.

14 Three towards the east, and three towards the south. And as for those towards the east, was of coloured stone, and one of pearl, and one of jacinth, and those towards the south of red stone.

15 But the middle one reached to heaven like the throne of God, of alabaster, and the summit of the throne was of sapphire.

16 And I saw a flaming fire. And beyond these mountains is a region the end of the great earth: there the heavens were completed.

17 And I saw a deep abyss, with columns of heavenly fire, and among them I saw columns of fire fall, which were beyond measure alike towards the height and towards the depth.

18 And beyond that abyss I saw a place which had no firmament of the heaven above, and no firmly founded earth beneath it: there was no water upon it, and no birds, but it was a waste and horrible place.

19   I saw there seven stars like great burning mountains, and to me, when I inquired regarding them. The angel said: "This place is the end of heaven and earth. This has become a prison for the stars and the host of heaven.

20   And the stars which roll over the fire are they which have transgressed the commandment of the Lord in the beginning of their rising, because they did not come forth at their appointed times.

21   And He was wroth with them, and bound them till the time when their guilt should be consummated for ten thousand years."

22   And Uriel said to me: "Here shall stand the angels who have connected themselves with women, and their spirits assuming many different forms are defiling mankind and shall lead them astray into sacrificing to demons as gods.

23   Here shall they stand, till the day of the great judgement in which they shall be judged till they are made an end of. And the women also of the angels who went astray shall become sirens."

24   And I, Enoch, alone saw the vision, the ends of all things: and no man shall see as I have seen.

Chapter 7 The Holy Angels

1   And these are the names of the holy angels who watch mankind.

2   Uriel, one of the holy angels, who is over the world and over Tartarus.

3   Raphael, one of the holy angels, who is over the spirits of men.

4   Raguel, one of the holy angels who takes vengeance on the world of the luminaries.

5   Michael, one of the holy angels, to wit, he that is set over the best part of mankind and over chaos.

6   Saraqael, one of the holy angels, who is set over the spirits, who sin in the spirit.

7   Gabriel, one of the holy angels, who is over Paradise and the serpents and the Cherubim.

8 Remiel, one of the holy angels, whom God set over those who rise.

9 And I proceeded to where things were chaotic. And I saw there something horrible: I saw neither a heaven above nor a firmly founded earth, but a place chaotic and horrible.

10 And there I saw seven stars of the heaven bound together in it, like great mountains and burning with fire.

11 Then I said: "For what sin are they bound, and on what account have they been cast in hither?"

12 Then said Uriel, one of the holy angels, who was with me, and was chief over them, and said: "Enoch, why dost thou ask, and why art thou eager for the truth? These are of the number of the stars of heaven, which have transgressed the commandment of the Lord, and are bound here till ten thousand years, the time entailed by their sins, are consummated."

13 And from thence I went to another place, which was still more horrible than the former, and I saw a horrible thing. A great fire there which burnt and blazed, and the place was cleft as far as the abyss, being full of great descending columns of fire. Neither its extent or magnitude could I see, nor could I conjecture.

14 Then I said: "How fearful is the place and how terrible to look upon!"

15 Then Uriel answered me, one of the holy angels who was with me, and said unto me: "Enoch, why hast thou such fear and affright?"

16 And I answered: "Because of this fearful place, and because of the spectacle of the pain."

17 And he said unto me: "This place is the prison of the angels, and here they will be imprisoned for ever."

18 And thence I went to another place, the mountain of hard rock.

19 And there was in it four hollow places, deep and wide and very smooth. How smooth are the hollow places and deep and dark to look at.

20   Then Raphael answered, one of the holy angels who was with me, and said unto me: "These hollow places have been created for this very purpose, that the spirits of the souls of the dead should assemble therein, yea that all the souls of the children of men should assemble here. And these places have been made to receive them till the day of their judgement and till their appointed period, till the great judgement upon them."

21   I saw a dead man making suit, and his voice went forth to heaven and made suit. And I asked Raphael the angel who was with me, and I said unto him: "This spirit which maketh suit, whose is it, whose voice goeth forth and maketh suit to heaven?"

22   And he answered me saying: "This is the spirit which went forth from Abel, whom his brother Cain slew, and he makes his suit against him till his seed is destroyed from the face of the earth, and his seed is annihilated from amongst the seed of men."

23   The I asked regarding it, and regarding all the hollow places: "Why is one separated from the other?"

24   And he answered me and said unto me: "These three have been made that the spirits of the dead might be separated. And such a division has been make for the spirits of the righteous, in which there is the bright spring of water. And such has been made for sinners when they die and are buried in the earth and judgement has not been executed on them in their lifetime.

25   Here their spirits shall be set apart in this great pain till the great day of judgement and punishment and torment of those who curse for ever and retribution for their spirits. There He shall bind them for ever. And such a division has been made for the spirits of those who make their suit, who make disclosures concerning their destruction, when they were slain in the days of the sinners.

26   Such has been made for the spirits of men who were not righteous but sinners, who were complete in transgression, and of the transgressors they shall be companions but their spirits shall not be slain in the day of judgement nor shall they be raised from thence."

27   The I blessed the Lord of glory and said: "Blessed be my Lord, the Lord of righteousness, who ruleth for ever."

28   From thence I went to another place to the west of the ends of the earth. And I saw a burning fire which ran without resting, and paused not from its course day or night but regularly.

29   And I asked saying: "What is this which rests not?"

30   Then Raguel, one of the holy angels who was with me, answered me and said unto me: "This course of fire which thou hast seen is the fire in the west which persecutes all the luminaries of heaven."

31   And from thence I went to another place of the earth, and he showed me a mountain range of fire which burnt day and night.

32   And I went beyond it and saw seven magnificent mountains all differing each from the other, and the stones were magnificent and beautiful, magnificent as a whole, of glorious appearance and fair exterior: three towards the east, one founded on the other, and three towards the south, one upon the other, and deep rough ravines, no one of which joined with any other.

33   And the seventh mountain was in the midst of these, and it excelled them in height, resembling the seat of a throne: and fragrant trees encircled the throne.

34   And amongst them was a tree such as I had never yet smelt, neither was any amongst them nor were others like it: it had a fragrance beyond all fragrance, and its leaves and blooms and wood wither not for ever: and its fruit is beautiful, and its fruit resembles the dates of a palm.

35   Then I said: "How beautiful is this tree, and fragrant, and its leaves are fair, and its blooms very delightful in appearance."

36   Then answered Michael, one of the holy and honored angels who was with me, and was their leader.

37   And he said unto me: "Enoch, why dost thou ask me regarding the fragrance of the tree, and why dost thou wish to learn the truth?"

38   Then I answered him saying: "I wish to know about everything, but especially about this tree."

39   And he answered saying: "This high mountain which thou hast seen, whose summit is like the throne of God, is His throne, where the Holy Great One, the Lord of Glory, the Eternal King, will sit, when He shall come down to visit the earth with goodness. And as for this fragrant tree no mortal is permitted to touch it till the great judgement, when He shall take vengeance on all and bring to its consummation for ever. It shall then be given to the righteous and holy. Its fruit shall be for food to the elect: it shall be transplanted to the holy place, to the temple of the Lord, the Eternal King.

40   Then shall they rejoice with joy and be glad, and into the holy place shall they enter; and its fragrance shall be in their bones, and they shall live a long life on earth. Such as thy fathers lived; and in their days shall no sorrow or plague or torment or calamity touch them."

41   Then blessed I the God of Glory, the Eternal King, who hath prepared such things for the righteous, and hath created them and promised to give to them.

42   And I went from thence to the middle of the earth, and I saw a blessed place in which there were trees with branches abiding and blooming.

43   And there I saw a holy mountain, and underneath the mountain to the east there was a stream and it flowed towards the south. And I saw towards the east another mountain higher than this, and between them a deep and narrow ravine: in it also ran a stream underneath the mountain.

44   And to the west thereof there was another mountain, lower than the former and of small elevation, and a ravine deep and dry between them: and another deep and dry ravine was at the extremities of the three mountains.

45   And all the ravines were deep and narrow, of hard rock, and trees were not planted upon them. And I marveled at the rocks, and I marveled at the ravine, yea, I marveled very much.

46   Then said I: "For what object is this blessed land, which is entirely filled with trees, and this accursed valley between?"

47 Then Uriel, one of the holy angels who was with me, answered and said: "This accursed valley is for those who are accursed for ever. Here shall all the accursed be gathered together who utter with their lips against the Lord unseemly words and of His glory speak hard things. Here shall they be gathered together, and here shall be their place of judgement.

48 In the last days there shall be upon them the spectacle of righteous judgement in the presence of the righteous for ever: here shall the merciful bless the Lord of glory, the Eternal King. In the days of judgement over the former, they shall bless Him for the mercy in accordance with which He has assigned them."

49 Then I blessed the Lord of Glory and set forth His glory and lauded Him gloriously.

50 And thence I went towards the east, into the midst of the mountain range of the desert, and I saw a wilderness and it was solitary, full of trees and plants. And water gushed forth from above. Rushing like a copious watercourse towards the north–west it caused clouds and dew to ascend on every side.

51 And thence I went to another place in the desert, and approached to the east of this mountain range. And there I saw aromatic trees exhaling the fragrance of frankincense and myrrh, and the trees also were similar to the almond tree.

52 And beyond these, I went afar to the east, and I saw another place, a valley of water. And therein there was a tree, the color of fragrant trees such as the mastic. And on the sides of those valleys I saw fragrant cinnamon. And beyond these I proceeded to the east.

53 And I saw other mountains, and amongst them were groves of trees, and there flowed forth from them nectar, which is named sarara and galbanum. And beyond these mountains I saw another mountain to the east of the ends of the earth, whereon were aloe–trees, and all the trees were full of stacte, being like almond–trees. And when one burnt it, it smelt sweeter than any fragrant odour.

54   And after these fragrant odours, as I looked towards the north over the mountains I saw seven mountains full of choice nard and fragrant trees and cinnamon and pepper.

55   And thence I went over the summits of all these mountains, far towards the east of the earth, and passed above the Erythraean sea and went far from it, and passed over the angel Zotiel.

56   And I came to the Garden of Righteousness, and from afar off I saw numerous trees, and these great—two trees there, very great, beautiful, and glorious, and magnificent, and the Tree of Knowledge, whose holy fruit they eat and know great wisdom.

57   That tree is in height like the strangler fig, and its leaves are like the Carob tree, and its fruit is like the clusters of the vine, very beautiful: and the fragrance of the tree penetrates afar.

58   Then I said: "How beautiful is the tree, and how attractive is its look!"

59   Then Raphael the holy angel, who was with me, answered me and said: "This is the tree of wisdom, of which thy father old and thy aged mother, who were before thee, have eaten, and they learnt wisdom and their eyes were opened, and they knew that they were naked and they were driven out of the garden."

60   And from thence I went to the ends of the earth and saw there great beasts, and each differed from the other; and birds also differing in appearance and beauty and voice, the one differing from the other.

61   And to the east of those beasts I saw the ends of the earth whereon the heaven rests, and the portals of the heaven open. And I saw how the stars of heaven come forth, and I counted the portals out of which they proceed, and wrote down all their outlets, of each individual star by itself, according to their number and their names, their courses and their positions, and their times and their months, as Uriel the holy angel who was with me showed me.

62   He showed all things to me and wrote them down for me; also their names he wrote for me, and their laws and their companies.

63 And from thence I went towards the north to the ends of the earth, and there I saw a great and glorious device at the ends of the whole earth.

64 And here I saw three portals of heaven open in the heaven: through each of them proceed north winds: when they blow there is cold, hail, frost, snow, dew, and rain. And out of one portal they blow for good: but when they blow through the other two portals, it is with violence and affliction on the earth, and they blow with violence.

65 And from thence I went towards the west to the ends of the earth, and saw there three portals of the heaven open such as I had seen in the east, the same number of portals, and the same number of outlets.

66 And from thence I went to the south to the ends of the earth, and saw there three open portals of the heaven: and thence there come dew, rain, and wind. And from thence I went to the east to the ends of the heaven, and saw here the three eastern portals of heaven open and small portals above them.

67 Through each of these small portals pass the stars of heaven and run their course to the west on the path which is shown to them.

68 And as often as I saw I blessed always the Lord of Glory, and I continued to bless the Lord of Glory who has wrought great and glorious wonders, to show the greatness of His work to the angels and to spirits and to men, that they might praise His work and all His creation: that they might see the work of His might and praise the great work of His hands and bless Him for ever.

12

Book 2: The Parables

Chapter 1 The First Parable

1 The second vision which he saw, the vision of wisdom, which Enoch the son of Jared, the son of Mahalaleel, the son of Cainan, the son of Enos, the son of Seth, the son of Adam, saw.

2 And this is the beginning of the words of wisdom which I lifted up my voice to speak and say to those which dwell on earth: "Hear, ye men of old time, and see, ye that come after, the words of the Holy One which I will speak before the Lord of Spirits. It were better to declare to the men of old times, but even from those that come after we will not withhold the beginning of wisdom."

3 Till the present day such wisdom has never been given by the Lord of Spirits as I have received according to my insight, according to the good pleasure of the Lord of Spirits by whom the lot of eternal life has been given to me. Now three Parables were imparted to me, and I lifted up my voice and recounted them to those that dwell on the earth.

4 The first Parable.
When the congregation of the righteous shall appear, and sinners shall be judged for their sins, and shall be driven from the face of the earth:

5 And when the Righteous One shall appear before the eyes of the righteous, whose elect works hang upon the Lord of Spirits, and light shall appear to the righteous and the elect who dwell on the earth, where then will be the dwelling of the sinners, and where the resting–place of those who have denied the Lord of Spirits? It had been good for them if they had not been born.

6   When the secrets of the righteous shall be revealed and the sinners judged, and the godless driven from the presence of the righteous and elect.

7   From that time those that possess the earth shall no longer be powerful and exalted: And they shall not be able to behold the face of the holy, for the Lord of Spirits has caused His light to appear on the face of the holy, righteous, and elect.

8   Then shall the kings and the mighty perish and be given into the hands of the righteous and holy.

9   And thenceforward none shall seek for themselves mercy from the Lord of Spirits for their life is at an end.

10   And it shall come to pass in those days that elect and holy children will descend from the high heaven, and their seed will become one with the children of men.

11   And in those days Enoch received books of zeal and wrath, and books of disquiet and expulsion.

12   And mercy shall not be accorded to them, saith the Lord of Spirits.

13   And in those days a whirlwind carried me off from the earth, and set me down at the end of the heavens.

14   And there I saw another vision, the dwelling–places of the holy, and the resting–places of the righteous.

15   Here mine eyes saw their dwellings with His righteous angels and their resting places with the holy.

16   And they petitioned and interceded and prayed for the children of men, and righteousness flowed before them as water, and mercy like dew upon the earth: Thus it is amongst them for ever and ever.

17   And in that place mine eyes saw the Elect One of righteousness and of faith, and I saw his dwelling–place under the wings of the Lord of Spirits.

18   And righteousness shall prevail in his days, and the righteous and elect shall be without number before Him for ever and ever.

19   And all the righteous and elect before Him shall be strong as fiery lights, and their mouth shall be full of blessing, and their lips extol the name of the Lord of Spirits, and righteousness before Him shall never fail.

20   There I wished to dwell, and my spirit longed for that dwelling place, and there heretofore hath been my portion. For so has it been established concerning me before the Lord of Spirits.

21   In those days I praised and extolled the name of the Lord of Spirits with blessings and praises, because He hath destined me for blessing and glory according to the good pleasure of the Lord of Spirits.

22   For a long time my eyes regarded that place, and I blessed Him and praised Him, saying: "Blessed is He, and may He be blessed from the beginning and for evermore. And before Him there is no ceasing. He knows before the world was created what is for ever and what will be from generation unto generation."

23   Those who sleep not bless Thee: they stand before Thy glory and bless, praise, and extol, saying: "Holy, holy, holy, is the Lord of Spirits: He filleth the earth with spirits."

24   And here my eyes saw all those who sleep not: they stand before Him and bless and say: "Blessed be Thou, and blessed be the name of the Lord for ever and ever." And my face was changed; for I could no longer behold.

25   And after that I saw thousands of thousands and ten thousand times ten thousand, I saw a multitude beyond number and reckoning, who stood before the Lord of Spirits.

26   And on the four sides of the Lord of Spirits I saw four presences, different from those that sleep not, and I learnt their names: for the angel that went with me made known to me their names, and showed me all the hidden things.

27   And I heard the voices of those four presences as they uttered praises before the Lord of glory.

28   The first voice blesses the Lord of Spirits for ever and ever.

29   And the second voice I heard blessing the Elect One and the elect ones who hang upon the Lord of Spirits.

30   And the third voice I heard pray and intercede for those who dwell on the earth and supplicate in the name of the Lord of Spirits.

31   And I heard the fourth voice fending off the Satans and forbidding them to come before the Lord of Spirits to accuse them who dwell on the earth.

32   After that I asked the angel of peace who went with me, who showed me everything that is hidden: "Who are these four presences which I have seen and whose words I have heard and written down?"

33   And he said to me: "This first is Michael, the merciful and long–suffering: and the second, who is set over all the diseases and all the wounds of the children of men, is Raphael: and the third, who is set over all the powers, is Gabriel: and the fourth, who is set over the repentance unto hope of those who inherit eternal life, is named Phanuel."

34   And these are the four angels of the Lord of Spirits and the four voices I heard in those days.

35   And after that I saw all the secrets of the heavens, and how the kingdom is divided, and how the actions of men are weighed in the balance.

36   And there I saw the mansions of the elect and the mansions of the holy, and mine eyes saw there all the sinners being driven from thence which deny the name of the Lord of Spirits, and being dragged off: and they could not abide because of the punishment which proceeds from the Lord of Spirits.

37   And there mine eyes saw the secrets of the lightning and of the thunder, and the secrets of the winds, how they are divided to blow over the earth, and the secrets of the clouds and dew, and these I saw from whence they proceed in that place and from whence they saturate the dusty earth.

38   And there I saw closed chambers out of which the winds are divided, the chamber of the hail and winds, the chamber of the mist, and

of the clouds, and the cloud thereof hovers over the earth from the beginning of the world.

39 And I saw the chambers of the sun and moon, whence they proceed and whither they come again, and their glorious return, and how one is superior to the other, and their stately orbit, and how they do not leave their orbit, and they add nothing to their orbit and they take nothing from it, and they keep faith with each other, in accordance with the oath by which they are bound together.

40 And first the sun goes forth and traverses his path according to the commandment of the Lord of Spirits, and mighty is His name for ever and ever.

41 And after that I saw the hidden and the visible path of the moon, and she accomplishes the course of her path in that place by day and by night—the one holding a position opposite to the other before the Lord of Spirits.

42 And they give thanks and praise and rest not. For unto them is their thanksgiving rest.

43 For the sun changes oft for a blessing or a curse, and the course of the path of the moon is light to the righteous and darkness to the sinners in the name of the Lord. Who made a separation between the light and the darkness, and divided the spirits of men, and strengthened the spirits of the righteous in the name of His righteousness.

44 For no angel hinders and no power is able to hinder; for He appoints a judge for them all and He judges them all before Him.

45 Wisdom found no place where she might dwell, then a dwelling−place was assigned her in the heavens.

46 Wisdom went forth to make her dwelling among the children of men and found no dwelling−place.

47 Wisdom returned to her place and took her seat among the angels.

48   And unrighteousness went forth from her chambers: Whom she sought not she found and dwelt with them, as rain in a desert and dew on a thirsty land.

49   And I saw other lightnings and the stars of heaven, and I saw how He called them all by their names and they hearkened unto Him.

50   And I saw how they are weighed in a righteous balance according to their proportions of light: the width of their spaces and the day of their appearing, and how their revolution produces lightning: and their revolution according to the number of the angels, and they keep faith with each other.

51   And I asked the angel who went with me who showed me what was hidden: "What are these?"

52   And he said to me: "The Lord of Spirits hath showed thee their parabolic meaning: these are the names of the holy who dwell on the earth and believe in the name of the Lord of Spirits for ever and ever."

53   Also another phenomenon I saw in regard to the lightnings: how some of the stars arise and become lightnings and cannot part with their new form.

Chapter 2
The Second Parable

1   And this is the second Parable concerning those who deny the name of the dwelling of the holy ones and the Lord of Spirits.

2   And into the heaven they shall not ascend, and on the earth they shall not come. Such shall be the lot of the sinners who have denied the name of the Lord of Spirits. Who are thus preserved for the day of suffering and tribulation.

3   On that day Mine Elect One shall sit on the throne of glory and shall try their works, and their places of rest shall be innumerable. And their souls shall grow strong within them when they see Mine Elect Ones.

4   And those who have called upon My glorious name: Then will I cause Mine Elect One to dwell among them.

5   And I will transform the heaven and make it an eternal blessing and light and I will transform the earth and make it a blessing: and I will cause Mine Elect Ones to dwell upon it: But the sinners and evil–doers shall not set foot thereon.

6   For I have provided and satisfied with peace My righteous ones and have caused them to dwell before Me: But for the sinners there is judgement impending with Me, so that I shall destroy them from the face of the earth.

7   And there I saw One who had a head of days, and His head was white like wool, and with Him was another being whose countenance had the appearance of a man, and his face was full of graciousness, like one of the holy angels.

8   And I asked the angel who went with me and showed me all the hidden things, concerning that Son of Man, who he was, and whence he was, and why he went with the Head of Days.

9   And he answered and said unto me: "This is the Son of Man who hath righteousness. With whom dwelleth righteousness, and who reveals all the treasures of that which is hidden. Because the Lord of Spirits hath chosen him,

and whose lot hath preeminence before the Lord of Spirits in uprightness for ever.

10   And this Son of Man whom thou hast seen shall raise up the kings and the mighty from their seats and shall loosen the reins of the strong, and break the teeth of the sinners. Because they do not extol and praise Him, Nor humbly acknowledge whence the kingdom was bestowed upon them.

11   And he shall put down the countenance of the strong, and shall fill them with shame. Darkness shall be their dwelling and worms shall be their bed. They shall have no hope of rising from their beds because they do not extol the name of the Lord of Spirits.

12   These are they who judge the stars of heaven, tread upon the earth, and dwell upon it.

13   All their deeds manifest unrighteousness and their power rests upon their riches.

14   Their faith is in the gods which they have made with their hands and they deny the name of the Lord of Spirits.

15   They persecute the houses of His congregations and the faithful who hang upon the name of the Lord of Spirits.

16   And in those days shall have ascended the prayer of the righteous and the blood of the righteous from the earth before the Lord of Spirits.

17   In those days the holy ones who dwell above in the heavens shall unite with one voice and supplicate and pray and praise, give thanks and bless the name of the Lord of Spirits on behalf of the blood of the righteous which has been shed.

18   And that the prayer of the righteous may not be in vain before the Lord of Spirits, that judgement may be done unto them and that they may not have to suffer for ever."

19   In those days I saw the Head of Days when He seated himself upon the throne of His glory, and the books of the living were opened before Him, and all His host which is in heaven above and His counselors stood before Him.

20   And the hearts of the holy were filled with joy because the number of the righteous had been offered, and the prayer of the righteous had been heard, and the blood of the righteous been required before the Lord of Spirits.

21   And in that place I saw the fountain of righteousness, which was inexhaustible; and around it were many fountains of wisdom. All the thirsty drank of them and were filled with wisdom and their dwellings were with the righteous and holy and elect.

22   And at that hour that Son of Man was named in the presence of the Lord of Spirits, and His name before the Head of Days.

23   Yea, before the sun and the signs were created, before the stars of the heaven were made, His name was named before the Lord of Spirits.

24   "He shall be a staff to the righteous whereon to stay themselves and not fall and he shall be the light of the Gentiles, and the hope of those who are troubled of heart.

25   All who dwell on earth shall fall down and worship before Him, and will praise and bless and celebrate with song the Lord of Spirits.

26   And for this reason hath He been chosen and hidden before Him, before the creation of the world and for evermore.

27   And the wisdom of the Lord of Spirits hath revealed Him to the holy and righteous for He hath preserved the lot of the righteous because they have hated and despised this world of unrighteousness and have hated all its works and ways in the name of the Lord of Spirits: For in his name they are saved and according to His good pleasure hath it been in regard to their life.

28   In these days downcast in countenance shall the kings of the earth have become and the strong who possess the land because of the works of their hands. For on the day of their anguish and affliction they shall not save themselves and I will give them over into the hands of Mine Elect.

29   As straw in the fire so shall they burn before the face of the holy: As lead in the water shall they sink before the face of the righteous and no trace of them shall any more be found.

30   And on the day of their affliction there shall be rest on the earth, and before them they shall fall and not rise again. There shall be no one to take them with his hands and raise them for they have denied the Lord of Spirits and His Anointed One. The name of the Lord of Spirits be blessed.

31 For wisdom is poured out like water, and glory faileth not before Him for evermore.

32   For He is mighty in all the secrets of righteousness and unrighteousness shall disappear as a shadow and have no continuance. Because

the Elect One standeth before the Lord of Spirits and His glory is for ever and ever and His might unto all generations.

33   And in Him dwells the spirit of wisdom, and the spirit which gives insight, and the spirit of understanding and of might, and the spirit of those who have fallen asleep in righteousness.

34   And He shall judge the secret things and none shall be able to utter a lying word before Him for He is the Elect One before the Lord of Spirits according to His good pleasure.

35   In those days a change shall take place for the Holy and Elect, and the Light of Days shall abide upon them and glory and honor shall turn to the holy.

36   On the day of affliction on which evil shall have been treasured up against the sinners. And the righteous shall be victorious in the name of the Lord of Spirits and He will cause the others to witness that they may repent and forgo the works of their hands.

37   They shall have no honor through the name of the Lord of Spirits yet through His name shall they be saved, and the Lord of Spirits will have compassion on them for His compassion is great.

38   And He is righteous also in His judgement and in the presence of His glory unrighteousness also shall not maintain itself: At His judgement the unrepentant shall perish before Him.

39   And from henceforth, I will have no mercy on them." saith the Lord of Spirits.

40   In those days shall the earth also give back that which has been entrusted to it. Sheol also shall give back that which it has received, and hell shall give back that which it owes.

41   For in those days the Elect One shall arise and He shall choose the righteous and holy from among them.

42   For the day has drawn nigh that they should be saved.

43   And the Elect One shall in those days sit on My throne and His mouth shall pour forth all the secrets of wisdom and counsel for the Lord of Spirits hath given to Him and hath glorified Him.

44   In those days shall the mountains leap like rams and the hills also shall skip like lambs satisfied with milk, and the faces of the angels in heaven shall be lighted up with joy.

45   And the earth shall rejoice and the righteous shall dwell upon it and the Elect shall walk thereon.

46   And after those days in that place where I had seen all the visions of that which is hidden, for I had been carried off in a whirlwind and they had borne me towards the west.

47   There mine eyes saw all the secret things of heaven that shall be, a mountain of iron, and a mountain of copper, and a mountain of silver, and a mountain of gold, and a mountain of soft metal, and a mountain of lead.

48   And I asked the angel who went with me, saying, "What things are these which I have seen in secret?"

49   And he said unto me: "All these things which thou hast seen shall serve the dominion of His Anointed that He may be potent and mighty on the earth."

50   And that angel of peace answered, saying unto me: "Wait a little, and there shall be revealed unto thee all the secret things which surround the Lord of Spirits.

51   And these mountains which thine eyes have seen, the mountain of iron, and the mountain of copper, and the mountain of silver, and the mountain of gold, and the mountain of soft metal, and the mountain of lead.

52   All these shall be in the presence of the Elect One as wax before the fire, and like the water which streams down from above and they shall become powerless before his feet.

53   And it shall come to pass in those days that none shall be saved either by gold or by silver and none be able to escape.

54   And there shall be no iron for war. Nor shall one clothe oneself with a breastplate. Bronze shall be of no service, and tin shall not be esteemed, and lead shall not be desired.

55   And all these things shall be destroyed from the surface of the earth."

56   And I looked and turned to another part of the earth, and saw there a deep valley with burning fire. And they brought the kings and the mighty, and began to cast them into this deep valley.

57   And there mine eyes saw how they made these their instruments, iron chains of immeasurable weight.

58   And I asked the angel of peace who went with me, saying: "For whom are these chains being prepared?"

59   And he said unto me: "These are being prepared for the hosts of Azazel, so that they may take them and cast them into the abyss of complete condemnation, and they shall cover their jaws with rough stones as the Lord of Spirits commanded."

60   And Michael, and Gabriel, and Raphael, and Phanuel shall take hold of them on that great day, and cast them on that day into the burning furnace, that the Lord of Spirits may take vengeance on them for their unrighteousness in becoming subject to Satan and leading astray those who dwell on the earth.

61   And in those days shall punishment come from the Lord of Spirits, and He will open all the chambers of waters which are above the heavens, and of the fountains which are beneath the earth.

62   And all the waters shall be joined with the waters: that which is above the heavens is the masculine, and the water which is beneath the earth is the feminine.

63   And they shall destroy all who dwell on the earth and those who dwell under the ends of the heaven. And when they have recognized their unrighteousness which they have wrought on the earth, then by these shall they perish.

64   And after that, the Head of Days repented and said: "In vain have I destroyed all who dwell on the earth."

65   And He sware by His great name: "Henceforth I will not do so to all who dwell on the earth and I will set a sign in the heaven and this

shall be a pledge of good faith between Me and them for ever. So long as heaven is above the earth and this is in accordance with My command.

66   When I have desired to take hold of them by the hand of the angels on the day of tribulation and pain because of this, I will cause My chastisement and My wrath to abide upon them." saith God, the Lord of Spirits.

67   Ye mighty kings who dwell on the earth, ye shall have to behold Mine Elect One. How He sits on the throne of glory and judges Azazel and all his associates, and all his hosts in the name of the Lord of Spirits.

68   And I saw there the hosts of the angels of punishment going and they held scourges and chains of iron and bronze.

69   And I asked the angel of peace who went with me, saying: "To whom are these who hold the scourges going?"

70   And he said unto me: "To their elect and beloved ones, that they may be cast into the chasm of the abyss of the valley."

71   And then that valley shall be filled with their elect and beloved, and the days of their lives shall be at an end, and the days of their leading astray shall not thenceforward be reckoned.

72   And in those days the angels shall return and hurl themselves to the east upon the Parthians and Medes.

73   They shall stir up the kings, so that a spirit of unrest shall come upon them and they shall rouse them from their thrones that they may break forth as lions from their lairs and as hungry wolves among their flocks.

74   And they shall go up and tread under foot the land of His elect ones but the city of the righteous shall be a hindrance to their horses.

75   And they shall begin to fight among themselves and their right hand shall be strong against themselves.

76   And a man shall not know his brother nor a son his father or his mother till there be no number of the corpses through their slaughter and their punishment be not in vain.

77   In those days Sheol shall open its jaws and they shall be swallowed up therein. Their destruction shall be at an end. Sheol shall devour the sinners in the presence of the elect."

78   And it came to pass after this that I saw another host of wagons, and men riding thereon, and coming on the winds from the east, and from the west to the south.

79   And the noise of their wagons was heard, and when this turmoil took place the holy ones from heaven remarked it, and the pillars of the earth were moved from their place, and the sound thereof was heard from the one end of heaven to the other, in one day.

80   And they shall all fall down and worship the Lord of Spirits. And this is the end of the second Parable.

Chapter 3 The Third Parable

1   And I began to speak the third Parable concerning the righteous and elect.

2   Blessed are ye, ye righteous and Elect for glorious shall be your lot.

3   And the righteous shall be in the light of the sun and the elect in the light of eternal life.

4   The days of their life shall be unending and the days of the holy without number.

5   And they shall seek the light and find righteousness with the Lord of Spirits.

6   There shall be peace to the righteous in the name of the Eternal Lord.

7   And after this it shall be said to the holy in heaven that they should seek out the secrets of righteousness, the heritage of faith.

8   For it has become bright as the sun upon earth and the darkness is past.

9   And there shall be a light that never ends and to a limit of days they shall not come.

10   For the darkness shall first have been destroyed and the light of uprightness established for ever before the Lord of Spirits.

11   In those days mine eyes saw the secrets of the lightnings, and of the lights, and the judgements they execute, and they lighten for a blessing or a curse as the Lord of Spirits willeth.

12   And there I saw the secrets of the thunder, and how when it resounds above in the heaven, the sound thereof is heard.

13   And He caused me to see the judgements executed on the earth, whether they be for well–being and blessing, or for a curse according to the word of the Lord of Spirits.

14   And after that, all the secrets of the lights and lightnings were shown to me, and they lighten for blessing and for satisfying.

15   In the year 500, in the seventh month, on the fourteenth day of the month in the life of Enoch.

16   In that parable I saw how a mighty quaking made the heaven of heavens to quake, and the host of the Most High, and the angels, a thousand thousands and ten thousand times ten thousand were disquieted with a great disquiet.

17   And the Head of Days sat on the throne of His glory, and the angels and the righteous stood around Him.

18   And a great trembling seized me, and fear took hold of me, and my loins gave way, and dissolved were my reins, and I fell upon my face.

19   And Michael sent another angel from among the holy ones and he raised me up, and when he had raised me up my spirit returned; for I had not been able to endure the look of this host, and the commotion and the quaking of the heaven.

20   And Michael said unto me: Why art thou disquieted with such a vision? Until this day lasted the day of His mercy; and He hath been merciful and long
–suffering towards those who dwell on the earth.

21   And when the day, and the power, and the punishment, and the judgement come, which the Lord of Spirits hath prepared for those who worship not the righteous law, and for those who deny the right-

eous judgement, and for those who take His name in vain, that day is prepared, for the elect a covenant, but for sinners an inquisition.

22   When the punishment of the Lord of Spirits shall rest upon them, it shall rest in order that the punishment of the Lord of Spirits may not come in vain, and it shall slay the children with their mothers and the children with their fathers.

23   Afterwards the judgement shall take place according to His mercy and His patience."

24   And on that day were two monsters parted, a female monster named Leviathan, to dwell in the abysses of the ocean over the fountains of the waters.

25   But the male is named Behemoth, who occupied with his breast a waste wilderness named Duidain, on the east of the garden where the elect and righteous dwell, where my grandfather was taken up, the seventh from Adam, the first man whom the Lord of Spirits created.

26   And I besought the other angel that he should show me the might of those monsters, how they were parted on one day and cast, the one into the abysses of the sea and the other unto the dry land of the wilderness.

27   And he said to me: "Thou son of man, herein thou dost seek to know what is hidden."

28   And the other angel who went with me and showed me what was hidden told me what is first and last in the heaven in the height, and beneath the earth in the depth, and at the ends of the heaven, and on the foundation of the heaven.

29   And the chambers of the winds, and how the winds are divided, and how they are weighed, and how the portals of the winds are reckoned, each according to the power of the wind, and the power of the lights of the moon, and according to the power that is fitting: and the divisions of the stars according to their names and how all the divisions are divided.

30   And the thunders according to the places where they fall, and all the divisions that are made among the lightnings that it may lighten, and their host that they may at once obey.

31   For the thunder has places of rest assigned to it while it is waiting for its peal; and the thunder and lightning are inseparable, and although not one and undivided, they both go together through the spirit and separate not.

32   For when the lightning lightens, the thunder utters its voice, and the spirit enforces a pause during the peal, and divides equally between them; for the treasury of their peals is like the sand, and each one of them as it peals is held in with a bridle, and turned back by the power of the spirit, and pushed forward according to the many quarters of the earth.

33   And the spirit of the sea is masculine and strong, and according to the might of his strength he draws it back with a rein, and in like manner it is driven forward and disperses amid all the mountains of the earth.

34   And the spirit of the hoarfrost is his own angel, and the spirit of the hail is a good angel.

35   And the spirit of the snow has forsaken his chambers on account of his strength; there is a special spirit therein, and that which ascends from it is like smoke, and its name is Frost.

36   And the spirit of the mist is not united with them in their chambers, but it has a special chamber; for its course is glorious both in light and in darkness, and in winter and in summer, and in its chamber is an angel.

37   And the spirit of the dew has its dwelling at the ends of the heaven, and is connected with the chambers of the rain, and its course is in winter and summer: and its clouds and the clouds of the mist are connected, and the one gives to the other.

38   And when the spirit of the rain goes forth from its chamber, the angels come and open the chamber and lead it out, and when it is dif-

fused over the whole earth it unites with the water on the earth. And whensoever it unites with the water on the earth.

39   For the waters are for those who dwell on the earth; for they are nourishment for the earth from the Most High who is in heaven: therefore there is a measure for the rain, and the angels take it in charge.

40   And these things I saw towards the Garden of the Righteous.

41   And the angel of peace who was with me said to me: "These two monsters, prepared conformably to the greatness of God, shall feed."

42   And I saw in those days how long cords were given to those angels, and they took to themselves wings and flew, and they went towards the north.

43   And I asked the angel, saying unto him: "Why have those angels taken these cords and gone off?"

44   And he said unto me: "They have gone to measure."

45   And the angel who went with me said unto me: "These shall bring the measures of the righteous and the ropes of the righteous to the righteous. That they may stay themselves on the name of the Lord of Spirits for ever and ever.

46   The elect shall begin to dwell with the elect, and those are the measures which shall be given to faith and which shall strengthen righteousness.

47   And these measures shall reveal all the secrets of the depths of the earth. And those who have been destroyed by the desert, and those who have been devoured by the beasts, and those who have been devoured by the fish of the sea. That they may return and stay themselves on the day of the Elect One; for none shall be destroyed before the Lord of Spirits, and none can be destroyed."

48   And all who dwell above in the heaven received a command and power and one voice and one light like unto fire.

49   And that One with their first words they blessed and extolled and lauded with wisdom.

50   And they were wise in utterance and in the spirit of life.

51   And the Lord of Spirits placed the Elect one on the throne of glory. And he shall judge all the works of the holy above in the heaven, and in the balance shall their deeds be weighed.

52   And thus the Lord commanded the kings and the mighty and the exalted, and those who dwell on the earth, and said: "Open your eyes and lift up your horns if ye are able to recognize the Elect One."

53   And the Lord of Spirits seated him on the throne of His glory and the spirit of righteousness was poured out upon Him.

54   And the word of his mouth slays all the sinners, and all the un-righteous are destroyed from before his face.

55   And there shall stand up in that day all the kings and the mighty, and the exalted and those who hold the earth, and they shall see and rec-ognize how He sits on the throne of His glory.

56   And righteousness is judged before him and no lying word is spoken before him.

57   Then shall pain come upon them as on a woman in travail when her child enters the mouth of the womb and she has pain in bringing forth.

58   And one portion of them shall look on the other and they shall be terrified, and they shall be downcast of countenance, and pain shall seize them when they see that Son of Man sitting on the throne of his glory.

59   And the kings and the mighty and all who possess the earth shall bless and glorify and extol him who rules over all, who was hidden.

60   For from the beginning the Son of Man was hidden and the Most High preserved Him in the presence of His might, and revealed Him to the elect.

61   And the congregation of the elect and holy shall be sown and all the elect shall stand before him on that day.

62   And all the kings and the mighty and the exalted and those who rule the earth shall fall down before Him on their faces and worship and

set their hope upon that Son of Man, and petition him and supplicate for mercy at his hands.

63   Nevertheless that Lord of Spirits will so press them that they shall hastily go forth from His presence, and their faces shall be filled with shame, and the darkness grow deeper on their faces.

64   And He will deliver them to the angels for punishment to execute vengeance on them because they have oppressed His children and His elect.

65   And they shall be a spectacle for the righteous and for His elect: They shall rejoice over them because the wrath of the Lord of Spirits resteth upon them and His sword is drunk with their blood.

66   And the righteous and elect shall be saved on that day, and they shall never thenceforward see the face of the sinners and unrighteous.

67   And the Lord of Spirits will abide over them, and with that Son of Man shall they eat and lie down and rise up for ever and ever.

68   And the righteous and elect shall have risen from the earth and ceased to be of downcast countenance.

69   And they shall have been clothed with garments of glory and these shall be the garments of life from the Lord of Spirits: And your garments shall not grow old. Nor your glory pass away before the Lord of Spirits.

70   In those days shall the mighty and the kings who possess the earth implore to grant them a little respite from His angels of punishment to whom they were delivered, that they might fall down and worship before the Lord of Spirits and confess their sins before Him.

71   And they shall bless and glorify the Lord of Spirits, and say: "Blessed is the Lord of Spirits and the Lord of kings, and the Lord of the mighty and the Lord of the rich, and the Lord of glory and the Lord of wisdom, and splendid in every secret thing is Thy power from generation to generation, and Thy glory for ever and ever.

72   Deep are all Thy secrets and innumerable, and Thy righteousness is beyond reckoning. We have now learnt that we should glorify and bless the Lord of kings and Him who is king over all kings."

73   And they shall say: "Would that we had rest to glorify and give thanks and confess our faith before His glory! And now we long for a little rest but find it not. We follow hard upon and obtain not, and light has vanished from before us, and darkness is our dwelling–place for ever and ever.

74   For we have not believed before Him nor glorified the name of the Lord of Spirits but our hope was in the sceptre of our kingdom, and in our own glory.

75   And in the day of our suffering and tribulation He saves us not and we find no respite for confession that our Lord is true in all His works, and in His judgements and His justice, and His judgements have no respect of persons.

76   And we pass away from before His face on account of our works and all our sins are reckoned up in righteousness."

77   Now they shall say unto themselves: "Our souls are full of unrighteous gain, but it does not prevent us from descending from the midst thereof into the burden of Sheol."

78   And after that their faces shall be filled with darkness and shame before that Son of Man, and they shall be driven from his presence, and the sword shall abide before his face in their midst.

79   Thus spake the Lord of Spirits: "This is the ordinance and judgement with respect to the mighty and the kings and the exalted and those who possess the earth before the Lord of Spirits."

80   And other forms I saw hidden in that place. I heard the voice of the angel saying: "These are the angels who descended to the earth, and revealed what was hidden to the children of men and seduced the children of men into committing sin."

13

Book 3: The Book of Noah

Chapter 1 Birth of Noah

1 And after some days my son Methuselah took a wife for his son Lamech, and she became pregnant by him and bore a son.

2 And his body was white as snow and red as the blooming of a rose, and the hair of his head and his long locks were white as wool, and his eyes beautiful. And when he opened his eyes, he lighted up the whole house like the sun, and the whole house was very bright.

3 And thereupon he arose in the hands of the midwife, opened his mouth, and conversed with the Lord of righteousness.

4 And his father Lamech was afraid of him and fled, and came to his father Methuselah.

5 And he said unto him: "I have begotten a strange son, diverse from and unlike man, and resembling the sons of the God of heaven; and his nature is different and he is not like us, and his eyes are as the rays of the sun, and his countenance is glorious.

6 And it seems to me that he is not sprung from me but from the angels, and I fear that in his days a wonder may be wrought on the earth. And now, my father, I am here to petition thee and implore thee that thou mayest go to Enoch, our father, and learn from him the truth, for his dwelling–place is amongst the angels."

7 And when Methuselah heard the words of his son, he came to me to the ends of the earth; for he had heard that I was there, and he cried aloud, and I heard his voice and I came to him.

8   And I said unto him: "Behold, here am I, my son, wherefore hast thou come to me?"

9   And he answered and said: "Because of a great cause of anxiety have I come to thee, and because of a disturbing vision have I approached.

10   And now, my father, hear me: unto Lamech my son there hath been born a son, the like of whom there is none, and his nature is not like mans nature, and the color of his body is whiter than snow and redder than the bloom of a rose, and the hair of his head is whiter than white wool, and his eyes are like the rays of the sun, and he opened his eyes and thereupon lighted up the whole house.

11   And he arose in the hands of the midwife, and opened his mouth and blessed the Lord of heaven.

12   And his father Lamech became afraid and fled to me, and did not believe that he was sprung from him, but that he was in the likeness of the angels of heaven; and behold I have come to thee that thou mayest make known to me the truth."

13   And I, Enoch, answered and said unto him: "The Lord will do a new thing on the earth, and this I have already seen in a vision, and make known to thee that in the generation of my father Jared some of the angels of heaven transgressed the word of the Lord.

14   And behold they commit sin and transgress the law, and have united themselves with women and commit sin with them, and have married some of them, and have begot children by them.

15   And they shall produce on the earth giants not according to the spirit, but according to the flesh, and there shall be a great punishment on the earth, and the earth shall be cleansed from all impurity.

16   Yea, there shall come a great destruction over the whole earth, and there shall be a deluge and a great destruction for one year.

17   And this son who has been born unto you shall be left on the earth, and his three children shall be saved with him: when all mankind that are on the earth shall die he and his sons shall be saved.

18   And now make known to thy son Lamech that he who has been born is in truth his son, and call his name Noah; for he shall be left to you, and he and his sons shall be saved from the destruction which shall come upon the earth on account of all the sin and all the unrighteousness, which shall be consummated on the earth in his days.

19   And after that there shall be still more unrighteousness than that which was first consummated on the earth; for I know the mysteries of the holy ones; for He, the Lord, has showed me and informed me, and I have read in the heavenly tablets.

20   And I saw written on them that generation upon generation shall transgress, till a generation of righteousness arises, and transgression is destroyed and sin passes away from the earth, and all manner of good comes upon it.

21   And now, my son, go and make known to thy son Lamech that this son, which has been born, is in truth his son, and that is no lie."

22   And when Methuselah had heard the words of his father Enoch–for he had shown to him everything in secret–he returned and showed to him and called the name of that son Noah; for he will comfort the earth after all the destruction.

Chapter 2 Calling Enoch

1   And in those days Noah saw the earth that it had sunk down and its destruction was nigh.

2   And he arose from thence and went to the ends of the earth, and cried aloud to his grandfather Enoch.

3   Noah said three times with an embittered voice: "Hear me, hear me, hear me."

4   And I said unto him: "Tell me what it is that is falling out on the earth that the earth is in such evil plight and shaken, lest perchance I shall perish with it?"

5   And thereupon there was a great commotion , on the earth, and a voice was heard from heaven, and I fell on my face.

6   And Enoch my grandfather came and stood by me, and said unto me: "Why hast thou cried unto me with a bitter cry and weeping?

7   A command has gone forth from the presence of the Lord concerning those who dwell on the earth that their ruin is accomplished because they have learnt all the secrets of the angels, and all the violence of the Satans, and all their powers, the most secret ones.

8   And all the power of those who practice sorcery, and the power of witchcraft, and the power of those who make molten images. For the whole earth: And how silver is produced from the dust of the earth, and how soft metal originates in the earth. For lead and tin are not produced from the earth like the first: it is a fountain that produces them, and an angel stands therein, and that angel is preeminent."

9   And after that my grandfather Enoch took hold of me by my hand and raised me up, and said unto me: "Go, for I have asked the Lord of Spirits as touching this commotion on the earth.

10   And He said unto me: "Because of their unrighteousness their judgement has been determined upon and shall not be withheld by Me for ever. Because of the sorceries which they have searched out and learnt, the earth and those who dwell upon it shall be destroyed."

11   And these, they have no place of repentance for ever, because they have shown them what was hidden, and they are the damned: but as for thee, my son, the Lord of Spirits knows that thou art pure, and guiltless of this reproach concerning the secrets.

12   And He has destined thy name to be among the holy and will preserve thee amongst those who dwell on the earth. And has destined thy righteous seed both for kingship and for great honors, and from thy seed shall proceed a fountain of the righteous and holy without number for ever."

13   And after that he showed me the angels of punishment who are prepared to come and let loose all the powers of the waters which are

beneath in the earth in order to bring judgement and destruction on all who dwell on the earth.

14 And the Lord of Spirits gave commandment to the angels who were going forth that they should not cause the waters to rise but should hold them in check; for those angels were over the powers of the waters.

15 And I went away from the presence of Enoch.

Chapter 3 Judgement of Angels

1 And in those days the word of God came unto me, and He said unto me: "Noah, thy lot has come up before Me, a lot without blame, a lot of love and uprightness.

2 And now the angels are working, and when they have completed their task I will place My hand upon it and preserve it, and there shall come forth from it the seed of life, and a change shall set in so that the earth will not remain without inhabitant.

3 And I will make fast thy seed before me for ever and ever, and I will spread abroad those who dwell with thee: it shall not be unfruitful on the face of the earth, but it shall be blessed and multiply on the earth in the name of the Lord."

4 And He will imprison those angels, who have shown unrighteousness in that burning valley which my grandfather Enoch had formerly shown to me in the west among the mountains of gold and silver and iron and soft metal and tin.

5 And I saw that valley in which there was a great convulsion and a convulsion of the waters.

6 And when all this took place, from that fiery molten metal and from the convulsion thereof in that place, there was produced a smell of sulphur, and it was connected with those waters, and that valley of the angels who had led astray burned beneath that land.

7 And through its valleys proceed streams of fire where these angels are punished who had led astray those who dwell upon the earth.

8 But those waters shall in those days serve for the kings and the mighty and the exalted, and those who dwell on the earth, for the heal-

ing of the body, but for the punishment of the spirit; now their spirit is full of lust, that they may be punished in their body.

9   For they have denied the Lord of Spirits and see their punishment daily, and yet believe not in His name.

10   And in proportion as the burning of their bodies becomes severe a corresponding change shall take place in their spirit for ever and ever; for before the Lord of Spirits none shall utter an idle word.

11   For the judgement shall come upon them because they believe in the lust of their body and deny the Spirit of the Lord.

12   And those same waters will undergo a change in those days; for when those angels are punished in these waters, these water–springs shall change their temperature, and when the angels ascend, this water of the springs shall change and become cold.

13   And I heard Michael answering and saying: "This judgement wherewith the angels are judged is a testimony for the kings and the mighty who possess the earth.

14   Because these waters of judgement minister to the healing of the body of the kings and the lust of their body; therefore they will not see and will not believe that those waters will change and become a fire which burns for ever."

Chapter 4 Secrets of the Parables

1   And after that my grandfather Enoch gave me the teaching of all the secrets in the book in the Parables which had been given to him, and he put them together for me in the words of the book of the Parables.

2   And on that day Michael answered Raphael and said: "The power of the spirit transports and makes me to tremble because of the severity of the judgement of the secrets, the judgement of the angels: who can endure the severe judgement which has been executed, and before which they melt away?"

3   And Michael answered again, and said to Raphael: "Who is he whose heart is not softened concerning it, and whose reins are not trou-

bled by this word of judgement that has gone forth upon them because of those who have thus led them out?"

4   And it came to pass when he stood before the Lord of Spirits, Michael said thus to Raphael: "I will not take their part under the eye of the Lord; for the Lord of Spirits has been angry with them because they do as if they were the Lord.

Therefore all that is hidden shall come upon them for ever and ever; for neither angel nor man shall have his portion, but alone they have received their judgement for ever and ever."

5   And after this judgement they shall terrify and make them to tremble because they have shown this to those who dwell on the earth.

6   And behold the names of those angels: the first of them is Samjaza, the second Artaqifa, and the third Armen, the fourth Kokabel, the fifth Turael, the sixth Rumjal, the seventh Danjal, the eighth Neqael, the ninth Baraqel, the tenth Azazel, the eleventh Armaros, the twelfth Batarjal, the thirteenth Busasejal, the fourteenth Hananel, the fifteenth Turel, and the sixteenth Simapesiel, the seventeenth Jetrel, the eighteenth Tumael, the nineteenth Turel, the twentieth Rumael, the twenty–first Azazel.

7   And these are the chiefs of their angels and their names, and their chief ones over hundreds and over fifties and over tens.

8   The name of the first Jeqon: that is, the one who led astray the sons of God, and brought them down to the earth, and led them astray through the daughters of men.

9   And the second was named Asbeel: he imparted to the holy sons of God evil counsel, and led them astray so that they defiled their bodies with the daughters of men.

10   And the third was named Gadreel: he it is who showed the children of men all the blows of death, and he led astray Eve, and showed the shield and the coat of mail, and the sword for battle, and all the weapons of death to the children of men. And from his hand they have proceeded against those who dwell on the earth from that day and for evermore.

11 And the fourth was named Penemue: he taught the children of men the bitter and the sweet, and he taught them all the secrets of their wisdom. And he instructed mankind in writing with ink and paper, and thereby many sinned from eternity to eternity and until this day. For men were not created for such a purpose, to give confirmation to their good faith with pen and ink. For men were created exactly like the angels, to the intent that they should continue pure and righteous, and death, which destroys everything, could not have taken hold of them but through this their knowledge they are perishing, and through this power it is consuming men.

12 And the fifth was named Kasdeja: this is he who showed the children of men all the wicked smithings of spirits and demons, and the smitings of the embryo in the womb, that it may pass away, and the bites of the serpent, and the smitings which befall through the noontide heat the son of the serpent named Tabaet.

13 And this is the task of Kasbeel, the chief of the oath which he showed to the holy ones when he dwelt high above in glory, and its name is Biqa.

14 This angel requested Michael to show him the hidden name, that he might enunciate it in the oath, so that those might quake before that name and oath who revealed all that was in secret to the children of men.

15 And this is the power of this oath, for it is powerful and strong, and he placed this oath Akae in the hand of Michael.

16 These are the secrets of this oath and they are strong through his oath: The heaven was suspended before the world was created, and for ever.

17 And through it the earth was founded upon the water and from the secret recesses of the mountains come beautiful waters from the creation of the world and unto eternity.

18 And through that oath the sea was created and as its foundation He set for it the sand against the time of anger, and it dare not pass beyond it from the creation of the world unto eternity.

19   And through that oath are the depths made fast and abide and stir not from their place from eternity to eternity.

20   And through that oath the sun and moon complete their course and deviate not from their ordinance from eternity to eternity.

21   And through that oath the stars complete their course and He calls them by their names, and they answer Him from eternity to eternity.

22   And this oath is mighty over them and through it their paths are preserved and their course is not destroyed.

23   And there was great joy amongst them, and they blessed and glorified and extolled because the name of that Son of Man had been revealed unto them.

24   And he sat on the throne of His glory and the sum of judgement was given unto the Son of Man, and He caused the sinners to pass away and be destroyed from off the face of the earth, and those who have led the world astray.

25   With chains shall they be bound and in their assemblage place of destruction shall they be imprisoned, and all their works vanish from the face of the earth.

26   And from henceforth there shall be nothing corruptible; For that Son of Man has appeared and has seated himself on the throne of His glory.

27   All evil shall pass away before His face and the word of that Son of Man shall go forth and be strong before the Lord of Spirits.

14

Book 4: The Kingdom of Heaven

Chapter 1 Enoch is Taken

1   And it came to pass after this that his name during his lifetime was raised aloft to that Son of Man and to the Lord of Spirits from amongst those who dwell on the earth.

2   And he was raised aloft on the chariots of the spirit and his name vanished among them.

3   And from that day I was no longer numbered amongst them and He set me between the two winds, between the North and the West, where the angels took the cords to measure for me the place for the elect and righteous.

4   And there I saw the first fathers and the righteous who from the beginning dwell in that place.

5   And it came to pass after this that my spirit was translated and it ascended into the heavens I saw the holy sons of God.

6   They were stepping on flames of fire: Their garments were white and their faces shone like snow.

7   And I saw two streams of fire and the light of that fire shone like hyacinth, and I fell on my face before the Lord of Spirits.

8   And the angel Michael seized me by my right hand and lifted me up and led me forth into all the secrets, and he showed me all the secrets of righteousness.

9   And he showed me all the secrets of the ends of the heaven, and all the chambers of all the stars, and all the luminaries, Whence they proceed before the face of the holy ones.

10   And he translated my spirit into the heaven of heavens and I saw there as it were a structure built of crystals and between those crystals tongues of living fire.

11   And my spirit saw the girdle which girt that house of fire and on its four sides were streams full of living fire, and they girt that house.

12   And round about were Seraphin, Cherubic, and Ophannin: And these are they who sleep not and guard the throne of His glory.

13   And I saw angels who could not be counted. A thousand thousands and ten thousand times ten thousand encircling that house.

14   And Michael, and Raphael, and Gabriel, and Phanuel, and the holy angels who are above the heavens go in and out of that house.

15   And they came forth from that house, and Michael and Gabriel, Raphael, and Phanuel, and many holy angels without number.

16   And with them the Head of Days, His head white and pure as wool, and His raiment indescribable.

17   And I fell on my face and my whole body became relaxed, and my spirit was transfigured; and I cried with a loud voice with the spirit of power and blessed and glorified and extolled.

18   And these blessings which went forth out of my mouth were well pleasing before that Head of Days.

19   And that Head of Days came with Michael and Gabriel, Raphael, and Phanuel, thousands and ten thousands of angels without number.

20   And He came to me and greeted me with His voice, and said unto me: "This is the Son of Man who is born unto righteousness, and righteousness abides over Him, and the righteousness of the Head of Days forsakes Him not."

21   And he said unto me: "He proclaims unto thee peace in the name of the world to come; for from hence has proceeded peace since the creation of the world, and so shall it be unto thee for ever and for ever and ever.

22   And all shall walk in his ways since righteousness never forsaketh Him.

23   With Him will be their dwelling places, and with Him their heritage, and they shall not be separated from Him for ever and ever and ever.

24   And so there shall be length of days with that Son of Man and the righteous shall have peace and an upright way in the name of the Lord of Spirits for ever and ever.

Chapter 2 The Luminaries

1   The book of the courses of the luminaries of the heaven, the relations of each, according to their classes, their dominion and their seasons, according to their names and places of origin, and according to their months, which Uriel, the holy angel, who was with me, who is their guide showed me.

2   And he showed me all their laws exactly as they are, and how it is with regard to all the years of the world and unto eternity, till the new creation is accomplished which dureth till eternity.

3   And this is the first law of the luminaries: the luminary the sun has its rising in the eastern portals of the heaven, and its setting in the western portals of the heaven.

4   And I saw six portals in which the sun rises, and six portals in which the sun sets and the moon rises and sets in these portals, and the leaders of the stars and those whom they lead: six in the east and six in the west, and all following each other in accurately corresponding order: also many windows to the right and left of these portals.

5   And first there goes forth the great luminary, named the sun, and his circumference is like the circumference of the heaven, and he is quite filled with illuminating and heating fire.

6   The chariot on which he ascends, the wind drives, and the sun goes down from the heaven and returns through the north in order to reach the east, and is so guided that he comes to the appropriate portal and shines in the face of the heaven.

7   In this way he rises in the first month in the great portal, which is the fourth. And in that fourth portal from which the sun rises in the

first month are twelve window–openings, from which proceed a flame when they are opened in their season.

8   When the sun rises in the heaven, he comes forth through that fourth portal thirty mornings in succession, and sets accurately in the fourth portal in the west of the heaven.

9   And during this period the day becomes daily longer and the night nightly shorter to the thirtieth morning.

10   On that day the day is longer than the night by a ninth part, and the day amounts exactly to ten parts and the night to eight parts.

11   And the sun rises from that fourth portal, and sets in the fourth and returns to the fifth portal of the east thirty mornings and rises from it and sets in the fifth portal.

12   And then the day becomes longer by two parts and amounts to eleven parts, and the night becomes shorter and amounts to seven parts.

13   And it returns to the east and enters into the sixth portal, and rises and sets in the sixth portal one–and–thirty mornings on account of its sign.

14   On that day the day becomes longer than the night, and the day becomes double the night, and the day becomes twelve parts, and the night is shortened and becomes six parts.

15   And the sun mounts up to make the day shorter and the night longer, and the sun returns to the east and enters into the sixth portal and rises from it and sets thirty mornings.

16   And when thirty mornings are accomplished, the day decreases by exactly one part, and becomes eleven parts, and the night seven.

17   And the sun goes forth from that sixth portal in the west, and goes to the east and rises in the fifth portal for thirty mornings, and sets in the west again in the fifth western portal.

18   On that day the day decreases by two parts, and amounts to ten parts and the night to eight parts.

19   And the sun goes forth from that fifth portal and sets in the fifth portal of the west, and rises in the fourth portal for one–and–thirty mornings on account of its sign, and sets in the west.

20   On that day the day is equalized with the night, and the night amounts to nine parts and the day to nine parts.

21   And the sun rises from that portal and sets in the west, and returns to the east and rises thirty mornings in the third portal and sets in the west in the third portal.

22   And on that day the night becomes longer than the day, and night becomes longer than night, and day shorter than day till the thirtieth morning, and the night amounts exactly to ten parts and the day to eight parts.

23   And the sun rises from that third portal and sets in the third portal in the west and returns to the east and for thirty mornings rises in the second portal in the east, and in like manner sets in the second portal in the west of the heaven.

24   And on that day the night amounts to eleven parts and the day to seven parts.

25   And the sun rises on that day from that second portal and sets in the west in the second portal, and returns to the east into the first portal for one–and–thirty mornings, and sets in the first portal in the west of the heaven.

26   And on that day the night becomes longer and amounts to the double of the day: and the night amounts exactly to twelve parts and the day to six.

27   And the sun has traversed the divisions of his orbit and turns again on those divisions of his orbit, and enters that portal thirty mornings and sets also in the west opposite to it.

28   And on that night has the night decreased in length by a ninth part, and the night has become eleven parts and the day seven parts.

29   And the sun has returned and entered into the second portal in the east, and returns on those his divisions of his orbit for thirty mornings, rising and setting.

30   And on that day the night decreases in length, and the night amounts to ten parts and the day to eight.

31   And on that day the sun rises from that portal, and sets in the west,

and returns to the east, and rises in the third portal for one–and–thirty mornings, and sets in the west of the heaven.

32   On that day the night decreases and amounts to nine parts, and the day to nine parts, and the night is equal to the day and the year is exactly as to its days three hundred and sixty–four.

33   And the length of the day and of the night, and the shortness of the day and of the night arise–through the course of the sun these distinctions are made.

34   So it comes that its course becomes daily longer, and its course nightly shorter.

35   And this is the law and the course of the sun, and his return as often as he returns sixty times and rises for ever and ever.

36   And that which rises is the great luminary, and is so named according to its appearance, according as the Lord commanded.

37   As he rises, so he sets and decreases not, and rests not, but runs day and night, and his light is sevenfold brighter than that of the moon; but as regards size they are both equal.

38   And after this law I saw another law dealing with the smaller luminary, which is named the Moon.

39   And her circumference is like the circumference of the heaven, and her chariot in which she rides is driven by the wind, and light is given to her in measure.

40   And her rising and setting change every month and her days are like the days of the sun, and when her light is uniform it amounts to the seventh part of the light of the sun.

41   And thus she rises. And her first phase in the east comes forth on the thirtieth morning: and on that day she becomes visible and constitutes for you the first phase of the moon on the thirtieth day together with the sun in the portal where the sun rises.

42   And the one half of her goes forth by a seventh part, and her whole circumference is empty, without light, with the exception of one–seventh part of it, the fourteenth part of her light.

43   And when she receives one–seventh part of the half of her light, her light amounts to one–seventh part and the half thereof.

44   And she sets with the sun, and when the sun rises the moon rises with him and receives the half of one part of light, and in that night in the beginning of her morning in the commencement of the lunar day the moon sets with the sun, and is invisible that night with the fourteen parts and the half of one of them.

45   And she rises on that day with exactly a seventh part, and comes forth and recedes from the rising of the sun, and in her remaining days she becomes bright in the thirteen parts.

46   And I saw another course, a law for her, how according to that law she performs her monthly revolution.

47   And all these Uriel, the holy angel who is the leader of them all showed to me, and their positions, and I wrote down their positions as he showed them to me, and I wrote down their months as they were, and the appearance of their lights till fifteen days were accomplished.

48   In single seventh parts she accomplishes all her light in the east, and in single seventh parts accomplishes all her darkness in the west.

49   And in certain months she alters her settings, and in certain months she pursues her own peculiar course.

50   In two months the moon sets with the sun: in those two middle portals the third and the fourth. She goes forth for seven days, and turns about and returns again through the portal where the sun rises, and accomplishes all her light and she recedes from the sun, and in eight days enters the sixth portal from which the sun goes forth.

51   And when the sun goes forth from the fourth portal she goes forth seven days, until she goes forth from the fifth and turns back again in seven days into the fourth portal and accomplishes all her light: and she recedes and enters into the first portal in eight days.

52   And she returns again in seven days into the fourth portal from which the sun goes forth.

53   Thus I saw their position, how the moons rose and the sun set in those days.

54   And if five years are added together the sun has an overplus of thirty days, and all the days which accrue to it for one of those five years, when they are full, amount to 364 days.

55   And the overplus of the sun and of the stars amounts to six days: in 5 years 6 days every year come to 30 days: and the moon falls behind the sun and stars to the number of 30 days.

56   And the sun and the stars bring in all the years exactly, so that they do not advance or delay their position by a single day unto eternity; but complete the years with perfect justice in 364 days.

57   In 3 years there are 1,092 days, and in 5 years 1,820 days, so that in 8 years there are 2,912 days.

58   For the moon alone the days amount in 3 years to 1,062 days, and in 5 years she falls 50 days behind to the sum there is 5 to be added 62 days.

59   And in 5 years there are 1,770 days, so that for the moon the days 6 in 8 years amount to 21,832 days.

60   For in 8 years she falls behind to the amount of 80 days, all the 17 days she falls behind in 8 years are 80.

61   And the year is accurately completed in conformity with their world–stations and the stations of the sun, which rise from the portals through which it rises and sets 30 days.

62   And the leaders of the heads of the thousands, who are placed over the whole creation and over all the stars, have also to do with the four intercalary days, being inseparable from their office, according to the reckoning of the year, and these render service on the four days which are not reckoned in the reckoning of the year.

63   And owing to them men go wrong therein, for those luminaries truly render service on the world–stations, one in the first portal, one in the third portal of the heaven, one in the fourth portal, and one in the sixth portal, and the exactness of the year is accomplished through its separate three hundred and sixty–four stations.

64   For the signs and the times and the years and the days the angel Uriel showed to me, whom the Lord of glory hath set for ever over all

the luminaries of the heaven, in the heaven and in the world that they should rule on the face of the heaven and be seen on the earth and be leaders for the day and the night and all the ministering creatures which make their revolution in all the chariots of the heaven.

65   In like manner twelve doors Uriel showed me open in the circumference of the suns chariot in the heaven, through which the rays of the sun break forth: and from them is warmth diffused over the earth, when they are opened at their appointed seasons.

66   And for the winds and the spirit of the dew when they are opened, standing open in the heavens at the ends.

67   As for the twelve portals in the heaven at the ends of the earth, out of which go forth the sun, moon, and stars, and all the works of heaven in the east and in the west.

68   There are many windows open to the left and right of them, and one window at its season produces warmth, corresponding to those doors from which the stars come forth according as He has commanded them and wherein they set corresponding to their number.

69   And I saw chariots in the heaven, running in the world, above those portals in which revolve the stars that never set.

70   And one is larger than all the rest and it is that that makes its course through the entire world.

71   And at the ends of the earth I saw twelve portals open to all the quarters from which the winds go forth and blow over the earth.

72   Three of them are open on the face of the heavens, and three in the west, and three on the right of the heaven, and three on the left.

73   And the three first are those of the east, and three are of the north, and three after those on the left of the south, and three of the west.

74   Through four of these come winds of blessing and prosperity and from those eight come hurtful winds: when they are sent, they bring destruction on all the earth and on the water upon it, and on all who dwell thereon, and on everything which is in the water and on the land.

75   And the first wind from those portals, called the east wind, comes forth through the first portal which is in the east, inclining towards the south: from it come forth desolation, drought, heat, and destruction.

76   And through the second portal in the middle comes what is fitting, and from it there come rain and fruitfulness and prosperity and dew; and through the third portal which lies toward the north come cold and drought.

77   And after these come forth the south winds through three portals: through the first portal of them inclining to the east comes forth a hot wind.

78   And through the middle portal next to it there come forth fragrant smells, and dew and rain, and prosperity and health.

79   And through the third portal lying to the west come forth dew and rain, locusts and desolation.

80   And after these the north winds: from the seventh portal in the east come dew and rain, locusts and desolation.

81   And from the middle portal come in a direct direction health and rain and dew and prosperity; and through the third portal in the west come cloud and hoarfrost, and snow and rain, and dew and locusts.

82   And after these four are the west winds: through the first portal adjoining the north come forth dew and hoarfrost, and cold and snow and frost.

83   And from the middle portal come forth dew and rain, and prosperity and blessing; and through the last portal which adjoins the south come forth drought and desolation, and burning and destruction.

84   And the twelve portals of the four quarters of the heaven are therewith completed and all their laws and all their plagues and all their benefactions have I shown to thee, my son Methuselah.

85   And the first quarter is called the east because it is the first. And the second, the south, because the Most High will descend there, yea, there in quite a special sense will He who is blessed for ever descend.

86   And the west quarter is named the diminished because there all the luminaries of the heaven wane and go down.

87   And the fourth quarter named the north, is divided into three parts: the first of them is for the dwelling of men: and the second contains seas of water, and the abysses and forests and rivers, and darkness and clouds; and the third part contains the garden of righteousness.

88   I saw seven high mountains, higher than all the mountains which are on the earth and thence comes forth hoarfrost, and days, seasons, and years pass away.

89   I saw seven rivers on the earth larger than all the rivers: one of them coming from the west pours its waters into the Great Sea.

90   And these two come from the north to the sea and pour their waters into the Erythraean Sea in the east.

91   And the remaining, four come forth on the side of the north to their own sea, two of them to the Erythraean Sea, and two into the Great Sea and discharge themselves there and some say, into the desert.

92   Seven great islands I saw in the sea and in the mainland: two in the mainland and five in the Great Sea.

93   And the names of the sun are the following: the first Orjares, and the second Tomas.

94   And the moon has four names: the first name is Asonja, the second Ebla, the third Benase, and the fourth Erae.

95   These are the two great luminaries: their circumference is like the circumference of the heaven, and the size of the circumference of both is alike.

96   In the circumference of the sun there are seven portions of light which are added to it more than to the moon, and in definite measures it is s transferred till the seventh portion of the sun is exhausted.

97   And they set and enter the portals of the west, and make their revolution by the north, and come forth through the eastern portals on the face of the heaven.

98   And when the moon rises one-fourteenth part appears in the heaven: the light becomes full in her : on the fourteenth day she accomplishes her light.

99   And fifteen parts of light are transferred to her till the fifteenth day her light is accomplished, according to the sign of the year, and she becomes fifteen parts, and the moon grows by fourteenth parts.

100   And in her waning decreases on the first day to fourteen parts of her light, on the second to thirteen parts of light, on the third to twelve, on the fourth to eleven, on the fifth to ten, on the sixth to nine, on the seventh to eight, on the eighth to seven, on the ninth to six, on the tenth to five, on the eleventh to four, on the twelfth to three, on the thirteenth to two, on the fourteenth to the half of a seventh, and all her remaining light disappears wholly on the fifteenth.

101   And in certain months the month has twenty-nine days and once twenty
-eight.

102   And Uriel showed me another law: when light is transferred to the moon, and on which side it is transferred to her by the sun.

103   During all the period during which the moon is growing in her light, she is transferring it to herself when opposite to the sun during fourteen daysher light is accomplished in the heaven, and when she is illumined throughout, her light is accomplished full in the heaven.

104   And on the first day she is called the new moon, for on that day the light rises upon her. She becomes full moon exactly on the day when the sun sets in the west, and from the east she rises at night, and the moon shines the whole night through till the sun rises over against her and the moon is seen over against the sun.

105   On the side whence the light of the moon comes forth, there again she wanes till all the light vanishes and all the days of the month are at an end and her circumference is empty, void of light.

106   And three months she makes of thirty days, and at her time she makes three months of twenty-nine days each, in which she accom-

plishes her waning in the first period of time, and in the first portal for one hundred and seventy–seven days.

107   And in the time of her going out she appears for three months thirty days each, and for three months she appears twenty–nine each.

108   At night she appears like a man for twenty days each time, and by day she appears like the heaven, and there is nothing else in her save her light.

109   And now, my son, I have shown thee everything, and the law of all the stars of the heaven is completed.

110   And he showed me all the laws of these for every day, and for every season of bearing rule, and for every year, and for its going forth, and for the order prescribed to it every month and every week: And the waning of the moon which takes place in the sixth portal: for in this 4 sixth portal her light is accomplished.

111   And after that there is the beginning of the waning which takes place in the first portal in its season, till one hundred and seventy–seven days are accomplished: reckoned according to weeks, twenty–five and two days.

112   She falls behind the sun and the order of the stars exactly five days in the course of one period, and when this place which thou seest has been traversed.

113   Such is the picture and sketch of every luminary which Uriel the archangel, who is their leader, showed unto me.

Chapter 3 Heavenly Tablets

1   And in those days the angel Uriel answered and said to me: "Behold, I have shown thee everything Enoch and I have revealed everything to thee that thou shouldst see this sun and this moon, and the leaders of the stars of the heaven and all those who turn them, their tasks and times and departures.

2   And in the days of the sinners the years shall be shortened and their seed shall be tardy on their lands and fields.

3   And all things on the earth shall alter and shall not appear in their time: The rain shall be kept back and the heaven shall withhold it.

4   And in those times the fruits of the earth shall be backward and shall not grow in their time, and the fruits of the trees shall be withheld in their time.

5   And the moon shall alter her order and not appear at her time.

6   And in those days the sun shall be seen and he shall journey in the evening on the extremity of the great chariot in the west and shall shine more brightly than accords with the order of light.

7   And many chiefs of the stars shall transgress the order and these shall alter their orbits and tasks and not appear at the seasons prescribed to them.

8   And the whole order of the stars shall be concealed from the sinners and the thoughts of those on the earth shall err concerning them. And they shall be altered from all their ways. Yea, they shall err and take them to be gods.

9   And evil shall be multiplied upon them, and punishment shall come upon them so as to destroy all."

10   And He said unto me: "Observe, Enoch, these heavenly tablets and read what is written thereon, and mark every individual fact."

11   And I observed the heavenly tablets, and read everything which was written and understood everything, and read the book of all the deeds of mankind, and of all the children of flesh that shall be upon the earth to the remotest generations.

12   And forthwith I blessed the great Lord the King of glory for ever, in that He has made all the works of the world.

13   And I extolled the Lord because of His patience and blessed Him because of the children of men.

14   And after that I said: "Blessed is the man who dies in righteousness and goodness concerning whom there is no book of unrighteousness written, and against whom no day of judgement shall be found."

15   And those seven holy ones brought me and placed me on the earth before the door of my house, and said to me: "Declare everything

to thy son Methuselah, and show to all thy children that no flesh is righteous in the sight of the Lord, for He is their Creator.

16 One year we will leave thee with thy son, till thou givest thy commands, that thou mayest teach thy children and record for them, and testify to all thy children; and in the second year they shall take thee from their midst.

17 Let thy heart be strong, for the good shall announce righteousness to the good; The righteous with the righteous shall rejoice and shall offer congratulation to one another.

18 But the sinners shall die with the sinners and the apostate go down with the apostate.

19 And those who practice righteousness shall die on account of the deeds of men and be taken away on account of the doings of the godless.

20 And in those days they ceased to speak to me, and I came to my people, blessing the Lord of the world.

Chapter 4
One Year to Record

1 And now, my son Methuselah, all these things I am recounting to thee and writing down for thee! and I have revealed to thee everything, and given thee books concerning all these: so preserve, my son Methuselah, the books from thy fathers hand, and see that thou deliver them to the generations of the world.

2 I have given wisdom to thee and to thy children and thy children that shall be to thee, that they may give it to their children for generations, this wisdom that passeth their thought.

3 And those who understand it shall not sleep but shall listen with the ear that they may learn this wisdom and it shall please those that eat thereof better than good food.

4 Blessed are all the righteous, blessed are all those who walk in the way of righteousness and sin not as the sinners.

5   In the reckoning of all their days in which the sun traverses the heaven, entering into and departing from the portals for thirty days with the heads of thousands of the order of the stars, together with the four which are intercalated which divide the four portions of the year, which lead them and enter with them four days.

6   Owing to them men shall be at fault and not reckon them in the whole reckoning of the year: yea, men shall be at fault, and not recognize them accurately.

7   For they belong to the reckoning of the year and are truly recorded for ever, one in the first portal and one in the third, and one in the fourth and one in the sixth, and the year is completed in three hundred and sixty–four days.

8   And the account thereof is accurate and the recorded reckoning thereof exact; for the luminaries, and months and festivals, and years and days, has Uriel shown and revealed to me, to whom the Lord of the whole creation of the world hath subjected the host of heaven.

9   And he has power over night and day in the heaven to cause the light to give light to men, sun, moon, and stars, and all the powers of the heaven which revolve in their circular chariots.

10   And these are the orders of the stars, which set in their places, and in their seasons and festivals and months.

11   And these are the names of those who lead them, who watch that they enter at their times, in their orders, in their seasons, in their months, in their periods of dominion, and in their positions.

12   Their four leaders who divide the four parts of the year enter first; and after them the twelve leaders of the orders who divide the months; and for the three hundred and sixty there are heads over thousands who divide the days; and for the four intercalary days there are the leaders which sunder the four parts of the year.

13   And these heads over thousands are intercalated between leader and leader, each behind a station, but their leaders make the division.

14   And these are the names of the leaders who divide the four parts of the year which are ordained: Milkiel, Helemmelek, and Melejal, and Narel.

15   And the names of those who lead them: Adnarel, and Ijasusael, and Elomeel - these three follow the leaders of the orders, and there is one that follows the three leaders of the orders which follow those leaders of stations that divide the four parts of the year.

16   In the beginning of the year Melkejal rises first and rules, who is named Tamaini and sun, and all the days of his dominion whilst he bears rule are ninety
—one days.

17   And these are the signs of the days which are to be seen on earth in the days of his dominion: sweat, and heat, and calms; and all the trees bear fruit, and leaves are produced on all the trees, and the harvest of wheat, and the rose
—flowers, and all the flowers which come forth in the field, but the trees of the winter season become withered.

18   And these are the names of the leaders which are under them: Berkael, Zelebsel, and another who is added a head of a thousand, called Hilujaseph: and the days of the dominion of this are at an end.

19   The next leader after him is Helemmelek, whom one names the shining sun, and all the days of his light are ninety—one days. And these are the signs of days on the earth: glowing heat and dryness, and the trees ripen their fruits and produce all their fruits ripe and ready, and the sheep pair and become pregnant, and all the fruits of the earth are gathered in, and everything that is in the fields, and the winepress: these things take place in the days of his dominion.

20   These are the names, and the orders, and the leaders of those heads of thousands: Gidaljal, Keel, and Heel, and the name of the head of a thousand which is added to them, Asfael: and the days of his dominion are at an end.

Chapter 5 Visions

1   And now, my son Methuselah, I will show thee all my visions which I have seen, recounting them before thee.

2   Two visions I saw before I took a wife, and the one was quite unlike the other. The first when I was learning to write: the second before I took thy mother I saw a terrible vision.

3   And regarding them I prayed to the Lord. I had laid me down in the house of my grandfather Mahalaleel I saw in a vision how the heaven collapsed and was borne off and fell to the earth.

4   And when it fell to the earth I saw how the earth was swallowed up in a great abyss, and mountains were suspended on mountains, and hills sank down on hills, and high trees were rent from their stems and hurled down and sunk in the abyss.

5   And thereupon a word fell into my mouth and I lifted up to cry aloud, and said: "The earth is destroyed!"

6   And my grandfather Mahalaleel waked me as I lay near him, and said unto me: "Why dost thou cry so my son, and why dost thou make such lamentation?"

7   And I recounted to him the whole vision which I had seen, and he said unto me: "A terrible thing hast thou seen, my son, and of grave moment is thy dream vision as to the secrets if all the sin of the earth: it must sink into the abyss and be destroyed with a great destruction.

8   And now, my son, arise and make petition to the Lord of glory, since thou art a believer that a remnant may remain on the earth, and that He may not destroy the whole earth. My son, from heaven all this will come upon the earth, and upon the earth there will be great destruction."

9   After that I arose and prayed and implored and besought, and wrote down my prayer for the generations of the world, and I will show everything to thee, my son Methuselah.

10   And when I had gone forth below and seen the heaven and the sun rising in the east, and the moon setting in the west, and a few stars, and the whole earth, and everything as He had known it in the beginning then I blessed the Lord of judgement and extolled Him because He

had made the sun to go forth from the windows of the east, and He ascended and rose on the face of the heaven, and set out and kept traversing the path shown unto Him.

11   And I lifted up my hands in righteousness and blessed the Holy and Great One and spake with the breath of my mouth, and with the tongue of flesh which God has made for the children of the flesh of men that they should speak therewith, and He gave them breath and a tongue and a mouth that they should speak therewith:

12   "Blessed be Thou, O Lord, King, Great and mighty in Thy greatness, Lord of the whole creation of the heaven, King of kings and God of the whole world.

13   And Thy power and kingship and greatness abide for ever and ever, and throughout all generations Thy dominion; and all the heavens are Thy throne for ever, and the whole earth Thy footstool for ever and ever.

14   For Thou hast made and Thou rulest all things and nothing is too hard for Thee.

15   Wisdom departs not from the place of Thy throne nor turns away from Thy presence.

16   And Thou knowest and seest and hearest everything and there is nothing hidden from Thee for Thou seest everything.

17   And now the angels of Thy heavens are guilty of trespass and upon the flesh of men abideth Thy wrath until the great day of judgement.

18   And now, O God and Lord and Great King, I implore and beseech Thee to fulfil my prayer to leave me a posterity on earth and not destroy all the flesh of man and make the earth without inhabitant so that there should be an eternal destruction.

19   And now, my Lord, destroy from the earth the flesh which has aroused Thy wrath but the flesh of righteousness and uprightness establish as a plant of the eternal seed and hide not Thy face from the prayer of Thy servant, O Lord."

20   And after this I saw another dream, and I will show the whole dream to thee, my son.

21   And Enoch lifted up and spake to his son Methuselah: "To thee, my son, will I speak: hear my words—incline thine ear to the dream—vision of thy father.

22   Before I took thy mother Edna, I saw in a vision on my bed, and behold a bull came forth from the earth, and that bull was white; and after it came forth a heifer, and along with this came forth two bulls, one of them black and the other red.

23   And that black bull gored the red one and pursued him over the earth, and thereupon I could no longer see that red bull.

24   But that black bull grew and that heifer went with him, and I saw that many oxen proceeded from him which resembled and followed him.

25   And that cow, that first one, went from the presence of that first bull in order to seek that red one, but found him not, and lamented with a great lamentation over him and sought him.

26   And I looked till that first bull came to her and quieted her, and from that time onward she cried no more.

27   And after that she bore another white bull, and after him she bore many bulls and black cows.

28   And I saw in my sleep that white bull likewise grow and become a great white bull, and from him proceeded many white bulls, and they resembled him. And they began to beget many white bulls, which resembled them, one following the other, many.

29   And again I saw with mine eyes as I slept, and I saw the heaven above, and behold a star fell from heaven, and it arose and eat and pastured amongst those oxen.

30   And after that I saw the large and the black oxen, and behold they all changed their stalls and pastures and their cattle, and began to live with each other.

31   And again I saw in the vision, and looked towards the heaven, and behold I saw many stars descend and cast themselves down from

heaven to that first star, and they became bulls amongst those cattle and pastured with them amongst them.

32   And I looked at them and saw, and behold they all let out their privy members, like horses, and began to cover the cows of the oxen, and they all became pregnant and bare elephants, camels, and asses.

33   And all the oxen feared them and were affrighted at them, and began to bite with their teeth and to devour, and to gore with their horns.

34   And they began, moreover, to devour those oxen; and behold all the children of the earth began to tremble and quake before them and to flee from them.

35   And again I saw how they began to gore each other and to devour each other, and the earth began to cry aloud.

36   And I raised mine eyes again to heaven, and I saw in the vision, and behold there came forth from heaven beings who were like white men: and four went forth from that place and three with them.

37   And those three that had last come forth grasped me by my hand and took me up away from the generations of the earth, and raised me up to a lofty place, and showed me a tower raised high above the earth and all the hills were lower.

38   And one said unto me: "Remain here till thou seest everything that befalls those elephants, camels, and asses, and the stars and the oxen, and all of them."

39   And I saw one of those four who had come forth first, and he seized that first star which had fallen from the heaven, and bound it hand and foot and cast it into an abyss.

40   Now that abyss was narrow and deep, and horrible and dark.

41   And one of them drew a sword, and gave it to those elephants and camels and asses: then they began to smite each other, and the whole earth quaked because of them.

42   And as I was beholding in the vision, lo, one of those four who had come forth stoned them from heaven, and gathered and took all the

great stars whose privy members were like those of horses and bound them all hand and foot, and cast them in an abyss of the earth.

43   And one of those four went to that white bull and instructed him in a secret without his being terrified: he was born a bull and became a man, and built for himself a great vessel and dwelt thereon; and three bulls dwelt with him in that vessel and they were covered in.

44   And again I raised mine eyes towards heaven and saw a lofty roof, with seven water torrents thereon and those torrents flowed with much water into an enclosure.

45   And I saw again, and behold fountains were opened on the surface of that great enclosure, and that water began to swell and rise upon the surface and I saw that enclosure till all its surface was covered with water.

46   And the water, the darkness, and mist increased upon it; and as I looked at the height of that water, that water had risen above the height of that enclosure, and was streaming over that enclosure, and it stood upon the earth.

47   And all the cattle of that enclosure were gathered together until I saw how they sank and were swallowed up and perished in that water.

48   But that vessel floated on the water, while all the oxen and elephants and camels and asses sank to the bottom with all the animals, so that I could no longer see them, and they were not able to escape, perished and sank into the depths.

49   And again I saw in the vision till those water torrents were removed from that high roof, and the chasms of the earth were leveled up and other abysses were opened.

50   Then the water began to run down into these, till the earth became visible; but that vessel settled on the earth, and the darkness retired and light appeared.

51   But that white bull which had become a man came out of that vessel, and the three bulls with him, and one of those three was white like that bull, and one of them was red as blood, and one black: and that white bull departed from them.

52   And they began to bring forth beasts of the field and birds, so that there arose different genera: lions, tigers, wolves, dogs, hyenas, wild boars, foxes, squirrels, swine, falcons, vultures, kites, eagles, and ravens; and among them was born a white bull.

53   And they began to bite one another; but that white bull which was born amongst them begat a wild ass and a white bull with it, and the wild asses multiplied. But that bull which was born from him begat a black wild boar and a white sheep; and the former begat many boars, but that sheep begat twelve sheep.

54   And when those twelve sheep had grown, they gave up one of them to the asses, and those asses again gave up that sheep to the wolves, and that sheep grew up among the wolves.

55   And the Lord brought the eleven sheep to live with it and to pasture with it among the wolves: and they multiplied and became many flocks of sheep.

56   And the wolves began to fear them, and they oppressed them until they destroyed - cry aloud on account of their little ones, and to complain unto their Lord.

57   And a sheep which had been saved from the wolves fled and escaped to the wild asses; and I saw the sheep how they lamented and cried, and besought their Lord with all their might, till that Lord of the sheep descended at the voice of the sheep from a lofty abode, and came to them and pastured them.

58   And He called that sheep which had escaped the wolves, and spake with it concerning the wolves that it should admonish them not to touch the sheep.

59   And the sheep went to the wolves according to the word of the Lord, and another sheep met it and went with it, and the two went and entered together into the assembly of those wolves, and spake with them and admonished them not to touch the sheep from henceforth.

60   And thereupon I saw the wolves, and how they oppressed the sheep exceedingly with all their power; and the sheep cried aloud.

61   And the Lord came to the sheep and they began to smite those wolves and the wolves began to make lamentation; but the sheep became quiet and forthwith ceased to cry out.

62   And I saw the sheep till they departed from amongst the wolves; but the eyes of the wolves were blinded, and those wolves departed in pursuit of the sheep with all their power.

63   And the Lord of the sheep went with them, as their leader, and all His sheep followed Him: and his face was dazzling and glorious and terrible to behold.

64   But the wolves began to pursue those sheep till they reached a sea of water. And that sea was divided, and the water stood on this side and on that before their face, and their Lord led them and placed Himself between them and the wolves.

65   And as those wolves did not yet see the sheep, they proceeded into the midst of that sea, and the wolves followed the sheep, and those wolves ran after them into that sea.

66   And when they saw the Lord of the sheep, they turned to flee before His face, but that sea gathered itself together, and became as it had been created, and the water swelled and rose till it covered those wolves.

67   And I saw till all the wolves who pursued those sheep perished and were drowned.

68   But the sheep escaped from that water and went forth into a wilderness, where there was no water and no grass; and they began to open their eyes and to see; and I saw the Lord of the sheep pasturing them and giving them water and grass, and that sheep going and leading them.

69   And that sheep ascended to the summit of that lofty rock, and the Lord of the sheep sent it to them.

70   And after that I saw the Lord of the sheep who stood before them, and His appearance was great and terrible and majestic, and all those sheep saw Him and were afraid before His face.

71 And they all feared and trembled because of Him, and they cried to that sheep with them which was amongst them: "We are not able to stand before our Lord or to behold Him."

72 And that sheep which led them again ascended to the summit of that rock, but the sheep began to be blinded and to wander from the way which he had showed them, but that sheep wot not thereof.

73 And the Lord of the sheep was wrathful exceedingly against them, and that sheep discovered it, and went down from the summit of the rock, and came to the sheep, and found the greatest part of them blinded and fallen away.

74 And when they saw it they feared and trembled at its presence, and desired to return to their folds.

75 And that sheep took other sheep with it, and came to those sheep which had fallen away, and began to slay them; and the sheep feared its presence, and thus that sheep brought back those sheep that had fallen away, and they returned to their folds.

76 And I saw in this vision till that sheep became a man and built a house for the Lord of the sheep, and placed all the sheep in that house.

77 And I saw till this sheep which had met that sheep which led them fell asleep: and I saw till all the great sheep perished and little ones arose in their place, and they came to a pasture, and approached a stream of water.

78 Then that sheep, their leader which had become a man, withdrew from them and fell asleep, and all the sheep sought it and cried over it with a great crying.

79 And I saw till they left off crying for that sheep and crossed that stream of water, and there arose the two sheep as leaders in the place of those which had led them and fallen asleep.

80 And I saw till the sheep came to a goodly place, and a pleasant and glorious land, and I saw till those sheep were satisfied; and that house stood amongst them in the pleasant land.

81   And sometimes their eyes were opened, and sometimes blinded, till another sheep arose and led them and brought them all back, and their eyes were opened.

82   And the dogs and the foxes and the wild boars began to devour those sheep till the Lord of the sheep raised up another sheep a ram from their midst, which led them. And that ram began to butt on either side those dogs, foxes, and wild boars till he had destroyed them all.

83   And that sheep whose eyes were opened saw that ram, which was amongst the sheep, till it forsook its glory and began to butt those sheep and trampled upon them, and behaved itself unseemly.

84   And the Lord of the sheep sent the lamb to another lamb and raised it to being a ram and leader of the sheep instead of that ram which had forsaken its glory.

85   And it went to it and spake to it alone, and raised it to being a ram, and made it the prince and leader of the sheep; but during all these things those dogs oppressed the sheep.

86   And the first ram pursued that second ram, and that second ram arose and fled before it; and I saw till those dogs pulled down the first ram.

87   And that second ram arose and led the little sheep. And those sheep grew and multiplied; but all the dogs, and foxes, and wild boars feared and fled before it, and that ram butted and killed the wild beasts, and those wild beasts had no longer any power among the 49sheep and robbed them no more of ought.

88   And that ram begat many sheep and fell asleep; and a little sheep became ram in its stead, and became prince and leader of those sheep and that house became great and broad, and it was built for those sheep.

89   A tower lofty and great was built on the house for the Lord of the sheep, and that house was low, but the tower was elevated and lofty, and the Lord of the sheep stood on that tower and they offered a full table before Him.

90   And again I saw those sheep that they again erred and went many

ways, and forsook that their house, and the Lord of the sheep called some from amongst the sheep and sent them to the sheep, but the sheep began to slay them.

91   And one of them was saved and was not slain, and it sped away and cried aloud over the sheep; and they sought to slay it, but the Lord of the sheep saved it from the sheep, and brought it up to me, and caused it to dwell there.

92   And many other sheep He sent to those sheep to testify unto them and lament over them.

93   And after that I saw that when they forsook the house of the Lord and His tower they fell away entirely, and their eyes were blinded; and I saw the Lord of the sheep how He wrought much slaughter amongst them in their herds until those sheep invited that slaughter and betrayed His place.

94   And He gave them over into the hands of the lions and tigers, and wolves and hyenas, and into the hand of the foxes, and to all the wild beasts, and those wild beasts began to tear in pieces those sheep.

95   And I saw that He forsook that their house and their tower and gave them all into the hand of the lions, to tear and devour them, into the hand of all the wild beasts.

96   And I began to cry aloud with all my power, and to appeal to the Lord of the sheep, and to represent to Him in regard to the sheep that they were devoured by all the wild beasts.

97   But He remained unmoved, though He saw it, and rejoiced that they were devoured and swallowed and robbed, and left them to be devoured in the hand of all the beasts.

98   And He called seventy shepherds, and cast those sheep to them that they might pasture them, and He spake to the shepherds and their companions: "Let each individual of you pasture the sheep henceforward, and everything that I shall command you that do ye. And I will deliver them over unto you duly numbered, and tell you which of them are to be destroyed and them destroy ye."

99   And He gave over unto them those sheep.

100   And He called another and spake unto him: "Observe and mark everything that the shepherds will do to those sheep; for they will destroy more of them than I have commanded them. And every excess and the destruction which will be wrought through the shepherds, record how many they destroy according to my command, and how many according to their own caprice: record against every individual shepherd all the destruction he effects. And read out before me by number how many they destroy, and how many they deliver over for destruction, that I may have this as a testimony against them, and know every deed of the shepherds, that I may comprehend and see what they do, whether or not they abide by my command which I have commanded them. But they shall not know it, and thou shalt not declare it to them, nor admonish them, but only record against each individual all the destruction which the shepherds effect each in his time and lay it all before me."

101   And I saw till those shepherds pastured in their season, and they began to slay and to destroy more than they were bidden, and they delivered those sheep into the hand of the lions.

102   And the lions and tigers eat and devoured the greater part of those sheep, and the wild boars eat along with them; and they burnt that tower and demolished that house.

103   And I became exceedingly sorrowful over that tower because that house of the sheep was demolished, and afterwards I was unable to see if those sheep entered that house.

104   And the shepherds and their associates delivered over those sheep to all the wild beasts, to devour them, and each one of them received in his time a definite number: it was written by the other in a book how many each one of them destroyed of them.

105   And each one slew and destroyed many more than was prescribed; and I began to weep and lament on account of those sheep.

106   And thus in the vision I saw that one who wrote, how he wrote down every one that was destroyed by those shepherds, day by day, and carried up and laid down and showed actually the whole book to the

Lord of the sheep – everything that they had done, and all that each one of them had made away with, and all that they had given over to destruction.

107   And the book was read before the Lord of the sheep, and He took the book from his hand and read it and sealed it and laid it down.

108   And forthwith I saw how the shepherds pastured for twelve hours, and behold three of those sheep turned back and came and entered and began to build up all that had fallen down of that house; but the wild boars tried to hinder them, but they were not able.

109   And they began again to build as before, and they reared up that tower, and it was named the high tower; and they began again to place a table before the tower, but all the bread on it was polluted and not pure.

110   And as touching all this the eyes of those sheep were blinded so that they saw not, and their shepherds likewise; and they delivered them in large numbers to their shepherds for destruction, and they trampled the sheep with their feet and devoured them.

111   And the Lord of the sheep remained unmoved till all the sheep were dispersed over the field and mingled with them and they did not save them out of the hand of the beasts.

112   And this one who wrote the book carried it up, and showed it and read it before the Lord of the sheep, and implored Him on their account, and besought Him on their account as he showed Him all the doings of the shepherds, and gave testimony before Him against all the shepherds.

113   And he took the actual book and laid it down beside Him and departed.

114   And I saw till that in this manner thirty–five shepherds undertook the pasturing, and they severally completed their periods as did the first; and others receive them into their hands, to pasture them for their period, each shepherd in his own period.

115   And after that I saw in my vision all the birds of heaven coming, the eagles, the vultures, the kites, the ravens; but the eagles led all the

birds; and they began to devour those sheep, and to pick out their eyes and to devour their flesh.

116 And the sheep cried out because their flesh was being devoured by the birds and as for me I looked and lamented in my sleep over that shepherd who pastured the sheep.

117 And I saw until those sheep were devoured by the dogs and eagles and kites, and they left neither flesh nor skin nor sinew remaining on them till only their bones stood there: and their bones too fell to the earth and the sheep became few.

118 And I saw until that twenty–three had undertaken the pasturing and completed in their several periods fifty–eight times.

119 But behold lambs were borne by those white sheep, and they began to open their eyes and to see, and to cry to the sheep.

120 Yea, they cried to them, but they did not hearken to what they said to them, but were exceedingly deaf, and their eyes were very exceedingly blinded.

121 And I saw in the vision how the ravens flew upon those lambs and took one of those lambs, and dashed the sheep in pieces and devoured them.

122 And I saw till horns grew upon those lambs, and the ravens cast down their horns; and I saw till there sprouted a great horn of one of those sheep, and their eyes were opened.

123 And it looked at them and their eyes opened, and it cried to the sheep, and the rams saw it and all ran to it.

124 And notwithstanding all this those eagles and vultures and ravens and kites still kept tearing the sheep and swooping down upon them and devouring them: still the sheep remained silent, but the rams lamented and cried out.

125 And those ravens fought and battled with it and sought to lay low its horn, but they had no power over it.

126 All the eagles and vultures and ravens and kites were gathered together and there came with them all the sheep of the field, yea, they all came together, and helped each other to break that horn of the ram.

127   And I saw till a great sword was given to the sheep, and the sheep proceeded against all the beasts of the field to slay them, and all the beasts and the birds of the heaven fled before their face.

128   And I saw that man, who wrote the book according to the command of the Lord, till he opened that book concerning the destruction which those twelve last shepherds had wrought, and showed that they had destroyed much more than their predecessors, before the Lord of the sheep.

129   And I saw till the Lord of the sheep came unto them and took in His hand the staff of His wrath, and smote the earth, and the earth clave asunder, and all the beasts and all the birds of the heaven fell from among those sheep, and were swallowed up in the earth and it covered them.

130   And I saw till a throne was erected in the pleasant land, and the Lord of the sheep sat Himself thereon, and the other took the sealed books and opened those books before the Lord of the sheep.

131   And the Lord called those men the seven first white ones, and commanded that they should bring before Him, beginning with the first star which led the way, all the stars whose privy members were like those of horses, and they brought them all before Him.

132   And He said to that man who wrote before Him, being one of those seven white ones, and said unto him: "Take those seventy shepherds to whom I delivered the sheep, and who taking them on their own authority slew more than I commanded them."

133   And behold they were all bound, I saw, and they all stood before Him.

134   And the judgement was held first over the stars, and they were judged and found guilty, and went to the place of condemnation, and they were cast into an abyss, full of fire and flaming, and full of pillars of fire.

135   And those seventy shepherds were judged and found guilty, and they were cast into that fiery abyss.

136   And I saw at that time how a like abyss was opened in the midst of the earth, full of fire, and they brought those blinded sheep, and they were all judged and found guilty and cast into this fiery abyss, and they burned; now this abyss was to the right of that house.

137   And I saw those sheep burning and their bones burning.

138   And I stood up to see till they folded up that old house; and carried off all the pillars, and all the beams and ornaments of the house were at the same time folded up with it, and they carried it off and laid it in a place in the south of the land.

139   And I saw till the Lord of the sheep brought a new house greater and loftier than that first, and set it up in the place of the first which had beer folded up: all its pillars were new, and its ornaments were new and larger than those of the first, the old one which He had taken away, and all the sheep were within it.

140   And I saw all the sheep which had been left, and all the beasts on the earth, and all the birds of the heaven, falling down and doing homage to those sheep and making petition to and obeying them in every thing.

141   And thereafter those three who were clothed in white and had seized me by my hand who had taken me up before, and the hand of that ram also seizing hold of me, they took me up and set me down in the midst of those sheep before the judgement took place.

142   And those sheep were all white, and their wool was abundant and clean.

143   And all that had been destroyed and dispersed, and all the beasts of the field, and all the birds of the heaven, assembled in that house, and the Lord of the sheep rejoiced with great joy because they were all good and had returned to His house.

144   And I saw till they laid down that sword, which had been given to the sheep, and they brought it back into the house, and it was sealed before the presence of the Lord, and all the sheep were invited into that house, but it held them not.

145   And the eyes of them all were opened, and they saw the good, and there was not one among them that did not see.

146   And I saw that that house was large and broad and very full.

147   And I saw that a white bull was born, with large horns and all the beasts of the field and all the birds of the air feared him and made petition to him all the time.

148   And I saw till all their generations were transformed, and they all became white bulls; and the first among them became a lamb, and that lamb became a great animal and had great black horns on its head; and the Lord of the sheep rejoiced over it and over all the oxen.

149   And I slept in their midst: and I awoke and saw everything.

150   This is the vision which I saw while I slept, and I awoke and blessed the Lord of righteousness and gave Him glory.

151   Then I wept with a great weeping and my tears stayed not till I could no longer endure it: when I saw, they flowed on account of what I had seen; for everything shall come and be fulfilled, and all the deeds of men in their order were shown to me.

152   On that night I remembered the first dream, and because of it I wept and was troubled–because I had seen that vision.

15

Book 5: Epistle of Enoch

Chapter 1
The Guidance of Enoch

1 And now, my son Methuselah, call to me all thy brothers and gather together to me all the sons of thy mother; For the word calls me, and the spirit is poured out upon me that I may show you everything that shall befall you for ever.

2 And there upon Methuselah went and summoned to him all his brothers and assembled his relatives.

3 And he spake unto all the children of righteousness and said: "Hear, ye sons of Enoch, all the words of your father, and hearken aright to the voice of my mouth for I exhort you and say unto you, beloved:

4 Love uprightness and walk therein.
And draw not nigh to uprightness with a double heart, And associate not with those of a double heart,
But walk in righteousness, my sons.

5 And it shall guide you on good paths, and righteousness shall be your companion.

6 For I know that violence must increase on the earth, And a great chastisement be executed on the earth, And all unrighteousness come to an end:
Yea, it shall be cut off from its roots, And its whole structure be destroyed.

7   And unrighteousness shall again be consummated on the earth,
And all the deeds of unrighteousness and of violence,
And transgression shall prevail in a twofold degree.

8   And when sin and unrighteousness and blasphemy, And violence in all kinds of deeds increase,
And apostasy and transgression and uncleanness increase,
A great chastisement shall come from heaven upon all these, And the holy Lord will come forth with wrath and chastisement,

To execute judgement on earth.

9   In those days violence shall be cut off from its roots, And the roots of unrighteousness together with deceit, And they shall be destroyed from under heaven.

10   And all the idols of the heathen shall be abandoned, And the temples burned with fire,
And they shall remove them from the whole earth, And they shall be cast into the judgement of fire,
And shall perish in wrath and in grievous judgement for ever.

11   And the righteous shall arise from their sleep, And wisdom shall arise and be given unto them.

12   And after that the roots of unrighteousness shall be cut off, and the sinners shall be destroyed by the sword and the blasphemers destroyed in every place, and those who plan violence and those who commit blasphemy shall perish by the sword.

13   And now I tell you, my sons, and show you the paths of righteousness and the paths of violence.

14   Yea, I will show them to you again that ye may know what will come to pass.

15   And now, listen to me, my sons, And walk in the paths of righteousness, And walk not in the paths of violence;
For all who walk in the paths of unrighteousness shall perish for ever."

Chapter 2 Wisdom of Enoch

1   The book written by Enoch – Enoch indeed wrote this complete doctrine of wisdom, praised of all men and a judge of all the earth for all my children who shall dwell on the earth. And for the future generations who shall observe uprightness and peace.

2   "Let not your spirit be troubled on account of the times; For the Holy and Great One has appointed days for all things.

3   And the righteous one shall arise from sleep, shall arise and walk in the paths of righteousness and all his path and conversation shall be in eternal goodness and grace.

4   He will be gracious to the righteous and give him eternal uprightness, and He will give him power so that he shall be with goodness and righteousness.

5   And he shall walk in eternal light.

6   And sin shall perish in darkness for ever and shall no more be seen from that day for evermore."

7   And after that Enoch both gave and began to recount from the books.

8   And Enoch said: "Concerning the children of righteousness and concerning the elect of the world, and concerning the plant of uprightness, I will speak these things.

9   Yea, I Enoch will declare unto you, my sons: According to that which appeared to me in the heavenly vision, and which I have known through the word of the holy angels, and have learnt from the heavenly tablets."

10   And Enoch began to recount from the books and said:

11   "I was born the seventh in the first week, while judgement and righteousness still endured.

12   And after me there shall arise in the second week great wickedness, and deceit shall have sprung up; and in it there shall be the first end.

13   And in it a man shall be saved; and after it is ended unrighteousness shall grow up, and a law shall be made for the sinners.

14   And after that in the third week at its close a man shall be elected as the plant of righteous judgement and his posterity shall become the plant of righteousness for evermore.

15   And after that in the fourth week, at its close, Visions of the holy and righteous shall be seen, and a law for all generations and an enclosure shall be made for them.

16   And after that in the fifth week, at its close, the house of glory and dominion shall be built for ever.

17   And after that in the sixth week all who live in it shall be blinded, and the hearts of all of them shall godlessly forsake wisdom.

18   And in it a man shall ascend; and at its close the house of dominion shall be burnt with fire, and the whole race of the chosen root shall be dispersed.

19   And after that in the seventh week shall an apostate generation arise, and many shall be its deeds, and all its deeds shall be apostate.

20   And at its close shall be elected, the elect righteous of the eternal plant of righteousness to receive sevenfold instruction concerning all His creation.

21   For who is there of all the children of men that is able to hear the voice of the Holy One without being troubled?

22   And who can think His thoughts?

23   And who is there that can behold all the works of heaven?

24   And how should there be one who could behold the heaven, and who is there that could understand the things of heaven and see a soul or a spirit and could tell thereof, or ascend and see all their ends and think them or do like them?

25   And who is there of all men that could know what is the breadth and the length of the earth, and to whom has been shown the measure of all of them?

26   Or is there any one who could discern the length of the heaven and how great is its height, and upon what it is founded, and how great is the number of the stars, and where all the luminaries rest?

27   And now I say unto you, my sons, love righteousness and walk therein; for the paths of righteousness are worthy of acceptation but the paths of unrighteousness shall suddenly be destroyed and vanish.

28   And to certain men of a generation shall the paths of violence and of death be revealed and they shall hold themselves afar from them, and shall not follow them.

29   And now I say unto you the righteous: Walk not in the paths of wickedness, nor in the paths of death, and draw not nigh to them, lest ye be destroyed.

30   But seek and choose for yourselves righteousness and an elect life, and walk in the paths of peace, and ye shall live and prosper.

31   And hold fast my words in the thoughts of your hearts and suffer them not to be effaced from your hearts; For I know that sinners will tempt men to evilly
—entreat wisdom so that no place may be found for her, and no manner of temptation may minish.

32   Woe to those who build unrighteousness and oppression and lay deceit as a foundation; For they shall be suddenly overthrown, and they shall have no peace.

33   Woe to those who build their houses with sin; For from all their foundations shall they be overthrown and by the sword shall they fall.

34   And those who acquire gold and silver in judgement suddenly shall perish.

35   Woe to you, ye rich, for ye have trusted in your riches and from your riches shall ye depart because ye have not remembered the Most High in the days of your riches.

36   Ye have committed blasphemy and unrighteousness, and have become ready for the day of slaughter, and the day of darkness and the day of the great judgement.

37   Thus I speak and declare unto you: He who hath created you will overthrow you and for your fall there shall be no compassion, and your Creator will rejoice at your destruction.

38   And your righteous ones in those days shall be a reproach to the sinners and the godless.

39   Oh that mine eyes were a cloud of waters that I might weep over you, and pour down my tears as a cloud of waters: That so I might rest from my trouble of heart!

40   Who has permitted you to practice reproaches and wickedness?

41   And so judgement shall overtake you, sinners.

42   Fear not the sinners, ye righteous; For again will the Lord deliver them into your hands, that ye may execute judgement upon them according to your desires.

43   Woe to you who fulminate anathemas which cannot be reversed: Healing shall therefore be far from you because of your sins.

44   Woe to you who requite your neighbor with evil; For ye shall be requited according to your works.

45   Woe to you, lying witnesses, and to those who weigh out injustice, for suddenly shall ye perish.

46   Woe to you, sinners, for ye persecute the righteous; for ye shall be delivered up and persecuted because of injustice, and heavy shall its yoke be upon you.

47   Be hopeful, ye righteous; for suddenly shall the sinners perish before you, and ye shall have lordship over them according to your desires.

48   And in the day of the tribulation of the sinners your children shall mount and rise as eagles, and higher than the vultures will be your nest, and ye shall ascend and enter the crevices of the earth, and the clefts of the rock for ever as coneys before the unrighteous, and the sirens shall sigh because of you and weep.

49   Wherefore fear not, ye that have suffered; For healing shall be your portion, and a bright light shall enlighten you, and the voice of rest ye shall hear from heaven.

50   Woe unto you, ye sinners, for your riches make you appear like the righteous but your hearts convict you of being sinners, and this fact shall be a testimony against you for a memorial of evil deeds.

51   Woe to you who devour the finest of the wheat and drink wine in large bowls, and tread under foot the lowly with your might.

52   Woe to you who drink water from every fountain; For suddenly shall ye be consumed and wither away because ye have forsaken the fountain of life.

53   Woe to you who work unrighteousness and deceit and blasphemy: It shall be a memorial against you for evil.

54   Woe to you, ye mighty, who with might oppress the righteous; For the day of your destruction is coming.

55   In those days many and good days shall come to the righteous—in the day of your judgement."

Chapter 3 Wisdom of Enoch

1   Believe, ye righteous, that the sinners will become a shame nd perish in the day of unrighteousness.

2   Be it known unto you that the Most High is mindful of your destruction and the angels of heaven rejoice over your destruction.

3   What will ye do, ye sinners, and whither will ye flee on that day of judgement when ye hear the voice of the prayer of the righteous?

4   Yea, ye shall fare like unto them against whom this word shall be a testimony: "Ye have been companions of sinners."

5   And in those days the prayer of the righteous shall reach unto the Lord and for you the days of your judgement shall come.

6   And all the words of your unrighteousness shall be read out before the Great Holy One and your faces shall be covered with shame, and He will reject every work which is grounded on unrighteousness.

7   Woe to you, ye sinners, who live on the mid ocean and on the dry land whose remembrance is evil against you.

8   Woe to you who acquire silver and gold in unrighteousness and say: "We have become rich with riches and have possessions and have

acquired everything we have desired. And now let us do what we purposed: For we have gathered silver and many are the husbandmen in our houses. And our granaries are full as with water."

9   Yea and like water your lies shall flow away for your riches shall not abide but speedily ascend from you; For ye have acquired it all in unrighteousness and ye shall be given over to a great curse.

10   And now I swear unto you, to the wise and to the foolish for ye shall have

manifold experiences on the earth.

11   For ye men shall put on more adornments than a woman and colored garments more than a virgin; In royalty and in grandeur and in power, and in silver and in gold and in purple, and in splendor and in food they shall be poured out as water.

12   Therefore they shall be wanting in doctrine and wisdom and they shall perish thereby together with their possessions.

13   And with all their glory and their splendour, and in shame and in slaughter and in great destitution their spirits shall be cast into the furnace of fire.

14   I have sworn unto you, ye sinners, as a mountain has not become a slave and a hill does not become the handmaid of a woman.

15   Even so, sin has not been sent upon the earth but man of himself has created it, and under a great curse shall they fall who commit it.

16   And barrenness has not been given to the woman but on account of the deeds of her own hands she dies without children.

17   I have sworn unto you, ye sinners, by the Holy Great One; That all your evil deeds are revealed in the heavens and that none of your deeds of oppression are covered and hidden.

18   And do not think in your spirit nor say in your heart that ye do not know and that ye do not see that every sin is every day recorded in heaven in the presence of the Most High.

19   From henceforth ye know that all your oppression wherewith ye oppress is written down every day till the day of your judgement.

20   Woe to you, ye fools, for through your folly shall ye perish: And ye transgress against the wise, and so good hap shall not be your portion.

21   And now, know ye that ye are prepared for the day of destruction: Wherefore do not hope to live, ye sinners, but ye shall depart and die; for ye know no ransom; for ye are prepared for the day of the great judgement, for the day of tribulation and great shame for your spirits.

22   Woe to you, ye obstinate of heart, who work wickedness and eat blood: Whence have ye good things to eat and to drink and to be filled? From all the good things which the Lord the Most High has placed in abundance on the earth; therefore ye shall have no peace.

23   Woe to you who love the deeds of unrighteousness: Wherefore do ye hope for good hap unto yourselves? Know that ye shall be delivered into the hands of the righteous, and they shall cut off your necks and slay you, and have no mercy upon you.

24   Woe to you who rejoice in the tribulation of the righteous; For no grave shall be dug for you.

25   Woe to you who set at nought the words of the righteous; For ye shall have no hope of life.

26   Woe to you who write down lying and godless words; For they write down their lies that men may hear them and act godlessly towards neighbors.

27   Therefore they shall have no peace but die a sudden death.

28   Woe to you who work godlessness and glory in lying and extol them: Ye shall perish, and no happy life shall be yours.

29   Woe to them who pervert the words of uprightness and transgress the eternal law, and transform themselves into what they were not into sinners: They shall be trodden under foot upon the earth.

30   In those days make ready, ye righteous, to raise your prayers as a memorial, and place them as a testimony before the angels that they may place the sin of the sinners for a memorial before the Most High.

31   In those days the nations shall be stirred up and the families of the nations shall arise on the day of destruction.

32   And in those days the destitute shall go forth and carry off their children and they shall abandon them, so that their children shall perish through them: Yea, they shall abandon their children sucklings, and not return to them and shall have no pity on their beloved ones.

33   And again I swear to you, ye sinners, that sin is prepared for a day of unceasing bloodshed.

34   And they who worship stones, and grave images of gold and silver and wood and clay, and those who worship impure spirits and demons, and all kinds of idols not according to knowledge, shall get no manner of help from them.

35   And they shall become godless by reason of the folly of their hearts and their eyes shall be blinded through the fear of their hearts and through visions in their dreams.

36   Through these they shall become godless and fearful; For they shall have wrought all their work in a lie and shall have worshiped a stone: Therefore in an instant shall they perish.

37   But in those days blessed are all they who accept the words of wisdom, and understand them, and observe the paths of the Most High, and walk in the path of His righteousness, and become not godless with the godless; For they shall be saved.

38   Woe to you who spread evil to your neighbors; For you shall be slain in Sheol.

39   Woe to you who make deceitful and false measures, and who cause bitterness on the earth; For they shall thereby be utterly consumed.

40   Woe to you who build your houses through the grievous toil of others, and all their building materials are the bricks and stones of sin; I tell you ye shall have no peace.

41   Woe to them who reject the measure and eternal heritage of their fathers and whose souls follow after idols; For they shall have no rest.

42   Woe to them who work unrighteousness and help oppression, and slay their neighbours until the day of the great judgement.

43   For He shall cast down your glory and bring affliction on your hearts, and shall arouse His fierce indignation and destroy you all with the sword; And all the holy and righteous shall remember your sins.

44   And in those days in one place the fathers together with their sons shall be smitten and brothers one with another shall fall in death till the streams flow with their blood.

45   For a man shall not withhold his hand from slaying his sons and his sons sons, and the sinner shall not withhold his hand from his honored brother: From dawn till sunset they shall slay one another.

46   And the horse shall walk up to the breast in the blood of sinners and the chariot shall be submerged to its height.

47   In those days the angels shall descend into the secret places and gather together into one place all those who brought down sin and the Most High will arise on that day of judgement to execute great judgement amongst sinners.

48   And over all the righteous and holy He will appoint guardians from amongst the holy angels to guard them as the apple of an eye until He makes an end of all wickedness and all sin, and though the righteous sleep a long sleep, they have nought to fear.

49   And the children of the earth shall see the wise in security, and shall understand all the words of this book, and recognize that their riches shall not be able to save them in the overthrow of their sins.

50   Woe to you, Sinners, on the day of strong anguish, Ye who afflict the righteous and burn them with fire: Ye shall be requited according to your works.

51   Woe to you, ye obstinate of heart, who watch in order to devise wickedness: Therefore shall fear come upon you and there shall be none to help you.

52   Woe to you, ye sinners, on account of the words of your mouth, and on account of the deeds of your hands which your godlessness as wrought; In blazing flames burning worse than fire shall ye burn.

53   And now, know ye that from the angels He will inquire as to your deeds in heaven, from the sun and from the moon and from the stars in reference to your sins because upon the earth ye execute judgement on the righteous.

54   And He will summon to testify against you every cloud and mist and dew and rain; for they shall all be withheld because of you from descending upon you, and they shall be mindful of your sins.

55   And now give presents to the rain that it be not withheld from descending upon you, nor yet the dew, when it has received gold and silver from you that it may descend.

56   When the hoarfrost and snow with their chilliness, and all the snow storms with all their plagues fall upon you, in those days ye shall not be able to stand before them.

Chapter 4 Wisdom of Enoch

1   Observe the heaven, ye children of heaven, and every work of the Most High, and fear ye Him and work no evil in His presence.

2   If He closes the windows of heaven, and withholds the rain and the dew from descending on the earth on your account, what will ye do then?

3   And if He sends His anger upon you because of your deeds, ye cannot petition Him; for ye spake proud and insolent words against His righteousness: therefore ye shall have no peace.

4   And see ye not the sailors of the ships, how their ships are tossed to and fro by the waves, and are shaken by the winds, and are in sore trouble?

5   And therefore do they fear because all their goodly possessions go into the sea with them, and they have evil forebodings of heart that the sea will swallow them and they will perish therein.

6   Are not the entire sea and all its waters, and all its movements, the work of the Most High, and has He not set limits to its doings, and confined it throughout by the sand?

7 And at His reproof it is afraid and dries up, and all its fish die and all that is in it; But ye sinners that are on the earth fear Him not.

8 Has He not made the heaven and the earth, and all that is therein?

9 Who has given understanding and wisdom to everything that moves on the earth and in the sea?

10 Do not the sailors of the ships fear the sea? Yet sinners fear not the Most High.

11 In those days when He hath brought a grievous fire upon you, whither will ye

flee, and where will ye find deliverance?

12 And when He launches forth His Word against you will you not be affrighted and fear? And all the luminaries shall be affrighted with great fear and all the earth shall be affrighted and tremble and be alarmed.

13 And all the angels shall execute their commandst and shall seek to hide themselves from the presence of the Great Glory, and the children of earth shall tremble and quake; and ye sinners shall be cursed for ever, and ye shall have no peace.

14 Fear ye not, ye souls of the righteous and be hopeful ye that have died in righteousness.

15 And grieve not if your soul into Sheol has descended in grief, and that in your life your body fared not according to your goodness but wait for the day of the judgement of sinners and for the day of cursing and chastisement.

16 And yet when ye die the sinners speak over you: "As we die, so die the righteous, and what benefit do they reap for their deeds? Behold, even as we, so do they die in grief and darkness and what have they more than we? From henceforth we are equal. And what will they receive and what will they see for ever? Behold, they too have died, And henceforth for ever shall they see no light."

17 I tell you, "Ye sinners, ye are content to eat and drink, and rob and sin, and strip men naked, and acquire wealth and see good days.

Have ye seen the righteous how their end falls out, that no manner of violence is found in them till their death?

18   Nevertheless they perished and became as though they had not been, and their spirits descended into Sheol in tribulation."

Chapter 5 Wisdom of Enoch

1   Another book which Enoch wrote for his son Methuselah and for those who will come after him, and keep the law in the last days.

2   Ye who have done good shall wait for those days till an end is made of those who work evil; and an end of the might of the transgressors.

3   And wait ye indeed till sin has passed away, for their names shall be blotted out of the book of life and out of the holy books, and their seed shall be destroyed for ever, and their spirits shall be slain, and they shall cry and make lamentation in a place that is a chaotic wilderness, and in the fire shall they burn; for there is no earth there.

4   And I saw there something like an invisible cloud; for by reason of its depth I could not look over, and I saw a flame of fire blazing brightly, and things like shining mountains circling and sweeping to and fro.

5   And I asked one of the holy angels who was with me and said unto him: "What is this shining thing? For it is not a heaven but only the flame of a blazing fire, and the voice of weeping and crying and lamentation and strong pain."

6   And he said unto me: "This place which thou seest—here are cast the spirits of sinners and blasphemers, and of those who work wickedness, and of those who pervert everything that the Lord hath spoken through the mouth of the prophets
– the things that shall be.

7   For some of them are written and inscribed above in the heaven, in order that the angels may read them and know that which shall befall the sinners, and the spirits of the humble, and of those who have afflicted their bodies, and been recompensed by God.

8   And of those who have been put to shame by wicked men: Who love God and loved neither gold nor silver nor any of the good things which are in the world, but gave over their bodies to torture.

9   Who, since they came into being, longed not after earthly food, but regarded everything as a passing breath, and lived accordingly, and the Lord tried them much, and their spirits were found pure so that they should bless His name.

10   And all the blessings destined for them I have recounted in the books.

11   And he hath assigned them their recompense, because they have been found to be such as loved heaven more than their life in the world, and though they were trodden under foot of wicked men and experienced abuse and reviling from them and were put to shame, yet they blessed Me.

12   And now I will summon the spirits of the good who belong to the generation of light, and I will transform those who were born in darkness, who in the flesh were not recompensed with such honor as their faithfulness deserved.

13   And I will bring forth in shining light those who have loved My holy name, and I will seat each on the throne of his honor.

14   And they shall be resplendent for times without number; for righteousness is the judgement of God; for to the faithful He will give faithfulness in the habitation of upright paths.

15   And they shall see those who were, born in darkness led into darkness, while the righteous shall be resplendent.

16   And the sinners shall cry aloud and see them resplendent, and they indeed will go where days and seasons are prescribed for them."

Chapter 6 Revelation of Enoch

1   I swear unto you that in heaven the angels remember you for good before the glory of the Great One: and your names are written before the glory of the Great One.

2   Be hopeful; for aforetime ye were put to shame through ill and affliction; but now ye shall shine as the lights of heaven, ye shall shine and ye shalll be seen, and the portals of heaven shall be opened to you.

3   And in your cry, cry for judgement, and it shall appear to you; for all your tribulation shall be visited on the rulers, and on all who helped those who plundered you.

4   Be hopeful, and cast not away your hopes for ye shall have great joy as the angels of heaven.

5   What shall ye be obliged to do?

6   Ye shall not have to hide on the day of the great judgement and ye shall not be found as sinners, and the eternal judgement shall be far from you for all the generations of the world.

7   And now fear not, ye righteous, when ye see the sinners growing strong and prospering in their ways, be not companions with them, but keep afar from their violence; For ye shall become companions of the hosts of heaven.

8   And, although the sinners say: "All our sins shall not be searched out and be written down," nevertheless they shall write down all your sins every day.

9   And now I show unto you that light and darkness, day and night, see all your sins.

10   Be not godless in your hearts, and lie not and alter not the words of uprightness, nor charge with lying the words of the Holy Great One, nor take account of your idols; for all your lying and all your godlessness issue not in righteousness but in great sin.

11   And now I know this mystery, that sinners will alter and pervert the words of righteousness in many ways, and will speak wicked words, and lie, and practice great deceits, and write books concerning their words.

12   But when they write down truthfully all my words in their languages, and do not change or minish ought from my words but write them all down truthfully – all that I first testified concerning them.

13   Then, I know another mystery, that books will be given to the righteous and the wise to become a cause of joy and uprightness and much wisdom.

14   And to them shall the books be given, and they shall believe in them and rejoice over them and then shall all the righteous who have learnt therefrom all the paths of uprightness be recompensed.

15   In those days the Lord bade to summon and testify to the children of earth concerning their wisdom: "Show unto them; for ye are their guides and a recompense over the whole earth.

16   For I and My son will be united with them for ever in the paths of uprightness in their lives; and ye shall have peace: rejoice, ye children of uprightness.

Amen."

The Emerald Tablets of Thoth

The Emerald Tablets of Thoth

The secrets of Atlantis. The path to enlightenment. The hidden wisdom of the ages.

The Emerald Tablets of Thoth is one of the most enigmatic and influential esoteric texts, said to contain the knowledge of an ancient, lost civilization. Allegedly written by Thoth, the Atlantean priest-king who became the Egyptian god of wisdom, these tablets reveal the secrets of immortality, cosmic laws, and the rise and fall of civilizations.

This mystical text includes:

The Fall of Atlantis – A lost civilization destroyed in a great cataclysm, its wisdom hidden for future generations.

The Path to Enlightenment – Teachings on self-mastery, higher consciousness, and spiritual awakening.

The Laws of the Universe – Insights into the balance of creation, the nature of reality, and the cycles of time.

The Power of the Spoken Word – The secrets of vibrational energy and manifestation.

The Role of the Initiate – How seekers of truth can unlock divine wisdom and transcend mortality.

Originally brought to light in the 20th century by Maurice Doreal, The Emerald Tablets of Thoth has been revered by alchemists, philosophers, and mystics for its profound insights. Is this truly the knowledge of an Atlantean priest-king? Does it hold the key to unlocking forgotten powers and hidden truths?

This edition presents the full text, allowing you to decipher its mysteries for yourself.

16

PREFACE

The history of the tablets translated in the following pages is strange and beyond the belief of modern scientists. Their antiquity is stupendous, dating back some 36,000 years B.C. The writer is Thoth, an Atlantean Priest-King, who founded a colony in ancient Egypt after the sinking of the mother country. He was the builder of the Great Pyramid of Giza, erroneously attributed to Cheops. (See The Great Pyramid by Doreal.) In it he incorporated his knowledge of the ancient wisdom and also securely secreted records and instruments of ancient Atlantis.

For some 16,000 years, he ruled the ancient race of Egypt, from approximately 50,000 B.C. to 36.000 B.C. At that time, the ancient barbarous race among which he and his followers had settled had been raised to a high degree of civilization. Thoth was an immortal, that is, he had conquered death, passing only when he willed and even then not through death. His vast wisdom made him ruler over the various Atlantean colonies, including the ones in South and Central America.

When the time came for him to leave Egypt, he erected the Great Pyramid over the entrance to the Great Halls of Amenti, placed in it his records, and appointed guards for his secrets from among the highest of his people. In later times, the descendants of these guards became the pyramid priests, by which Thoth was deified as the God of Wisdom, The Recorder, by those in the age of darkness which followed his passing. In legend, the halls of Amenti became the underworld, the Halls of the Gods, where the soul passed after death for judgment.

During later ages, the ego of Thoth passed into the bodies of men in the manner described in the tablets. As such, he incarnated three times, in his last being known as Hermes, the thrice-born. In this incarnation, he left the writings known to modern occultists as the Emerald Tablets, a later and far lesser exposition of the ancient mysteries.

The tablets translated in this work are ten which were left in the Great Pyramid in the custody of the pyramid priests. The ten are divided into thirteen parts for the sake of convenience. The last two are so great and far- reaching in their import that at present it is forbidden to release them to the world at large. However, in those contained herein are secrets which will prove of inestimable value to the serious student. They should be read, not once, but a hundred times for only thus can the true meaning be revealed. A casual reading will give glimpses of beauty, but more intensive study will oven avenues of wisdom to the seeker.

But now a word as to how these mighty secrets came to be revealed to modern man after being hidden so long.

Some thirteen hundred years B.C., Egypt, the ancient Khem, was in turmoil and many delegations of priests were sent to other parts of the world. Among these were some of the pyramid priests who carried with them the Emerald Tablets as a talisman by which they could exercise authority over the less advanced priest-craft of races descended from other Atlantean colonies. The tablets were understood from legend to give the bearer authority from Thoth.

The particular group of priests bearing the tablets emigrated to South America where they found a flourishing race, the Mayas who remembered much of the ancient wisdom. Among these, the priests settled and remained. In the tenth century, the Mayas had thoroughly settled the Yucatan, and the tablets were placed beneath the altar of one of the great temples of the Sun God. After the conquest of the Mayas by the Spaniards, the cities were abandoned and the treasures of the temples forgotten.

It should be understood that the Great Pyramid of Egypt has been and still is a temple of initiation into the mysteries. Jesus, Solomon,

Apollonius and others were initiated there. The writer (who has a connection with the Great White Lodge which also works through the pyramid priesthood) was instructed to recover and return to the Great Pyramid the ancient tablets. This, after adventures which need not be detailed here, was accomplished. Before returning them, he was given permission to translate and retain a copy of the wisdom engraved on the tablets. This was done in 1925 and only now has permission been given for part to be published. It is expected that many will scoff. Yet the true student will read between the lines and gain wisdom. If the light is in you, the light which is engraved in these tablets will respond.

Now, a word as to the material aspect of the tablets. They consist of twelve tablets of emerald green, formed from a substance created through alchemical transmutation. They are imperishable, resistant to all elements and substances. In effect, the atomic and cellular structure is fixed, no change ever taking place. In this respect, they violate the material law of ionization. Upon them are engraved characters in the ancient Atlantean language: characters which respond to attuned thought waves, releasing the associated mental vibration in the mind of the reader. The tablets are fastened together with hoops of golden-colored alloy suspended from a rod of the same material. So much for the material appearance. The wisdom contained therein is the foundation of the ancient mysteries. And for the one who reads with open eyes and mind, his wisdom shall be increased a hundred-fold.

Read. Believe or not, but read. And the vibration found therein will awaken a response in your soul. In Cosmic Harmony,
Doreal
Supreme Voice of the Brotherhood

17

INTRODUCTION

An Interpretation of the Emerald Tablets
      In the following pages, I will reveal some of the mysteries which as yet have only been touched upon lightly either by myself or other teachers or students of truth.

Man's search for understanding of the laws which regulate his life has been unending, yet always just beyond the veil which shields the higher planes from material man's vision the truth has existed, ready to be assimilated by those who enlarge their vision by turning inward, not outward, in their search.

In the silence of material senses lies the key to the unveiling of wisdom. He who talks does not know; he who knows does not talk. The highest knowledge is unutterable, for it exists as an entity in lanes which transcend all material words or symbols.

All symbols are but keys to doors leading to truths, and many times the door is not opened because the key seems so great that the things which are beyond it are not visible. If we can understand that all keys, all material symbols are manifestations, are but extensions of a great law and truth, we will begin to develop the vision which will enable us to penetrate beyond the veil.

All things in all universes move according to law, and the law which regulates the movement of the planets is no more immutable than the law which regulates the material expressions of man.

One of the greatest of all Cosmic Laws is that which is responsible for the formation of man as a material being. The great aim of the mystery schools of all ages has been to reveal the workings of the Law which connect man the material and man the spiritual. The connecting link between the material man and the spiritual man is the intellectual man, for the mind partakes of both the material and immaterial qualities. The aspirant for higher knowledge must develop the intellectual side of his nature and so strengthen his will that is able to concentrate all powers of his being on and in the plane he desires.

The great search for light, life and love only begins on the material plane. Carried to its ultimate, its final goal is complete oneness with the universal consciousness. The foundation in the material is the first step; then comes the higher goal of spiritual attainment.

In the following pages, I will give an interpretation of the Emerald Tablets and their secret, hidden and esoteric meanings. Concealed in the words of Thoth are many meanings that do not appear on the surface. Light of knowledge brought to bear upon the Tablets will open many new fields for thought. "Read and be wise" but only if the light of your own consciousness awakens the deep-seated understanding which is an inherent quality of the soul.

In the Threefold Light Doreal

18

EMERALD TABLET I

The History of Thoth, The Atlantean

I, Thoth, the Atlantean, master of mysteries, keeper of records, mighty king, magician, living from generation to generation, being about to pass into the Halls of Amenti, set down for the guidance of those that are to come after, these records of the mighty wisdom of Great Atlantis.

In the great city of Keor on the island of Undal in a time far past, I began this incarnation. Not as the little men of the present age did the mighty ones of Atlantis live and die, but rather from aeon to aeon did they renew their life in the Halls of Amenti where the river of life flows eternally onward.

A hundred times ten have I descended the dark way that led into light, and as many times have I ascended from the darkness into the light, my strength and power renewed.

Now for a time I descend, and the men of Khem shall know me no more. But in a time yet unborn will I rise again, mighty and potent, requiring an accounting of those left behind me. Then beware, O men of Khem, if ye have falsely betrayed my teaching, for I shall cast ye down from your high estate into the darkness of the caves from whence ye came. Betray not my secrets to the men of the North or the men of the South lest my curse fall upon ye. Remember and heed my words, for surely will I return again and require of thee that which ye guard. Aye, even from beyond time and from beyond death will I return, rewarding or punishing as ye have requited your trust. Great were my people in the ancient days, great beyond the conception of the little people now around me; knowing the wisdom of old, seeking far within the heart of infinity knowledge that belonged to Earth's youth. Wise were we with the wisdom of the Children of Light who dwelt among us. Strong were we with the power drawn from the eternal fire. And of all these, greatest among the children of men was my father, Thotme, keeper of the great temple, link between the Children of Light who dwelt within the temple and the races of men who inhabited the ten islands. Mouthpiece, after the three, of the Dweller of Unal, speaking to the Kings with the voice that must be obeyed.

Grew I there from a child into manhood, being taught by my father the elder mysteries, until in time there grew within the fire of wisdom, until it burst into a consuming flame. Naught desired I but the attainment of wisdom. Until on a great day the command came from the Dweller of the Temple that I be brought before him. Few there were among the children of men who had looked upon that mighty face and lived, for not as the sons of men are the Children of Light when they are not incarnate in a physical body.

Chosen was I from the sons of men, taught by the Dweller so that his purposes might be fulfilled, purposes yet unborn in the womb of time. Long ages I dwelt in the Temple, learning ever and yet ever more wisdom, until I, too, approached the light emitted from the great fire. Taught me he, the path to Amenti, the underworld where the great king sits upon his throne of might. Deep I bowed in homage before the Lords of Life and the Lords of Death, receiving as my gift the key of Life. Free was I of the Halls of Amenti, bound not by death to the circle of life. Far to the stars I journeyed until space and time became as naught. Then having drunk deep of the cup of wisdom, I looked into the hearts of men and there found I greater mysteries and was glad. For only in the Search for Truth could my Soul be stilled and the flame within be quenched.

Down through the ages I lived, seeing those around me taste of the cup of death and return again in the light of life. Gradually from the Kingdoms of Atlantis passed waves of consciousness that had been one with me, only to be replaced by spawn of a lower star.

In obedience to the law, the word of the Master grew into flower. Downward into darkness turned the thoughts of the Atlanteans, until at last in his wrath arose from his Agwanti, the Dweller, (this word has no English equivalent; it means a state of detachment) speaking The Word, calling the power. Deep in Earth's heart, the sons of Amenti heard, and hearing, directed the changing of the flower of fire that burns eternally, changing and shifting, using the Logos, until that great fire changed its direction.

Over the world then broke the great waters, drowning and sinking, changing Earth's balance until only the Temple of Light was left standing on the great mountain on Undal still rising out of the water; some there were who were living, saved from the rush of the fountains.
Called to me then the Master, saying: "Gather ye together my people. Take them by the arts ye have learned of far across the waters, until ye reach the land of the hairy barbarians, dwelling in caves of the desert. Follow there the plan that ye know of."

Gathered I then my people and entered the great ship of the Master. Upward we rose into the morning. Dark beneath us lay the Temple. Suddenly over it rose the waters. Vanished from Earth, until the time appointed, was the great Temple.
Fast we fled toward the sun of the morning, until beneath us lay the land of the children of Khem. Raging, they came with cudgels and spears lifted in anger seeking to slay and utterly destroy the Sons of Atlantis. Then raised I my staff and directed a ray of vibration, striking them still in their tracks as fragments of stone of the mountain. Then spoke I to them in words calm and peaceful, telling them of the might of Atlantis, saying we were children of the Sun and its messengers. Cowed I them by my display of magic-science, until at my feet they groveled, when I released them.
Long dwelt we in the land of Khem, long and yet long again. Until obeying the commands of the Master, who while sleeping yet lives eternally,

I sent from me the Sons of Atlantis, sent them in many directions, that from the womb of time wisdom might rise again in her children.

Long time dwelt I in the land of Khem, doing great works by the wisdom within me. Upward grew into the light of knowledge the children of Khem, watered by the rains of my wisdom. Blasted I then a path to Amenti so that I might retain my powers, living from age to age a Sun of Atlantis, keeping the wisdom, preserving the records.

Great grew the sons of Khem, conquering the people around them, growing slowly upwards in Soul force. Now for a time I go from among them into the dark halls of Amenti, deep in the halls of the Earth, before the Lords of the Powers, face to face once again with the Dweller.

Raised I high over the entrance, a doorway, a gateway leading down to Amenti. Few there would be with courage to dare it, few pass the portal to dark Amenti. Raised over the passage, I, a mighty pyramid, using the power that overcomes Earth force (gravity). Deep and yet deeper placed I a force-house or chamber; from it carved I a circular passage reaching almost to the great summit. There in the apex, set I the crystal, sending the ray into the "Time-Space", drawing the force from out of the ether, concentrating upon the gateway to Amenti. (See The Great Pyramid by Doreal.)

Other chambers I built and left vacant to all seeming, yet hidden within them are the keys to Amenti. He who in courage would dare the dark realms, let him be purified first by long fasting. Lie in the sarcophagus of stone in my chamber. Then to reveal I to him the great mysteries. Soon shall he follow to where I shall meet him, even in the darkness of Earth shall I meet him, I, Thoth, Lord of Wisdom, meet him and hold him and dwell with him always.

Built I the Great Pyramid, patterned after the pyramid of earth force, burning eternally so that it, too, might remain through the ages. In it, I built my knowledge of "Magic-Science" so that it might be here when again I return from Amenti. Aye, while I sleep in the Halls of Amenti, my Soul roaming free will incarnate, dwell among men in this form or another. (Hermes, thrice-born.)

Emissary on Earth am I of the Dweller, fulfilling his commands so man might be lifted. Now return I to the Halls of Amenti, leaving behind me some of my wisdom. Preserve ye and keep ye the command of the Dweller: Lift ever upwards your eyes toward the light. Surely in time, ye are one with the Master, surely by right ye are one with the Master, surely by right ye are one with the All.

Now I depart from ye. Know my commandments, keep them and be them, and I will be with you, helping and guiding you into the Light.

Now before me opens the portal. Go I down in the darkness of night.

19

EMERALD TABLET II

The Halls of Amenti
    Deep in the Earth's heart lie the Halls of Amenti, far 'neath the islands of sunken Atlantis, Halls of the Dead and halls of the living, bathed in the fire of the infinite ALL.

Far in a past time, lost in the space time, the Children of Light looked down on the world. See the children of men in their bondage, bound by the force that came from beyond. Knew they that only by freedom from bondage could man ever rise from the Earth to the Sun. Down they descended and created bodies, taking the semblance of men as their own. The masters of everything said after their forming: "We are they who were formed from the space-dust, partaking of life from the infinite ALL; living in the world as children of men, like and yet unlike the children of men."

Then for a dwelling place, far 'neath the earth crust, blasted great spaces they by their power, spaces apart from the children of men. Surrounded them by forces and power, shielded from harm they the Halls of the Dead.

Side by side then, placed they other spaces, filled them with Life and with Light from above. Builded they then the Halls of Amenti, that they might dwell eternally there living with life to eternity's end.

Thirty and two were there of the children, sons of Light who had come among men, seeking to free from the bondage of darkness those who were bound by the force from beyond.

Deep in the Halls of Life grew a flower, flaming, expanding, driving backward the night. Placed in the center, a ray of great potence, Life giving, Light giving, filling with power all who came near it. Placed they around it thrones, two and thirty, places for each of the Children of Light, placed so that they were bathed in the radiance, filled with the Life from the eternal Light. There time after time placed they their first created bodies so that they might be filled with the Spirit of Life. One hundred years out of each thousand must the Life- giving Light flame forth on their bodies. Quickening, awakening the Spirit of Life.

There in the circle from aeon to aeon, sit the Great Masters, living a life not known among men. There in the Halls of Life they lie sleeping; free flows their Soul through the bodies of men. Time after time, while their bodies lie sleeping, incarnate they in the bodies of men. Teaching and guiding onward and upward, out of the darkness into the Light. There in the Hall of Life, filled with their wisdom, known not to the races of man, living forever 'neath the cold fire of life, sit the Children of Light. Times there are when they awaken, come from the depths to be lights among men, infinite they among finite.

He who by progress has grown from the darkness, lifted himself from the night into light, free is he made of the Halls of Amenti, free of the Flower of Light and of Life. Guided he then, by wisdom and knowledge, passes from man, to the Master of Life. There he may dwell as one with the Masters, free from the bonds of the darkness of night.
Seated within the flower of radiance sit seven Lords from the Space-Time above us, helping and guiding through infinite Wisdom, the pathway through time of the children of men. Mighty and strange, they, veiled with their power, silent, all-knowing, drawing the Life force, different yet one with the children of men. Aye, different, and yet one with the Children of Light.

Custodians and watchers of the force of man's bondage, ready to loose when the light has been reached. First and most mighty, sits the Veiled Presence, Lord of Lords, the infinite Nine, over the others from each Cosmic cycle, weighing and watching the progress of men.

Under HE, sit the Lords of the Cycles; Three, Four, Five, and Six, Seven, Eight, each with his mission, each with his power, guiding, directing the destiny of man. There sit they, mighty and potent, free of all time and space. Not of this world they, yet akin to it, Elder Brothers they, of the children of men. Judging and weighing, they with their wisdom, watching the progress Light among men.

There before them was I led by the Dweller, watched him blend with ONE from above. Then from HE came forth a voice saying: "Great art thou, Thoth, among children of men. Free henceforth of the Halls of Amenti, Master of Life among children of men. Taste not of death except as thou will it, drink thou of Life to Eternity's end. Henceforth forever is Life, thine for the taking. Henceforth is Death at the call of thy hand. Dwell here or leave here when thou desireth, free is Amenti to the Sun of man. Take thou up Life in what form thou desireth, Child of the Light that has grown among men. Choose thou thy work, for all souls must labor, never be free from the pathway of Light. One step thou has gained on the long pathway upward, infinite now is the mountain of Light. Each step thou taketh but heightens the mountain; all of thy progress but lengthens the goal. Approach ye ever the infinite Wisdom, ever before thee recedes the goal. Free are ye made now of the Halls of Amenti to walk hand in hand with the Lords of the world, one in one purpose, working together, bringers of Light to the children of men."

Then from his throne came one of the Masters, taking my hand and leading me onward, through all the Halls of the deep hidden land. Led he me through the Halls of Amenti, showing the mysteries that are known not to man. Through the dark passage, downward he led me into the Hall where sits the dark Death. Vast as space lay the great Hall before me, walled by darkness but yet filled with Light.

Before me arose a great throne of darkness, veiled on it seated a figure of night. Darker than darkness sat the great figure, dark with a darkness not of the night. Before it then paused the Master, speaking The Word that brings about Life, saying: "Oh, master of darkness, guide of the way from Life unto Life, before thee I bring a Sun of the morning. Touch

him not ever with the power of night. Call not his flame to the darkness
of night. Know him, and see him, one of our brothers, lifted from darkness into the Light. Release thou his flame from its bondage, free let it
flame through the darkness of night." Raised then the hand of the figure, forth came a flame that grew clear and bright. Rolled back swiftly
the curtain of darkness, unveiled the Hall from the darkness of night.
Then grew in the great space before me, flame after flame, from the veil
of the night. Uncounted millions leaped they before me, some flaming forth as flowers of fire. Others there were that shed a dim radiance,
glowing but faintly from out of the night. Some there were that faded
swiftly; others that grew from a small spark of light. Each surrounded
by its dim veil of darkness, yet flaming with the light that could never be
quenched. Coming and going like fireflies in springtime, filled they the
space with Light and with Life.

Then spoke a voice, mighty and solemn, saying: "These are lights that
are souls among men, growing and fading, existing forever, changing yet
living, through death into life. When they have bloomed into flower,
reached the zenith of growth in their life, swiftly then send I my veil of
darkness, shrouding and changing to new forms of life. Steadily upward
throughout the ages, growing, expanding into yet greater flame, lighting
the darkness with yet greater power, quenched yet unquenched by the
veil of the night. So grows the soul of man ever upward, quenched yet
unquenched by the darkness of night.

I, Death, come, and yet I remain not, for life eternal exists in the All;
only an obstacle, I in the pathway, quick to be conquered by the infinite
light. Awaken, O flame that burns ever inward, flame forth and conquer
the veil of the night."

Then in the midst of the flames in the darkness grew there one that
drove forth the night, flaming, expanding, ever brighter, until at last was
nothing but Light. Then spoke my guide, the voice of the master: "See
your own soul as it grows in the light, free now forever from the Lord of
the night."

Forward he led me through many great spaces filled with the mysteries of the Children of Light; mysteries that man may never yet know of until he, too, is a Sun of the Light. Backward then HE led me into the Light of the Hall of the Light. Knelt I then before the great Masters, Lords of ALL from the cycles above.

Spoke HE then with words of great power saying: "Thou has been made free of the Halls of Amenti. Choose thou thy work among the children of men."

Then spoke I: "O, great master, let me be a teacher of men, leading them onward and upward until they too, are lights among men; freed from the veil of the night that surrounds them, flaming with light that shall shine among men."

Spoke to me then the voice: "Go, as ye will. So be it decreed. Master are ye of your destiny, free to take or reject at will. Take ye the power, take ye the wisdom. Shine as a light among the children of men."

Upward then, led me the Dweller. Dwelt I again among children of men, teaching and showing some of my wisdom; Sun of the Light, a fire among men.

Now again I tread the path downward, seeking the light in the darkness of night. Hold ye and keep ye, preserve my record, guide shall it be to the children of men.

20

EMERALD TABLET III

The Key of Wisdom
     I, Thoth, the Atlantean, give of my wisdom, give of my knowledge, give of my power. Freely I give to the children of men. Give that they, too, might have wisdom to shine through the world from the veil of the night. Wisdom is power and power is wisdom, one with each other, perfecting the whole.
Be thou not proud, O man, in thy wisdom. Discourse with the ignorant as well as the wise. If one comes to thee full of knowledge, listen and heed, for wisdom is all.
     Keep thou not silent when evil is spoken for Truth like the sunlight shines above all.
     He who over-steppeth the Law shall be punished, for only through Law comes the freedom of men. Follow thine heart during thy lifetime. Do thou more than is commanded of thee.
When thou has gained riches, follow thou thine heart, for all these are of no avail if thine heart be weary.
Diminish thou not the time of following thine heart. It is abhorred of the soul.
     They that are guided go not astray, but they that are lost cannot find a straight path. If thou go among men, make for thyself, Love, the beginning and end of the heart.
     If one cometh unto thee for council, let him speak freely, that the thing for which he hath come to thee may be done. If he hesitates to open his heart to thee, it is because thou, the judge, doeth the wrong.

Repeat thou not extravagant speech, neither listen thou to it, for it is the utterance of one not in equilibrium. Speak thou not of it, so that he before thee may know wisdom.

Silence is of great profit. An abundance of speech profiteth nothing.

Exalt not thine heart above the children of men, lest it be brought lower than the dust. If thou be great among men, be honored for knowledge and gentleness.

If thou seeketh to know the nature of a friend, ask not his companion, but pass a time alone with him. Debate with him, testing his heart by his words and his bearing.

That which goeth into the store-house must come forth, and the things that are thine must be shared with a friend.

Knowledge is regarded by the fool as ignorance, and the things that are profitable are to him hurtful. He liveth in death. It is therefore his food.

The wise man lets his heart overflow but keeps silent his mouth.

O man, list to the voice of wisdom; list to the voice of light. Mysteries there are in the Cosmos that unveiled fill the world with their light. Let he who would be free from the bonds of darkness first divine the material from the immaterial, the fire from the earth; for know ye that as earth descends to earth, so also fire ascends unto fire and becomes one with fire. He who knows the fire that is within himself shall ascend unto the eternal fire and dwell in it eternally.

Fire, the inner fire, is the most potent of all force, for it overcometh all things and penetrates to all things of the Earth.

Man supports himself only on that which resists. So Earth must resist man else he existeth not.

All eyes do not see with the same vision, for to one an object appears of one form and color and to a different eye of another. So also the infinite fire, changing from color to color, is never the same from day to day.

Thus, speak I, Thoth, of my wisdom, for man is a fire burning bright through the night; never is quenched in the veil of the darkness, never is quenched by the veil of the night.

Hark ye, O man, and list to this wisdom: where do name and form cease? Only in consciousness, invisible, an infinite force of radiance bright. The forms that ye create by brightening thy vision are truly effects that follow thy cause.

Man is a star bound to a body, until in the end, he is freed through his strife. Only struggle and toiling thy utmost shall the star within thee bloom out in new life. He who knows the commencement of all things, free is his star from the realms of night.

Remember, O man, that all which exists is only another form of that which exists not. Everything that has being is passing into yet other being and thou thyself are not an exception.

Consider the Law, for all is Law. Seek not that which is not of the Law, for such exists only in the illusions of the senses.

Wisdom cometh to all her children even as they cometh unto wisdom.

All through the ages, the light has been hidden. Awake, O man, and be wise.

Deep in the mysteries of life have I traveled, seeking and searching for that which is hidden. List ye, O man, and be wise.
Far 'neath the earth crust, in the Halls of Amenti, mysteries I saw that are hidden from men.
Oft have I journeyed the deep hidden passage, looked on the Light that is Life among men. There 'neath the Flowers of Life ever living, searched I the hearts and the secrets of men. Found I that man is but living in darkness, light of the great fire is hidden within.

Before the Lords of hidden Amenti learned I the wisdom I give unto men. Masters are they of the great Secret Wisdom, brought from the future of infinity's end. Seven are they, the Lords of Amenti, overlords they of the Children of Morning, Suns of the Cycles, Masters of Wisdom. Formed are not they as the children of men? Three, Four, Five and Six, Seven, Eight, Nine are the titles of the Masters of men.
Far from the future, formless yet forming, came they as teachers for the children of men. Live they forever, yet not of the living, bound not to

life and yet free from death. Rule they forever with infinite wisdom, bound yet not bound to the dark Halls of Death. Life they have in them, yet life that is not life, free from all are the Lords of the ALL.

Forth from them came forth the Logos, instruments they of the power o'er all. Vast is their countenance, yet hidden in smallness, formed by a forming, known yet unknown.

Three holds the key of all hidden magic, creator he of the Halls of the Dead; sending forth power, shrouding with darkness, binding the souls of the children of men; sending the darkness, binding the soul force; director of negative to the children of men.

Four is he who looses the power. Lord, he, of Life to the children of men.

Light is his body, flame is his countenance; freer of souls to the children of men.

Five is the master, the Lord of all magic-Key to The Word that resounds among men. Six is the Lord of Light, the hidden pathway, part of the souls of the children of men. Seven is he who is Lord of the vastness, master of Space and the key of the Times. Eight is he who orders the progress; weighs and balances the journey of men.

Nine is the father, vast he of countenance, forming and changing from out of the formless. Meditate on the symbols I give thee. Keys are they, though hidden from men.

Reach ever upward, O Soul of the morning. Turn thy thoughts upward to Light and to Life. Find in the keys of the numbers I bring thee, light on the pathway from life unto life.

Seek ye with wisdom. Turn thy thoughts inward. Close not thy mind to the Flower of Light. Place in thy body a thought-formed picture. Think of the numbers that lead thee to Life.

Clear is the pathway to he who has wisdom. Open the door to the Kingdom of Light. Pour forth thy flame as a Sun of the morning. Shut out the darkness and live in the day.

Take thee, O man! As part of thy being, the Seven who are but are not as they seem. Opened, O man! Have I my wisdom. Follow the path in the way I have led.

Masters of Wisdom, Sun of the Morning Light and Life to the children of men.

21

EMERALD TABLET IV

The Space Born

List ye, O man, to the voice of wisdom, list to the voice of Thoth, the Atlantean. Freely I give to thee of my wisdom gathered from the time and space of this cycle; master of mysteries, Sun of the morning, Thoth the teacher of men, is of ALL.

Long time ago, I in my childhood, lay 'neath the stars on long-buried Atlantis, dreaming of mysteries far above men. Then in my heart grew there a great longing to conquer the pathway that led to the stars. Year after year, I sought after wisdom, seeking new knowledge, following the way, until at last my Soul, in great travail, broke from its bondage and bounded away. Free was I from the bondage of earth-men. Free from the body, I flashed through the night. Unlocked at last for me was the starspace. Free was I from the bondage of night. Now to the end of space sought I wisdom, far beyond knowledge of finite man.

Far into space, my Soul traveled freely into infinity's circle of light. Strange, beyond knowledge, were some of the planets, great and gigantic, beyond dreams of men. Yet found I Law, in all of its beauty, working through and among them as here among men. Flashed forth my soul through infinity's beauty, far through space I flew with my thoughts.

Rested I there on a planet of beauty. Strains of harmony filled all the air. Shapes there were, moving in Order, great and majestic as stars in the night; mounting in harmony, ordered equilibrium, symbols of the Cosmic, like unto Law.

Many the stars I passed in my journey, many the races of men on their worlds; some reaching high as stars of the morning, some falling low in the blackness of night. Each and all of them struggling upward, gaining the heights and plumbing the depths, moving at times in realms of brightness, living through darkness, gaining the Light.
Know, O man, that Light is thine heritage. Know that darkness is only a veil. Sealed in thine heart is brightness eternal, waiting the moment of freedom to conquer, waiting to rend the veil of the night.

Some I found who had conquered the ether. Free of space were they while yet they were men. Using the force that is the foundation of ALL things, far in space constructed they a planet, drawn by the force that flows through the ALL; condensing, coalescing the ether into forms that grew as they willed. Outstripping in science, they, all of the races, mighty in wisdom, sons of the stars.

Long time I paused, watching their wisdom. Saw them create from out of the ether cities gigantic of rose and gold. Formed forth from the primal element, base of all matter, the ether far flung.

Far in the past, they had conquered the ether, freed themselves from the bondage of toil; formed in their mind only a picture and swiftly created, it grew.

Forth then, my soul sped, throughout the Cosmos, seeing ever, new things and old; learning that man is truly space-born, a Sun of the Sun, a child of the stars.
Know ye, O man, whatever form ye inhabit, surely it is one with the stars. Thy bodies are nothing but planets revolving around their central suns. When ye have gained the light of all wisdom, free shall ye be to shine in the ether-one of the Suns that light outer darkness-one of the space-born grown into Light. Just as the stars in time lose their brilliance, light passing from them into the great source, so, O man, thy soul passes onward, leaving behind the darkness of night.

Formed forth ye, from the primal ether, filled with the brilliance that flows from the source, bound by the ether coalesced around, yet ever it flames until at last it is free. Lift up your flame from out of the darkness, fly from they night and ye shall be free.

Traveled I through the space-time, knowing my soul at last was set free, knowing that now might I pursue wisdom. Until at last, I passed to a plane, hidden from knowledge, known not to wisdom, extension beyond all that we know. Now, O man, when I had this knowing, happy my soul grew, for now I was free. Listen, ye space-born, list to my wisdom: know ye not that ye, too, will be free.

List ye again, O man, to my wisdom, that hearing, ye too, might live and be free. Not of the earth are ye- earthy, but child of the Infinite Cosmic Light.

Now, to ye, I give knowledge, freedom to walk in the path I have trod, showing ye truly how by my striving, I trod the path that leads to the stars.

Hark ye, O man, and know of thy bondage, know how to free thyself from the toils. Out of the darkness shall ye rise upward, one with the Light and one with the stars. Follow ye ever the path of wisdom. Only by this can ye rise from below. Ever man's destiny leads him onward into the Curves of Infinity's ALL.

Know ye, O man, that all space is ordered. Only by Order are ye One with the ALL. Order and balance are the Law of the Cosmos. Follow and ye shall be One with the ALL.

He who would follow the pathway of wisdom, open must be to the Flower of Life, extending his consciousness out of the darkness, flowing through time and space in the ALL.

Deep in the silence, first ye must linger until at last ye are free from desire, free from the longing to speak in the silence. Conquer by silence, the bondage of words. Abstaining from eating until ye have conquered desire for food, that is bondage of soul.

Then lie ye down in the darkness. Close ye your eyes from the rays of the Light.

Center thy soul-force in the place of thine consciousness, shaking it free from the bonds of the night. Place in thy mind-place the image thou desireth. Picture the place thou desireth to see. Vibrate back and forth with thy power. Loosen the soul from out of its night. Fiercely must thou shake with all of thy power until at last thy soul shall be free.

Mighty beyond words is the flame of the Cosmic, hanging in planes, unknown to man; mighty and balanced, moving in Order, music of harmonies, far beyond man. Speaking with music, singing with color, flame from the beginning of Eternity's ALL.

Spark of the flame art thou, O my children, burning with color and living with music. List to the voice and thou shalt be free. Consciousness free is fused with the Cosmic, One with the Order and Law of the ALL.

Knew ye not man, that out of the darkness, Light shall flame forth, a symbol of ALL.

Pray ye this prayer for attaining of wisdom. Pray for the coming of Light to the ALL. "Mighty Spirit of Light that shines through the Cosmos, draw my flame closer in harmony to thee. Lift up my fire from out of the darkness, magnet of fire that is One with the ALL. Lift up my soul, thou mighty and potent. Child of the Light, turn not away. Draw me in power to melt in thy furnace; One with all things and all things in One, fire of the life-strain and One with the Brain."

When ye have freed thy soul from its bondage, know that for ye the darkness is gone. Ever through space ye may seek wisdom, bound not by fetters forged in flesh.

Onward and upward into the morning, free flash, O Soul, to the realms of Light. Move thou in Order, move thou in Harmony, freely shalt move with the Children of Light.

Seek ye and know ye, my Key of Wisdom. Thus, O man, ye shall surely be free.

22

EMERALD TABLET V

The Dweller of Unal

Oft dream I of buried Atlantis, lost in the ages that have passed into night. Aeon on aeon thou existed in beauty, a shining through the darkness of night.

Mighty in power, ruling the earth-born, Lord of the Earth in Atlantis' day. King of the nations, master of wisdom, Light through Suntal, Keeper of the Way, dwelt in his Temple, the Master of Unal, Light of the Earth in Atlantis' day.

Master, He, from a cycle beyond us, living in bodies as one among men. Not as the earth-born, He from beyond us, Sun of a cycle, advanced beyond men.

Know ye, O man, that Horlet the Master, was never one with the children of men. Far in the past time when Atlantis first grew as a power, appeared there one with the Key of Wisdom, showing the way of Light to all.

Showed he to all men the path of attainment, way of the Light that flows among men. Mastering darkness, leading the Man-Soul, upward to heights that were One with the Light.

Divided the Kingdoms, He into sections. Ten were they, ruled by children of men. Upon another, built He a Temple, built but not by the children of men.

Out of the Ether called He its substance, moulded and formed by the power of Ytolan into the forms He built with His mind. Mile upon mile it covered the island, space upon space it grew in its might. Black, yet not black, but dark like the space-time, deep in its heart the Essence of Light. Swiftly the Temple grew into being, moulded an shaped by the Word of the Dweller, called from the formless into a form.

Builded He then, within it, great chambers, filled them from forms called forth from the Ether, filled them with wisdom called forth by His mind.

Formless was He within his Temple, yet was He formed in the image of man. Dwelling among them yet not of them, strange and far different was He from the children of men.

Chose He then from among the people, Three who became his gateway. Chose He the Three from the Highest to become his links with Atlantis. Messengers they, who carried his councel, to the kings of the children of men.

Brought He forth others and taught them wisdom; teachers, they, to the children of men. Placed He them on the island of Undal to stand as teachers of Light to men.

Each of those who were thus chosen, taught must he be for years five and ten. Only thus could he have understanding to being Light to the children of men. Thus there came into being the Temple, a dwelling place for the Master of man.

I, Thoth, have ever sought wisdom, searching in darkness and searching in Light. Long in my youth I traveled the pathway, seeking ever new knowledge to gain. Until after much striving, one of the Three, to me brought the Light. Brought He to me the commands of the Dweller, called me from darkness into the Light.

Brought He me, before the Dweller, deep in the Temple before the great Fire.

There on the great throne, beheld I, the Dweller, clothed with the Light and flashing with fire. Down I knelt before that great wisdom, feeling the Light flowing through me in waves. Heard I then the voice of the Dweller: "O darkness, come into the Light. Long have ye sought the pathway to the Light. Each soul on earth that loosens its fetters shall soon be made free from the bondage of night. Forth from the darkness have ye arisen, closer approached the Light of your goal. Here ye shall dwell as one of my children, keeper of records gathered by wisdom, instrument thou of the Light from beyond. Ready be thou made to do what is needed, perserver of wisdom though the ages of darkness that shall come fast on the children of men. Live thee here and drink of all wisdom. Secrets and mysteries unto thee shall unveil."

Then answered I, the Master of Cycles, saying: "O Light, that descended to men, give thou to me of thy wisdom that I might be a teacher of men. Give thou of thy Light that I may be free."

Spoke then to me again, the Master: "Age after age shall ye live through your wisdom. Aye, when o'er Atlantis the ocean waves roll, holding the Light, though hidden in darkness, ready to come when e'er thou shalt call. Go thee now and learn greater wisdom. Grow thou through Light to Infinity's ALL."

Long then dwelt I in the Temple of the Dweller until at last I was One with the Light.

Followed I then the path to the star planes, followed I then the pathway to Light. Deep into Earth's heart I followed the pathway, learning the secrets, below as above; learning the pathway to the Halls of Amenti; learning the Law that balances the world. To earth's hidden chambers pierced I by my wisdom, deep through the Earth's crust, into the pathway, hidden for ages from the children of men. Unveiled before me, ever more wisdom until I reached a new knowledge: found that all is part of an ALL, great and yet greater than all that we know. Searched I Infinity's heart through the ages. Deep and yet deeper, more mysteries I found.

Now, as I look back through the ages, know I that wisdom is boundless, ever grown greater throughout the ages, One with Infinity's greater than all.

Light there was in ancient Atlantis. Yes, darkness, too, was hidden in all. Fell from the Light into the darkness, some who had risen to heights among men. Proud they became because of their knowledge, proud were they of their place among men. Deep delved they into the forbidden, opened the gateway that led to below. Sought they to gain ever more knowledge but seeking to bring it up from below.

He who descends below must have balance, else he is bound by lack of our Light. Opened, they then, by their knowledge, pathways forbidden to man.

But, in His Temple, all-seeing, the Dweller, lay in his Agwanti, which through Atlantis His soul roamed free. Saw He the Atlanteans, by their magic, opening the gateway that would bring to Earth a great woe. Fast fled His soul then, back to His body. Up He arose from His Agwanti. Called He the Three mighty messengers.
Gave the commands that shattered the world.

Deep 'neath Earth's crust to the Halls of Amenti, swiftly descended the Dweller. Called He then on the powers of the Seven Lords wielded; changed the Earth's balance. Down sank Atlantis beneath the dark waves.

Shattered the gateway that had been opened; shattered the doorway that led down below. All of the islands were shattered except Unal, and part of the island of the sons of the Dweller. Preserved He them to be the teachers, Lights on the path for those to come after, Lights for the lesser children of man.

Called He then, I Thoth, before him, gave me commands for all I should do, saying: "Take thou, O Thoth, all of your wisdom. Take all your records. Take all your magic. Go thou forth preserving the records until in time Light grows among men. Light shalt thou be all through the ages, hidden yet found by enlightened men. Over all Earth, give WE ye power, free thou to give or take it away. Gather thou now the sons of Atlantis. Take them and flee to the people of the rock caves. Fly to the land of the Children of Khem."
Then gathered I the sons of Atlantis. Into the spaceship I brought all my records, brought the records of sunken Atlantis. Gathered I all of my powers, instruments many of mighty magic.

Up then we rose on wings of the morning. High we arose above the Temple, leaving behind the three and Dweller, deep in the Halls 'neath the Temple. Down 'neath the waves sank the great Temple, closing the pathway to the Lords of the Cycles. Yet ever to him who has knowing, open shall be the path to Amenti.

Fast fled we then on the wings of the morning, fled to the land of the children of Khem. There by my power, I conquered and ruled them. Raised I to Light, the children of Khem.

Deep 'neath the rocks, I buried my spaceship, waiting the time when man might be free. Over the spaceship, erected a marker in the form of a lion yet like unto man. There 'neath the image rests yet my spaceship, forth to be brought when need shall arise.

Know ye, O man, that far in the future invaders shall come from out of the deep. Then awake, ye who have wisdom. Bring forth my ship and conquer with ease.

Deep 'neath the image lies my secret. Search and find in the pyramid I built. Each to the other is the Keystone; each the gateway that leads into Life. Follow the Key I leave behind me. Seek and the doorway to Life shall be thine. Seek thou in my pyramid, deep in the passage that ends in a wall. Use thou the Key of the Seven, and open to thee the pathway will fall.

Now unto thee I have given my wisdom. Now unto thee I have given my way. Follow the pathway. Solve thou my secrets. Unto thee I have shown the way.

23

EMERALD TABLET VI

Hark ye, O man, to the wisdom of magic. Hark to the knowledge of powers forgotten. Long, long ago in the days of the first man, warfare began between darkness and light. Men, then as now, were filled with both darkness and light; and while in some darkness held sway, in others light filled the soul.

Aye, age old is this warfare, the eternal struggle between darkness and light. Fiercely is it fought all through the ages, using strange powers hidden to man.

Adepts have there been filled with the blackness, struggling always against the light; but others there are who, filled with brightness, have ever conquered the darkness of night. Where e'er ye may be in all ages and planes, surely ye shall know of the battle with night. Long ages ago, the Suns of the Morning, descending, found the world filled with night. There in that past time began the struggle, the age old battle of darkness and Light.

Many in that time were so filled with darkness that only feebly flamed the light from the night.

Some there were, masters of darkness, who sought to fill all with their darkness; sought to draw others into their night. Fiercely withstood they, the masters of brightness; fiercely fought they from the darkness of night. Sought they ever to tighten the fetters, the chains that bind man to the darkness of night. Used they always the dark magic, brought into man by the power of darkness; magic that enshrouded man's soul with darkness.

Banded together in as order, Brothers of Darkness, they through the ages, antagonists they to the children of men. Walked they always secret and hidden, found yet not found by the children of men. Forever they walked and worked in darkness, hiding from the light in the darkness of night. Silently, secretly, use they their power, enslaving and binding the souls of men.

Unseen they come and unseen they go. Man in his ignorance calls Them from below.

Dark is the way the Dark Brothers travel, dark with a darkness not of the night, traveling o'er Earth they walk through man's dreams. Power have they gained from the darkness around them to call other dwellers from out of their plane in ways that are dark and unseen by man. Into man's mind-space reach the Dark Brothers. Around it, they close the veil of their night. There through its lifetime that soul dwells in bondage, bound by the fetters of the Veil of the night. Mighty are they in the forbidden knowledge, forbidden because it is one with the night. Hark ye, O man, and list to my warning: be ye free from the bondage of night. Surrender not your soul to the Brothers of Darkness. Keep thy face ever turned toward the Light. Know ye not, O man, that your sorrow only has come through the Veil of the night? Aye, man, heed ye my warning: strive ever upward, turn your soul toward the Light. For well know they that those who have traveled far towards the Sun on their pathway of Light have great and yet greater power to bind with darkness the children of Light.

List ye, O man, to he who comes to you. But weigh in the balance if his words be of Light. For many there are who walk in Dark Brightness and yet are not the children of Light. Easy it is to follow their pathway, easy to follow the path that they lead. But yes, O man, heed ye my warning: Light comes only to him who strives. Hard is the pathway that leads to the Wisdom, hard is the pathway that leads to the Light. Many shall ye find, the stones in your pathway; many the mountains to climb toward the Light. Yet know ye, O man, to him that o'ercometh, free will he be of the pathway of Light. Follow ye not the Dark Brothers ever. Always be ye a child of the Light. For know ye, O man, in the end Light must conquer and darkness and night be banished from Light.

Listen, O man, and heed ye this wisdom; even as darkness, so is the Light.
When darkness is banished and all Veils are rendered, out there shall flash from the darkness, the Light.

Even as exist among men the Dark Brothers, so there exists the Brothers of Light. Antagonists they of the Brothers of Darkness, seeking to free men from the night. Powers have they, mighty and potent. Knowing the Law, the planets obey. Work they ever in harmony and order, freeing the man-soul from its bondage of night. Secret and hidden, walk they also. Known not are they to the children of men. Yet know that ever they walk with thee, showing the Way to the children of men. Ever have They fought the Dark Brothers, conquered and conquering time without end. Yet always Light shall in the end be master, driving away the darkness of night.

Aye, man, know ye this knowing: always beside thee walk the Children of Light.

Masters they of the Sun power, ever unseen yet the guardians of men. Open to all is their pathway, open to he who will walk in the Light. Free are They of Dark Amenti, free of the Halls where Life regins supreme.
Suns are they and Lords of the morning, Children of Light to shine among men. Like man are they and yet are unlike. Never divided were they in the past. One have they been in Oneness eternal, throughout all space since the beginning of time. Up did they come in Oneness with the All One, up from the first-space, formed and unformed.

Given to man have they secrets that shall guard and protect him from all harm. He who would travel the path of a master, free must he be from the bondage of night. Conquer must he the formless and shapeless; conquer must he the phantom of fear. Knowing, must he gain of all the secrets, travel the pathway that leads through the darkness, yet ever before him keep the light of his goal. Obstacles great shall he meet in the pathway, yet press on to the Light of the Sun.

Hear ye, O man, the Sun is the symbol of the Light that shines at the end of thy road. Now to thee give I the secrets: how to meet the dark power, meet and conquer the fear from the night. Only by knowing can ye conquer; only by knowing can ye have Light.

Now I give unto thee the knowledge, known to the Masters; the knowing that conquers all the dark fears. Use this, the wisdom I give thee. Master thou shalt be of the Brothers of Night.

When unto thee there comes a feeling, drawing thee nearer to the dark gate, examine thine heart and find if the feeling thou hast has come from within. If thou shalt find the darkness thine own thoughts, banish them forth from place in thy mind. Send through thy body a wave of vibration, irregular first and regular second, repeating time after time until free. Start the Wave Force in thy Brain Center. Direct it in waves from thine head to thy foot.

But if thou findest thine heart is not darkened, be sure that a force is directed to thee. Only by knowing can thou overcome it. Only by wisdom can thou hope to be free. Knowledge brings wisdom and wisdom is power. Attain and ye shall have power o'er all.

Seek ye first a place bound with darkness. Place ye a circle around about thee. Stand erect in the midst of the circle. Use thou this formula, and thou shalt be free. Raise thou thine hands to the dark space above thee. Close thou thine eyes and draw in the Light. Call to the Spirit of Light through the Space-Time, using these words and thou shalt be free: "Fill thou my body with Spirit of Light. Come from the Flower that shines through the darkness. Come from the Halls where the Seven Lords rule. Name them by name, I, the Seven: Three, Four, Five and Six, Seven, Eight-Nine. By their names I call them to aid me, free me and save me from the darkness of night: Untanas, Quertas, Chietal, and Goyana, Huertal, Semveta-Ardal. By their names I implore thee, free me from darkness and fill me with Light."

Know ye, O man, that when ye have done this, ye shall be free from the fetters that bind ye, cast off the bondage of the Brothers of Night. See ye not that the names have the power to free by vibration the fetters that bind? Use them at need to free thou thine brother so the he, too, may come forth from the night.

Thou, O man, art thy brother's helper. Let him not lie in the bondage of night. Now unto thee, give I my magic. Take it and dwell on the pathway of Light. Light unto thee, Life unto thee, Sun may thou be on the cycle above.

24

EMERALD TABLET VII

The Seven Lords

    Hark ye, O man, and list to my Voice. Open thy mind-space and drink of my wisdom. Dark is the pathway of Life that ye travel. Many the pitfalls that lie in thy way. Seek ye ever to gain greater wisdom. Attain and it shall be light on thy way.

Open thy Soul, O man, to the Cosmic and let it flow in as one with thy Soul. Light is eternal and darkness is fleeting. Seek ye ever, O man, for the Light. Know ye that ever as Light fills thy being, darkness for thee shall soon disappear.

Open thy soul to the Brothers of Brightness. Let them enter and fill thee with Light. Lift up thine eyes to the Light of the Cosmos. Keep thou ever thy face to the goal. Only by gaining the light of all wisdom, art thou one with the Infinite goal. Seek ye ever the Oneness eternal. Seek ye ever the Light of the goal.

Light is infinite and Light is finite, separate only by darkness in man. Seek ye to rend the Veil of the Darkness. Bring thou together the Light into One.

Hear ye, O man, list to my Voice singing the song of Light and of Life. Throughout all space, Light is prevalent, encompassing ALL with its banners of flame. Seek ye forever in the Veil of the Darkness, somewhere ye shall surely find Light. Hidden and buried, lost to man's knowledge, deep in the finite the Infinite exists. Lost, but existing, flowing through all things, living in ALL is the Infinite Brain. In all space, there is only One wisdom. Though seeming divided, it is One in the

One. All that exists comes forth from the Light, and the Light comes forth from the ALL.

Everything created is based upon Order: Law rules the space where the Infinite dwells. Forth from equilibrium came the great cycles, moving in harmony toward Infinity's end.

Know ye, O man, that far in the space-time, Infinity itself shall pass into change. Here ye and list to the Voice of Wisdom: Know that ALL is of ALL evermore. Know that through time thou may pursue wisdom and find ever more light on the way. Aye, thou shalt find that ever receding, thy goal shall elude thee from day unto day.

Long time ago, in the Halls of Amenti, I, Thoth, stood before the Lords of the cycles. Mighty, They in their aspects of power; mighty, They in the wisdom unveiled.

Led by the Dweller, first did I see them. But afterwards free was I of their presence, free to enter their conclave at will. Oft did I journey down the dark pathway unto the Hall where the Light ever glows.

Learned I of the Masters of cycles, wisdom brought from the cycles above us, knowledge brought from Infinity's All. Many the questions I asked of the Lords of the cycles. Great was the wisdom they gave unto me. Now unto thee I give of this wisdom, drawn from the flame of Infinity's fire.

Deep in the Dark Halls sit the Seven, units of consciousness from cycles above. Manifest They in this cycle as guide of man to the knowledge of All. Seven are they, mighty in power, speaking these words through me to men. Time after time, stood I before them listening to words that came not with sound.

Once said They unto me: "O man, wouldst thou gain wisdom? Seek for it in the heart of the flame. Wouldst thou gain knowledge of power? Seek ye it in the heart of the flame. Wouldst be one with the heart of the flame? Seek then within thine own hidden flame."

Many the times spoke They to me, teaching me wisdom not of the world; showing me ever new paths to brightness; teaching me wisdom brought from above. Giving knowledge of operation, learning of Law, the order of ALL.

Spoke to me again, the Seven, saying: "From far beyond time are We come, O man. Traveled We from beyond the Space-Time, aye, from the place of Infinity's end. When ye and all of thy brethren were formless, formed forth were We from the order of ALL. Not as men are We though once We, too, were as men. Out of the Great Void were We formed forth in order and by Law. For know ye that that which is formed truly is formless, having form only to thine eyes."

And again, unto me spoke the Seven, saying: "Child of the Light, O Thoth, art thou, free to travel the bright path upward until at the last All Ones become One.

Forth were We formed after our order: Three, Four, Five and Six, Seven, Eight-Nine. Know ye that these are the number of cycles that We descend from unto man. Each having here a duty to fulfill; each having here a force to control. Yet are We, One, with the Soul of our cycle. Yet are We, too, seeking a goal. Far beyond man's conception, Infinity extends into a greater than All. There, in a time that is yet not a time, we shall ALL become ONE with a greater than ALL. Time and space are moving in circles. Know ye their law, and ye, too, shall be free. Aye, free shall ye be to move through the cycles-pass the guardians that dwell at the door."

Then to me spoke He of Nine, saying: "Aeons and aeons have I existed, knowing not Life, and tasting not death. For know ye, O man, that far in the future, life and death shall be one with the All. Each so perfected by balancing the other that neither exists in the Oneness of All. In men of this cycle, the life force is rampant, but life in its growth becomes one with the All. Here, I manifest in this your cycle, but yet am I there in your future of time. Yet to me, time exists not, for in my world time exists not, for formless are We. Life have We not but yet have existence, fuller and greater and freer than thee.

Man is a flame bound to a mountain, but We in our cycle shall ever be free. Know ye, O man, that when ye have progressed into the cycles that lengthen above, life itself will pass to the darkness and only the essence of Soul shall remain."

Then to me spoke the Lord of the Eight saying: "All that ye know is but part of little. Not as yet have ye touched on the Great. Far out in space where Light reigns supreme, came I into the Light. Formed was I also but not as ye are.

Body of Light was my formless form formed. Know I not Life and know I not Death, yet master am I of all that exists. Seek ye to find the path through the barriers. Travel the road that leads to the Light."

Spoke again to me the Nine saying: "Seek ye to find the path to beyond. Not impossible is it to grow to a consciousness above. For when Two have become One and One has become the All, know ye the barrier has lifted, and ye are made free of the road. Grow thou from form to the formless. Free may thou be of the road."

Thus, through ages I listened, learning the way to the All. Now lift I my thought to the All-Thing. List ye and hear when it calls. "O Light, all pervading, One with All and All with One, flow thou to me through the channel. Enter thou so that I may be free. Make me One with the All-Soul, shining from the blackness of night. Free let me be of all space-time, free from the Veil of the night. I, a child of the Light, command: Free from the darkness to be."

Formless am I to the Light-Soul, formless yet shining with Light. Know I the bonds of the darkness must shatter and fall before light.

Now give I this wisdom. Free may ye be, O man, living in light and in brightness. Turn not thy face from the Light. Thy soul dwells in realms of brightness. Ye are a child of the Light.

Turn thy thoughts inward not outward. Find thou the Light-Soul within. Know that thou are the Master. All else is brought from within. Grow thou to realms of brightness. Hold thou thy thought on the Light. Know thou are one with the Cosmos, a flame and a Child of the Light.

Now to thee give I warning: Let not thy thought turn away. Know that the brightness flows through thy body for aye. Turn not to the

Dark-Brightness that comes from the Brothers of Black. But keep thine eyes ever lifted, thy soul in tune with the Light.

Take ye this wisdom and heed it. List to my Voice and obey. Follow the pathway to brightness, and thou shalt be One with the way.

EMERALD TABLET VIII

The Key of Mysteries
Unto thee, O man, have I given my knowledge. Unto thee have I given of Light. Hear ye now and receive my wisdom brought from space planes above and beyond.

Not as man am I for free have I become of dimensions and planes. In each, take I on a new body. In each, I change in my form. Know I now that the formless is all there is of form.

Great is the wisdom of the Seven. Mighty are they from beyond. Manifest They through their power, filled by force from beyond.

Here ye these words of wisdom. Hear ye and make them thine own. Find in them the formless. Find ye the key to beyond. Mystery is but hidden knowledge. Know and ye shall unveil. Find the deep buried wisdom and be master of darkness and Light.

Deep are the mysteries around thee, hidden the secrets of Old. Search through the Keys of my Wisdom. Surely shall ye find the way. The gateway to power is secret, but he who attains shall receive. Look to the Light! O my brother. Open and ye shall receive. Press on through the valley of darkness. Overcome the dweller of the night. Keep ever thine eyes to the Light-Plane, and thou shalt be One with the Light.

Man is in process of changing to forms that are not of this world. Grows he in time to the formless, a plane on the cycle above. Know ye, ye must become formless before ye are one with the Light.

List ye, O man, to my voice, telling of the pathways to Light, showing the way of attainment when ye shall be One with the Light. Search ye the mysteries of Earth's heart. Learn of the Law that exists, holding the stars in their balance by the force of the primordial mist. Seek ye the flame of the Earth's Life. Bathe in the glare of its flame. Follow the three-cornered pathway until thou, too, art a flame.

Speak thou in words without voice to those who dwell down below. Enter the blue-litten Temple and bathe in the fire of all life.

Know, O man, thou art complex, a being of earth and of fire. Let thy flame shine out brightly. Be thou only the fire.

Wisdom is hidden in darkness. When lit by the flame of the Soul, find thou the wisdom and be Light-Born, a Sun of the Light without form. Seek thee ever more wisdom. Find it in the heart of the flame. Know that only by striving can Light pour into thy brain. Now have I spoken with wisdom. List to my Voice and obey. Tear open the Veils of the darkness. Shine a Light on the Way.

Speak I of Ancient Atlantis, speak of the days of the Kingdom of Shadows, speak of the coming of the children of shadows. Out of the great deep were they called by the wisdom of earth-men, called for the purpose of gaining great power.

Far in the past before Atlantis existed, men there were who delved into darkness, using dark magic, calling up beings from the great deep below us. Forth came they into this cycle. Formless were they of another vibration, existing unseen by the children of earth-men. Only through blood could they have formed being. Only through man could they live in the world.

In ages past were they conquered by the Masters, driven below to the place whence they came. But some there were who remained, hidden in spaces and planes unknown to man. Lived they in Atlantis as shadows, but at times they appeared among men. Aye, when the blood was offered, forth came they to dwell among men.

In the form of man moved they amongst us, but only to sight where they as are men. Serpent-headed when the glamour was lifted but appearing to man as men among men. Crept they into the Councils, taking forms that were like unto men. Slaying by their arts the chiefs of the kingdoms, taking their form and ruling o'er man. Only by magic could they be discovered. Only by sound could their faces be seen. Sought they from the kingdom of shadows to destroy man and rule in his place.

But, know ye, the Masters were mighty in magic, able to lift the Veil from the face of the serpent, able to send him back to his place. Came they to man and taught him the secret, the Word that only a man can pronounce. Swift then they lifted the Veil from the serpent and cast him forth from place among men.

Yet, beware, the serpent still liveth in a place that is open at times to the world. Unseen they walk among thee in places where the rites have been said. Again as time passes onward shall they take the semblance of men.

Called may they be by the master who knows the white or the black, but only the white master may control and bind them while in the flesh.

Seek not the kingdom of shadows, for evil will surely appear. For only the master of brightness shall conquer the shadow of fear.

Know ye, O my brother, that fear is an obstacle great. Be master of all in the brightness, the shadow will soon disappear. Hear ye and heed my wisdom, the voice of Light is clear. Seek not the valley of shadow, and Light only will appear.

List ye, O man, to the depth of my wisdom. Speak I of knowledge hidden from man. Far have I been on my journey though Space-Time, even to the end of the space of this cycle. Found I there the great barrier, holding man from leaving this cycle. Aye, glimpsed the Hounds of the Barrier, laying in wait for he who would pass them. In that space where time exists not, faintly I sensed the guardians of cycles. Move they only through angles. Free are they not of the curved dimensions.

Strange and terrible are the Hounds of the Barrier. Follow they consciousness to the limits of space. Think not to escape by entering your body, for follow they fast the Soul through angles. Only the circle will give ye protection, safe from the claws of the Dweller in Angles.

Once, in a time past, I approached the great Barrier, and saw on the shores where time exists not, the formless forms of the Hounds of the Barrier. Aye, hiding in the mist beyond time I found them; and They, scenting me afar off, raised themselves and gave the great bell cry that can be heard from cycle to cycle and moved through space toward my Soul.

Fled I then fast before them, back from time's unthinkable end. But ever after me pursued they, moving in strange angles not known to man. Aye, on the gray shore of Time-Space's end found I the Hounds of the Barrier, ravening for the Soul who attempts the beyond.

Fled I through circles back to my body. Fled, and fast after me they followed. Aye, after me the devourers followed, seeking through angles to devour my Soul.

Aye, know ye man, that the Soul who dares the Barrier may be held in bondage by the Hounds from beyond time, held till this cycle is all completed and left behind when the consciousness leaves.

Entered I my body. Created the circles that know not angles, created the form that from my form was formed. Made my body into a circle and lost the pursuers in the circles of time. But, even yet, when free from my body, cautious ever must I be not to move through angles, else my Soul might never be free.

Know ye, the Hounds of the Barrier move only through angles and never through curves of space. Only by moving through curves can ye escape them, for in angles they will pursue thee. O man, heed ye my warning; Seek not to break open the gate to beyond. Few there are who have succeeded in passing the Barrier to the greater Light that shines beyond. For know ye, ever the dwellers, seek such Souls to hold in their thrall.

Listen, O man, and heed ye my warning; seek ye to move not in angles but curves. And if while free from thy body, thou hearest the sound like the bay of a hound ringing clear and bell-like through thy being, flee back to thy body through circles, penetrate not the mist before.

When thou hast entered the form thou hast dwelt in, use thou the cross and the circle combined. Open thy mouth and use thou thy Voice. Utter the Word and thou shalt be free. Only the one who of Light has the fullest can hope to pass by the guards of the way. And then must he move through strange curves and angles that are formed in direction not known to man.

List ye, O man, and heed ye my warning: attempt not to pass the guards in the way. Rather should ye seek to gain of thine own Light and make thyself ready to pass on the way.

Light is thine ultimate end, O my brother. Seek and find ever the Light on thy way.

26

EMERALD TABLET IX

The Key of Freedom of Space

    List ye, O man, hear ye my voice, teaching of Wisdom and Light in this cycle; teaching ye how to banish the darkness, teaching ye how to bring Light in thy life.

Seek ye, O man, to find the great pathway that leads to eternal Life as a Sun. Draw ye away from the veil of the darkness. Seek to become a Light in the world. Make of thyself a vessel for Light, a focus for the Sun of this space.

Lift thou thine eyes to the Cosmos. Lift thou thine eyes to the Light. Speak in the words of the Dweller, the chant that calls down the Light. Sing thou the song of freedom. Sing thou the song of the Soul. Create the high vibration that will make thee One with the Whole. Blend all thyself with the Cosmos. Grow into One with the Light. Be thou a channel of order, a pathway of Law to the world.

Thy Light, O man, is the great Light, shining through the shadow of flesh. Free must thou rise from the darkness before thou art One with the Light.

Shadows of darkness surround thee. Life fills thee with its flow. But know, O man, thou must arise and forth from thy body go far to the planes that surround thee and yet are One with thee, too.

Look all around thee, O man. See thine own light reflected. Aye, even in the darkness around thee, thine own Light pours forth through the veil.

Seek thou for wisdom always. Let not thine body betray. Keep in the path of the Light wave. Shun thou the darkened way. Know thee that wisdom is lasting, existing since the All-Soul began, creating harmony from chaos by the Law that exists in the Way.

List ye, O man, to the teaching of wisdom. List to the voice that speaks of the past-time. Aye, I shall tell thee knowledge forgotten, tell ye of wisdom hidden in past-time, lost in the mist of darkness around me.

Know ye, man, ye are the ultimate of all things. Only the knowledge of this is forgotten, lost when man was cast into bondage, bound and fettered by the chains of the darkness.

Long, long ago, I cast off my body. Wandered I free through the vastness of ether, circled the angles that hold man in bondage. Know ye, O man, ye are only a spirit. The body is nothing. The Soul is All. Let not your body be a fetter. Cast off the darkness and travel in Light. Cast off your body, O man, and be free, truly a Light that is One with the Light.

When ye are free from the fetters of darkness and travel in space as a Sun of the Light, then ye shall know that space is not boundless but truly bounded by angles and curves. Know ye, O man, that all that exists is only an aspect of greater things yet to come. Matter is fluid and flows like a stream, constantly changing from one thing to another.

All through the ages has knowledge existed; never been changed, though buried in darkness; never been lost, though forgotten by man.

Know ye that throughout the space that ye dwell in are others as great as your own, interlaced through the heart of your matter yet separate in space of their own.

Once in a time long forgotten, I, Thoth, opened the doorway, penetrated into other spaces and learned of the secrets concealed. Deep in the essence of matter are many mysteries concealed.

Nine are the interlocked dimensions, and Nine are the cycles of space. Nine are the diffusions of consciousness, and Nine are the worlds within worlds. Aye, Nine are the Lords and the cycles that come from above and below.

Space is filled with concealed ones, for space is divided by time. Seek ye the key to the time-space, and ye shall unlock the gate. Know ye that throughout the time-space consciousness surely exists. Though from our knowledge it is hidden, yet still it forever exists.

The key to worlds within thee are found only within. For man is the gateway of mystery and the key that is One within One.

Seek ye within the circle. Use the Word I shall give. Open the gateway within thee, and sure thou, too, shalt live. Man, ye think that ye liveth, but know it is life within death. For as sure as ye are bound to your body, for you no life exists. Only the Soul is space-free, has life that is really a life. All else is only a bondage, a fetter from which to be free.

Think not that man is earth-born, though come from the earth he may be. Man is a light-born spirit. But, without knowing, he can never be free. Darkness fetters the Soul. Only the one who is seeking may ever hope to be free.
Shadows around thee are falling. Darkness fills all the spaces. Shine forth, O Light of the man-soul. Fill thou the darkness of space. Ye are a Sun of the Great Light. Remember and ye shall be free. Stay not thou in the shadows. Spring forth from the darkness of night. Light, let thy Soul be, O Sun-Born, filled with glory of Light, freed from the bonds of darkness, a Soul that is One with the Light.

Thou art the key to all wisdom. Within thee is all time and space. Live not in bondage to darkness. Free thou thy Light-form from night.

"Great Light that fills all the Cosmos, flow thou fully to man. Make of his body a light-torch that shall never be quenched among men."

Long in the past, sought I wisdom, knowledge not known to man. Far to the past I traveled into the space where time began. Sought I ever new knowledge to add to the wisdom I know. Yet only, I found, did the future hold the key to the wisdom I sought.

Down to the Halls of Amenti I journeyed, the greater knowledge to seek. Asked of the Lords of the Cycles, the way to the wisdom I sought. Asked the Lords this question: "Where is the source of ALL?" Answered, in tones that were mighty, the voice of the Lord of the Nine:

"Free thou thy Soul from thy body and come forth with me to the Light."

Forth I came from my body, a glittering flame in the night. Stood I before the Lords, bathed in the fire of Life. Seized was I then by a force, great beyond knowledge of man. Cast was I to the Abyss through spaces unknown to man.

Saw I moulding of Order from the chaos and angles of night. Saw I the Light spring from Order and heard the voice of the Light. Saw I the flame of the Abyss, casting forth Order and Light. Saw Order spring out of chaos. Saw Light giving forth Life.

Then heard I the voice: "Hear thou and understand. The flame is the source of all things, containing all things in potentiality. The Order that sent forth light is the Word and from the Word comes Life and the existence of all." And again spoke the voice saying: "The Life in thee is the Word. Find thou the Life within thee, and have powers to use of the Word."

Long I watched the Light-flame, pouring forth from the Essence of Fire, realizing that Life is but Order and that man is one with the fire.

Back I came to my body. Stood again with the Nine, listened to the voice of the Cycles, vibrate with powers they spoke: "Know ye, O Thoth, that Life is but the Word of the Fire. The Life force ye seek before thee is but the Word in the World as a fire. Seek ye the path to the Word and powers shall surely be thine."

Then asked I of the Nine: "O Lord, show me the path. Give me the path to the wisdom. Show me the way to the Word." Answered, me then, the Lord of the Nine: "Through Order, ye shall find the way. Saw ye not that the Word came from Chaos? Saw ye not that Light came from Fire? Look in thy life for disorder. Balance and order thy life. Quell all the Chaos of emotions and thou shalt have order in Life. Order brought forth from Chaos will bring thee the Word of the Source, will give thee the power of Cycles, and make of thy Soul a force that free will extend through the ages, a perfected Sun from the Source."

Listened I to the voice and deep sank the words in my heart. For ever have I sought for order that I might draw on the word. Know ye that he who attains it must ever in Order be. For use of the Word through disorder has never and can never be.

Take ye these words, O man. As part of thy life, let them be. Seek thee to conquer disorder, and One with the Word thou shalt be.

Put forth thy effort in gaining Light on the pathway of Life. Seek to be One with the Sun-State. Seek to be solely the Light. Hold thou thy thought on the Oneness of Light with the body of man. Know that all is Order from Chaos born into Light.

27

EMERALD TABLET X

The Key of Time

List ye, O man. Take of my wisdom. Learn of the deep hidden mysteries of space. Learn of the Thought that grew in the abyss, bringing Order and Harmony in space.

Know ye, O man, that all that exists has being only because of the Law. Know ye the Law and ye shall be free, never be bound by the fetters of night.

Far, through strange spaces, have I journeyed into the depth of the abyss of time, learning strange and yet stranger mysteries, until in the end all was revealed. Know ye that mystery is only mystery when it is knowledge unknown to man. When you have plumbed the heart of all mystery, knowledge and wisdom will surely be thine.

Seek ye and learn that Time is the secret whereby ye may be free of this space.

Long have I, Thoth, sought wisdom; aye, and shall seek to eternity's end for know I that ever before receding shall move the goal I seek to attain. Even the Lords of the Cycles know that not yet have They reached the goal, for with all of their wisdom, they know that Truth ever grows.

Once, in a past time, I spoke to the Dweller. Asked of the mystery of time and space. Asked him the question that surged in my being, saying: "O Master, what is time?"

Then to me spoke He, the Master: "Know ye, O Thoth, in the beginning there was void and nothingness: a timeless, spaceless, nothingness. And into the nothingness came a thought, purposeful, all-pervading, and It filled the Void. There existed no matter, only force, a movement, a vortex of vibration of the purposeful thought that filled the Void."

And I questioned the Master, saying: "Was this thought eternal?" And answered me the Dweller, saying: "In the beginning, there was eternal thought, and for thought to be eternal, time must exist. So into the all- pervading thought grew the Law of Time. Aye, time which exists through all space, floating in a smooth, rhythmic movement that is eternally in a state of fixation. Time changes not, but all things change in time. For time is the force that holds events separate, each in its proper place. Time is not in motion, but ye move through time as your consciousness moves from one event to another. Aye, by time ye exist, all in all, an eternal One existence. Know ye that even though in time ye are separate, yet still are One in all times existent." Ceased then the voice of the Dweller, and departed I to ponder on time. For knew I that in these words lay wisdom and a way to explore the mysteries of time.

Oft did I ponder the words of the Dweller. Then sought I to solve the mystery of time. Found I that time moves through strange angles. Yet only by curves could I hope to attain the key that would give me access to the time-space. Found I that only by moving upward and yet again by moving to right-ward could I be free from the time of this movement.

Forth I came from out of my body, moved in the movements that changed me in time. Strange were the sights I saw in my journeys, many the mysteries that opened to view. Aye, saw I man's beginning, learned from the past that nothing is new.

Seek ye, O man, to learn the pathway that leads through the spaces that are formed forth in time. Forget not, O man, with all of thy seeking that Light is the goal ye shall seek to attain. Search ye ever for

Light on thy pathway and ever for thee the goal shall endure. Let not thine heart turn ever to darkness. Light let thine Soul be, a sun on the way. Know ye that in the eternal brightness, ye shall ever find thy Soul hid in the Light, never fettered by bondage to darkness, ever it shines forth a Sun of the Light.

Aye, know, though hidden in darkness, your Soul, a spark of the true flame, exists. Be ye One with the greatest of all Lights. Find at the Source, the End of thy goal.

Light is life, for without the great Light nothing can ever exist. Know ye, that in all formed matter, the heart of Light always exists. Aye, even though bound in the darkness, inherent Light always exists.

Once I stood in the Halls of Amenti and heard the voice of the Lords of Amenti, saying in tones that rang through the silence, words of power, mighty and potent. Chanted they the song of the cycles, the words that opened the path to beyond. Aye, I saw the great path opened and looked for an instant into the beyond. Saw I the movements of the cycles, vast as the thought of the Source could convey.
Knew I then that even Infinity is moving on to some unthinkable end. Saw I that the Cosmos is Order and part of a movement that extends to all space, a part of an Order of Orders, constantly moving in a harmony of space. Saw I the wheeling of cycles like vast circles across the sky. Knew I then that all that has being is growing to meet yet other being in a far-off grouping of space and of time. Knew I then that in Words are power to open the planes that are hidden from man. Aye, that even in Words lies hidden the key that will open above and below.

Hark ye now, man, this word I leave with thee. Use it and ye shall find power in its sound. Say ye, the word: "Zin-Uru" and power ye shall find. Yet must ye understand that man is of Light and Light is of man.

List ye, O man, and hear a mystery stranger than all that lies 'neath the Sun. Know ye, O man, that all space is filled by worlds within worlds; aye, one within the other yet separate by Law.

Once in my search for deep buried wisdom, I opened the door that bars Them from man. Called I from other planes of being, one who was fairer than the daughters of men. Aye, I called her from out of the spaces to shine as a Light in the world of men.

Used I the drum of the Serpent. Wore I the robe of the purple and gold. Placed on my head, I, the crown of Silver. Around me the circle of cinnabar shone. Raised I my arms and cried the invocation that opens the path to the planes beyond, cried to the Lords of the Signs in their houses: "Lords of the two horizons, watchers of the treble gates, stand ye One at the right and One at the left as the Star rises to his throne and rules over his sign. Aye, thou dark prince of Arulu, open the gates of the dim, hidden land and release her whom ye keep imprisoned.

Hear ye, hear ye, hear ye, dark Lords and Shining Ones, and by their secret names, names which I know and can pronounce, hear ye and obey my will."

Lit I then with flame my circle and called Her in the space-planes beyond. "Daughter of Light return from Arulu. Seven times and seven times have I passed through the fire. Food have I not eaten. Water have I not drunk. I call thee from Arulu, from the realm of Ekershegal, I summon thee, Lady of Light."

Then before me rose the dark figures; aye, the figures of the Lords of Arulu. Parted they before me and forth came the Lady of Light. Free was she now from the Lords of the night, free to live in the Light of the earth Sun, free to live as a child of Light.

Here ye and listen, O my children. Magic is knowledge and only is Law. Be not afraid of the power within thee for it follows Law as the stars in the sky.

Know ye that to he without knowledge, wisdom is magic and not of the Law. But know ye that ever ye by your knowledge can approach closer to a place in the Sun.

List ye, my children, follow my teaching. Be ye ever seeker of Light. Shine in the world of men all around thee, a Light on the path that shall shine among men.

Follow ye and learn of my magic. Know that all force is thine if thou wilt. Fear not the path that leads thee to knowledge, but rather shun ye the dark road.

Light is thine, O man, for the taking. Cast off the fetters and thou shalt be free. Know ye that thy Soul is living in bondage fettered by fear that holds ye in thrall. Open thy eyes and see the great Sun-Light. Be not afraid for all is thine own. Fear is the Lord of dark Arulu to he who has never faced the dark fear. Aye, know that fear has existence created by those who are bound by their fears.

Shake off thy bondage, O children, and walk in the Light of the glorious day. Never turn thy thoughts to the darkness and surely ye shall be One with the Light.

Man is only what he believeth, a brother of darkness or a child of the Light. Come thou into the Light my Children. Walk in the pathway that leads to the Sun.

Hark ye now and list to the wisdom. Use thou the word I have given unto thee. Use it and surely thou shalt find power and wisdom and Light to walk in the way. Seek thee and find the key I have given and ever shalt thou be a Child of the Light.

28

EMERALD TABLET XI

The Key to Above and Below

Hear ye and list ye, O children of Khem, to the words that I give that shall bring ye to the Light. Ye know, O men, that I knew your fathers, aye, your fathers in a time long ago. Deathless have I been through all the ages, living among ye since your knowledge began. Leading ye upward to the Light of the Great Soul have I ever striven, drawing ye from out of the darkness of night.

Know ye, O people amongst whom I walk, that I, Thoth, have all of the knowledge and all of the wisdom known to man since the ancient days. Keeper have I been of the secrets of the great race, holder of the key that leads into life. Bringer up have I been to ye, O my children, even from the darkness of the Ancient of Days. List ye now to the words of my wisdom. List ye now to the message I bring. Hear ye now the words I give thee, and ye shall be raised from the darkness to Light.

Far in the past, when first I came to thee, found I thee in caves of rocks. Lifted I thee by my power and wisdom until thou didst shine as men among men. Aye, found I thee without any knowing. Only a little were ye raised beyond beasts. Fanned I ever the spark of thy consciousness until at last ye flamed as men.

Now shall I speak to thee knowledge ancient beyond the thought of thy race. Know ye that we of the Great Race had and have knowledge that is more than man's. Wisdom we gained from the star-born races, wisdom and knowledge far beyond man's. Down to us had descended the masters of wisdom as far beyond us as I am from thee. List ye now while I give ye wisdom. Use it and free thou shalt be.

Know ye that in the pyramid I builded are the Keys that shall show ye the Way into life. Aye, draw ye a line from the great image I builded, to the apex of the pyramid, built as a gateway. Draw ye another opposite in the same angle and direction. Dig ye and find that which I have hidden. There shall ye find the underground entrance to the secrets hidden before ye were men.

Tell ye I now of the mystery of cycles that move in movements that are strange to the finite, for infinite are they beyond knowledge of man. Know ye that there are nine of the cycles; aye, nine above and fourteen below, moving in harmony to the place of joining that shall exist in the future of time. Know ye that the Lords of the Cycles are units of consciousness sent from the others to unify This with the All. Highest are They of the consciousness of all the Cycles, working in harmony with the Law. Know They that in time all will be perfected, having none above and none below, but all One in a perfected Infinity, a harmony of all in the Oneness of All.

Deep 'neath Earth's surface in the Halls of Amenti sit the Seven, the Lords of the Cycles, aye, and another, the Lord from below. Yet know thee that in Infinity there is neither above nor below. But ever there is and ever shall be Oneness of All when all is complete. Oft have I stood before the Lords of the All. Oft at the fount of their wisdom have drunken and filled both my body and Soul with their Light.

Spake they to me and told me of cycles and the Law that gives them the means to exist. Aye, spake to me the Lord of the Nine saying: "O, Thoth, great are ye among Earth's children, but mysteries exist of which ye know not. Ye know that ye came from a space-time below this and know ye shall travel to a space-time beyond. But little ye know of the mysteries within them, little ye know of the wisdom beyond. Know ye that ye as a whole in this consciousness are only a cell in the process of growth.

The consciousness below thee is ever-expanding in different ways from those known to thee. Aye, it, though in space-time below thee, is ever growing in ways that are different from those that were part of the ways of thine own. For know that it grows as a result of thy growth but not in the same way that thou didst grow. The growth that thou had and have in the present have brought into being a cause and effect. No consciousness follows the path of those before it, else all would be repetition and vain. Each consciousness in the cycle it exists in follows its own path to the ultimate goal. Each plays its part in the Plan of the Cosmos. Each plays its part in the ultimate end. The farther the cycle, the greater its knowledge and ability to blend the Law of the whole.

Know ye, that ye in the cycles below us are working the minor parts of the Law, while we of the cycle that extends to Infinity take of the striving and build greater Law.

Each has his own part to play in the cycles. Each has his work to complete in his way. The cycle below thee is yet not below thee but only formed for a need that exists. For know ye that the fountain of wisdom that sends forth the cycles is eternally seeking new powers to gain. Ye know that knowledge is gained only by practice, and wisdom comes forth only from knowledge, and thus are the cycles created by Law. Means are they for the gaining of knowledge for the Plane of Law that is the Source of the All. The cycle below is not truly below but only different in space and in time. The consciousness there is working and testing lesser things than those ye are. And know, just as ye are working on greater, so above ye are those who are also working as ye are on yet other laws. The difference that exists between the cycles is only in ability to work with the Law. We, who have being in cycles beyond thee, are those who first came forth from the Source and have in the passage through time-space gained ability to use Laws of the Greater that are far beyond the conception of man. Nothing there is that is really below thee but only a different operation of Law.

Look thee above or look thee below, the same shall ye find. For all is but part of the Oneness that is at the Source of the Law. The consciousness below thee is part thine own as we are a part of thine.

Ye, as a child had not the knowledge that came to ye when ye became a man. Compare ye the cycles to man in his journey from birth unto death, and see in the cycle below thee the child with the knowledge he has; and see ye yourself as the child grown older, advancing in knowledge as time passes on. See ye, We, also, the child grown to manhood with the knowledge and wisdom that came with the years. So also, O Thoth, are the cycles of consciousness, children in different stages of growth, yet all from the one Source, the Wisdom, and all to the Wisdom returning again."

Ceased then He from speaking and sat in the silence that comes to the Lords. Then again spake He unto me, saying: "O Thoth, long have We sat in Amenti, guarding the flame of life in the Halls. Yet know, we are still part of our Cycles with our Vision reaching unto them and beyond. Aye, know we that of all, nothing else matters excepting the growth we can gain with our Soul. Know we the flesh is fleeting. The things men count great are nothing to us. The things we seek are not of the body but are only the perfected state of the Soul. When ye as men can learn that nothing but progress of Soul can count in the end, then truly ye are free from all bondage, free to work in a harmony of Law.

Know, O man, ye should aim at perfection, for only thus can ye attain to the goal. Though ye should know that nothing is perfect, yet it should be thy aim and thy goal." Ceased again the voice of the Nine, and into my consciousness the words had sunk. Now, seek I ever more wisdom that I may be perfect in Law with the All.

Soon go I down to the Halls of Amenti to live 'neath the cold flower of life. Ye whom I have taught shall nevermore see me. Yet live I forever in the wisdom I taught.

All that man is is because of his wisdom. All that he shall be is the result of his cause.

List ye, now to my voice and become greater than common man. Lift thine eyes upward, let Light fill thy being, be thou ever Children of Light. Only by effort shall ye grow upward to the plane where Light is the All of the All. Be ye the master of all that surrounds thee. Never be mastered by the effects of thy life. Create then ever more perfect causes and in time shalt thou be a Sun of the Light.

Free, let thine soul soar ever upward, free from the bondage and fetters of night. Lift thine eyes to the Sun in the sky-space. For thee, let it be a symbol of life. Know that thou art the Greater Light, perfect in thine own sphere, when thou art free. Look not ever into the blackness. Lift up thine eyes to the space above. Free let thine Light flame upward and shalt thou be a Child of the Light.

29

EMERALD TABLET XII

The Law of Cause and Effect
List ye, O man, to the words of my wisdom, list to the voice of Thoth, the Atlantean. Conquered have I the Law of the time-space. Knowledge have I gained of the future of time. Know I that man in his movement through space-time shall ever be ONE with the ALL.

Know ye, O man, that all of the future is an open book to him who can read. All effect shall bring forth its causes as all effects grew from the first cause. Know ye the future is not fixed or stable but varies as cause brings forth an effect. Look in the cause thou shalt bring into being, and surely thou shalt see that all is effect.
In the great beginning, there grew the First Cause that brought into being all that exists. Thou, thyself, art the effect of causation and in turn are the cause of yet other effects.

So, O man, be sure the effects that ye bring forth are ever causes of more perfect effects. Know ye the future is never in fixation but follows man's free will as it moves through the movements of time-space toward the goal where a new time begins. Man can only read the future through the causes that bring the effects. Seek ye within the causation and surely ye shall find the effects.

List ye, O man, while I speak of the future, speak of the effect that follows the cause. Know ye that man in his journey light-ward is ever seeking escape from the night. Aye, from the blackness of night that surrounds him, like the shadows that surround the stars in the sky and like the stars in the sky-space, he, too, shall shine from the shadows of night.

Ever his destiny shall lead him onward until he is ONE with the Light. Aye, though his way lies midst the shadows, ever before him glows the Great Light.

Dark thou the way be yet shall he conquer the shadows that flow around him like night.

Far in the future, I see men as Light-born, free from the darkness that fetters the Soul, living in Light without the bonds of the darkness to cover the Light that is Light of their Soul. Know ye, O man, before ye attain this that many the dark shadows shall fall on your Light striving to quench with the shadows of darkness the Light of the Soul that strives to be free.

Great is the struggle between Light and darkness, age old and yet ever new. Yet, know in a time, far in the future, Light shall be All and darkness shall fall.

List ye, O man, to my words of wisdom. Prepare and ye shall not bind your Light. Man has risen and man has fallen as ever new waves of consciousness flow from the great abyss below us toward the Sun of their goal.

Ye, my children, have risen from a state that was little above the beast, until now of all men ye are greatest. Yet before thee were others greater than thee. Yet tell I thee as before thee others have fallen, so also shall ye come to an end. And upon the land where ye dwell now, barbarians shall dwell and in turn rise to Light. Forgotten shall be the ancient-wisdom, yet ever shall live though hidden from men.

Aye, in the land thou callest Khem, races shall rise and races shall fall. Forgotten shalt thou be of the children of men. Yet thou shalt have moved to a star-space beyond this leaving behind this place where thou hast dwelt.

The Soul of man moves ever onward, bound not be any one star. But ever moving to the great goal before him where he is dissolved in the Light of the All. Know ye that ye shall ever go onward, moved by the Law of cause and effect until in the end both become One.

Aye, man, after ye have gone, others shall move in the places ye lived.

Knowledge and wisdom shall all be forgotten, and only a memory of Gods shall survive. As I to thee am a God by my knowledge, so ye, too, shall be Gods of the future because of your knowledge far above theirs. Yet know ye that all through the ages, man shall have access to Law when he will.

Ages to comes shall see revival of wisdom to those who shall inherit thy place on this star. They shall, in turn, comes into wisdom and learn to banish the darkness by Light. Yet greatly must they strive through the ages to bring unto themselves the freedom of Light. Many who are bound in darkness shall strive to hold others from Light. Then shall there come unto man the great warfare that shall make the Earth tremble and shake in its course. Aye, then shall the Dark Brothers open the warfare between Light and the night.

When man again shall conquer the ocean and fly in the air on wings like the birds; when he has learned to harness the lightning, then shall the time of warfare begin. Great shall the battle be twixt the forces, great the warfare of darkness and Light. Nation shall rise against nation using the dark forces to shatter the Earth.

Weapons of force shall wipe out the Earth-men until half of the races of men shall be gone. Then shall come forth the Sons of the Morning and give their edict to the children of men, saying: "O men, cease from thy striving against they brother. Only thus can ye come to the Light. Cease from thy unbelief, O my brother, and follow the path and know ye are right."

Then shall men cease from their striving, brother against brother and father against son. Then shall the ancient home of my people rise from its place 'neath the dark ocean waves. Then shall the Age of Lights be unfolded with all men seeking the Light of the goal. Then shall the Brothers of Light rule the people.

Banished shall be the darkness of night.

Aye, the children of men shall progress onward and upward to the great goal. Children of Light shall they become. Flame of the flame shall their Souls ever be. Knowledge and wisdom shall be man's in the great age for he shall approach the eternal flame, the SOURCE of all wisdom, the place of beginning, that is yet ONE with the end of all things. Aye, in a time that is yet unborn, all shall be ONE and ONE shall be All. Man, a perfect flame of this Cosmos, shall move forward to a place in the stars. Aye, shall move even from out of this space-time into another beyond the stars.

Long have ye listened to me, O my children, long have ye listened to the wisdom of Thoth. Now I depart from ye into the darkness. Now go I to the HALLS of AMENTI, there to dwell in the future [when] Light shall come again to man. Yet, know ye, my Spirit shall ever be with thee, guiding thy feet in the pathway of Light.
Guard ye the secrets I leave with thee, are surely my spirit will guard thee through life. Keep thine eyes ever on the pathway to wisdom. Keep the Light as thy goal evermore. Fetter not thy Soul in bondage of darkness; free let it wing in its flight to the stars.

Now I depart thee to dwell in Amenti. Be thou my children in this life and the next. The time will come when ye, too, shall be deathless, living from age to age a Light among men.

Guard ye the entrance to the HALLS of AMENTI. Guard ye the secrets I have hidden among ye. Let not the wisdom be cast to barbarians. Secret shall thou keep it for those who seek Light. Now depart I. Receive thou my blessing. Take thou my way and follow the Light.

Blend thou thy Soul in the Great Essence. ONE with the Great Light let thy consciousness be. Call thou on my when thou dost need me. Use my name three times in a row: CHEQUETET, ARELICH, VOMA-LITES.

30

EMERALD TABLET XIII

The Keys of Life and Death

List ye, O man, hear ye the wisdom. Hear ye the Word that shall fill thee with Life. Hear ye the Word that shall banish the darkness. Hear ye the voice that shall banish the night.

Mystery and wisdom have I brought to my children; knowledge and power descended from old. Know ye not that all shall be opened when ye shall find the oneness of all? One shall ye be with the Masters of Mystery, Conquerors of Death and Masters of Life. Aye, ye shall learn of the flower of Amenti the blossom of life that shines in the Halls. In Spirit shall ye reach that Halls of Amenti and bring back the wisdom that liveth in Light. Know ye the gateway to power is secret. Know ye the gateway to life is through death. Aye, through death but not as ye know death, but a death that is life and is fire and is Light.

Desireth thou to know the deep, hidden secret? Look in thy heart where the knowledge is bound. Know that in thee the secret is hidden, the source of all life and the source of all death.

List ye, O man, while I tell the secret, reveal unto thee the secret of old.

Deep in Earth's heart lies the flower, the source of the Spirit that binds all in its form. For know ye that the Earth is living in body as thou art alive in thine own formed form. The Flower of Life is as thine own place of Spirit and streams through the Earth as thine flows through thy form; giving of life to the Earth and its children, renewing the Spirit from form unto form. This is the Spirit that is form of thy body, shaping and moulding into its form.

Know ye, O man, that thy form is dual, balanced in polarity while formed in its form. Know that when fast on thee Death approaches, it is only because thy balance is shaken. It is only because one pole has been lost.

Know that thy body when in perfect balance may never be touched by the finger of Death. Aye, even accident may only approach when the balance is gone. When ye are in a balanced equilibrium, ye shall live on in time and not taste of Death. Know that thou art the balanced completion, existing because of thy balance of poles. As, in thee, one pole is drawn downward, fast from thee goes the balance of life. Then unto thee cold Death approaches, and change must come to thine unbalanced life.

Know that the secret of life in Amenti is the secret of restoring the balance of poles. All that exists has form and is living because of the Spirit of life in its poles.

See ye not that in Earth's heart is the balance of all things that exist and have being on its face? The source of thy Spirit is drawn from Earth's heart, for in thy form thou are one with the Earth.

When thou hast learned to hold thine own balance, then shalt thou draw on the balance of Earth. Exist then shalt thou while Earth is existing, changing in form, only when Earth, too, shalt change: Tasting not of death, but one with this planet, holding thy form till all pass away.

List ye, O man, whilst I give the secret so that ye, too, shalt taste not of change. One hour each day shalt thou lie with thine head pointed to the place of the positive pole (north). One hour each day shalt thy head be pointed to the place of the negative pole (south). Whilst thy head is placed to the northward, hold thou thy consciousness from the chest to the head. And when thy head is placed southward, hold thou thy thought from chest to the feet. Hold thou in balance once in each seven, and thy balance will retain the whole of its strength. Aye, if thou be old, thy body will freshen and thy strength will become as a youth's.

This is the secret known to the Masters by which they hold off the fingers of Death. Neglect not to follow the path I have shown, for when thou hast passed beyond years to a hundred to neglect it will mean the coming of Death.

Hear ye, my words, and follow the pathway. Keep thou thy balance and live on in life.

Hear ye, O man, and list to my voice. List to the wisdom that gives thee of Death. When at the end of thy work appointed, thou may desire to pass from this life, pass to the plane where the Suns of the Morning live and have being as Children of Light. Pass without pain and pass without sorrow into the plane where is eternal Light.

First lie at rest with thine head to the eastward. Fold thou thy hands at the Source of thy life (solar plexus). Place thou thy consciousness in the life seat. Whirl it and divide to north and to south. Send thou the one out toward the northward. Send thou the other out to the south. Relax thou thy hold upon thy being. Forth from they form will thy silver spark fly, upward and onward to the Sun of the morning, blending with Light, at one with its source. There it shall flame till desire shall be created. Then shall return to a place in a form. Know ye, O men, that thus pass the great Souls, changing at will from life unto life. Thus ever passes the Avatar, willing his Death as he wills his own life.

List ye, O man, drink of my wisdom. Learn ye the secret that is Master of Time. Learn ye how those ye call Masters are able to remember the lives of the past. Great is the secret yet easy to master, giving to thee the mastery of time. When upon thee death fast approaches, fear not but know ye are master of Death. Relax thy body, resist not with tension. Place in thy heart the flame of thy Soul. Swiftly then sweep it to the seat of the triangle. Hold for a moment, then move to the goal. This, thy goal, is the place between thine eyebrows, the place where the memory of life must hold sway. Hold thou thy flame here in thy brain-seat until the fingers of Death grasp thy Soul. Then as thou pass through the state of transition, surely the memories of life shall pass, too. Then shalt the past be as one with the present. Then shall the memory of all be retained.

Free shalt thou be from all retrogression. The things of the past shall live in today.

Man, ye have heard the voice of my wisdom. Follow and ye shall live through the ages as I.

List ye, O man, hear ye the wisdom. Hear ye the Word that shall fill thee with Life. Hear ye the Word that shall banish the darkness. Hear ye the voice that shall banish the night.

Mystery and wisdom have I brought to my children; knowledge and power descended from old. Know ye not that all shall be opened when ye shall find the oneness of all? One shall ye be with the Masters of Mystery, Conquerors of Death and Masters of Life. Aye, ye shall learn of the flower of Amenti the blossom of life that shines in the Halls. In Spirit shall ye reach that Halls of Amenti and bring back the wisdom that liveth in Light. Know ye the gateway to power is secret. Know ye the gateway to life is through death. Aye, through death but not as ye know death, but a death that is life and is fire and is Light.

Desireth thou to know the deep, hidden secret? Look in thy heart where the knowledge is bound. Know that in thee the secret is hidden, the source of all life and the source of all death.

List ye, O man, while I tell the secret, reveal unto thee the secret of old.

Deep in Earth's heart lies the flower, the source of the Spirit that binds all in its form. For know ye that the Earth is living in body as thou art alive in thine own formed form. The Flower of Life is as thine own place of Spirit and streams through the Earth as thine flows through thy form; giving of life to the Earth and its children, renewing the Spirit from form unto form. This is the Spirit that is form of thy body, shaping and moulding into its form.

Know ye, O man, that thy form is dual, balanced in polarity while formed in its form. Know that when fast on thee Death approaches, it is only because thy balance is shaken. It is only because one pole has been lost.

Know that thy body when in perfect balance may never be touched by the finger of Death. Aye, even accident may only approach when the balance is gone. When ye are in a balanced equilibrium, ye shall live on in time and not taste of Death. Know that thou art the balanced completion, existing because of thy balance of poles. As, in thee, one pole is drawn downward, fast from thee goes the balance of life. Then unto thee cold Death approaches, and change must come to thine unbalanced life.

Know that the secret of life in Amenti is the secret of restoring the balance of poles. All that exists has form and is living because of the Spirit of life in its poles.

See ye not that in Earth's heart is the balance of all things that exist and have being on its face? The source of thy Spirit is drawn from Earth's heart, for in thy form thou are one with the Earth.
When thou hast learned to hold thine own balance, then shalt thou draw on the balance of Earth. Exist then shalt thou while Earth is existing, changing in form, only when Earth, too, shalt change: Tasting not of death, but one with this planet, holding thy form till all pass away.

List ye, O man, whilst I give the secret so that ye, too, shalt taste not of change. One hour each day shalt thou lie with thine head pointed to the place of the positive pole (north). One hour each day shalt thy head be pointed to the place of the negative pole (south). Whilst thy head is placed to the northward, hold thou thy consciousness from the chest to the head. And when thy head is placed southward, hold thou thy thought from chest to the feet. Hold thou in balance once in each seven, and thy balance will retain the whole of its strength. Aye, if thou be old, thy body will freshen and thy strength will become as a youth's. This is the secret known to the Masters by which they hold off the fingers of Death. Neglect not to follow the path I have shown, for when thou hast passed beyond years to a hundred to neglect it will mean the coming of Death.

Hear ye, my words, and follow the pathway. Keep thou thy balance and live on in life.
Hear ye, O man, and list to my voice. List to the wisdom that gives thee of Death. When at the end of thy work appointed, thou may desire to

pass from this life, pass to the plane where the Suns of the Morning live and have being as Children of Light. Pass without pain and pass without sorrow into the plane where is eternal Light.

First lie at rest with thine head to the eastward. Fold thou thy hands at the Source of thy life (solar plexus). Place thou thy consciousness in the life seat. Whirl it and divide to north and to south. Send thou the one out toward the northward. Send thou the other out to the south. Relax thou thy hold upon thy being. Forth from they form will thy silver spark fly, upward and onward to the Sun of the morning, blending with Light, at one with its source. There it shall flame till desire shall be created. Then shall return to a place in a form. Know ye, O men, that thus pass the great Souls, changing at will from life unto life. Thus ever passes the Avatar, willing his Death as he wills his own life.

List ye, O man, drink of my wisdom. Learn ye the secret that is Master of Time. Learn ye how those ye call Masters are able to remember the lives of the past. Great is the secret yet easy to master, giving to thee the mastery of time. When upon thee death fast approaches, fear not but know ye are master of Death. Relax thy body, resist not with tension. Place in thy heart the flame of thy Soul. Swiftly then sweep it to the seat of the triangle. Hold for a moment, then move to the goal. This, thy goal, is the place between thine eyebrows, the place where the memory of life must hold sway. Hold thou thy flame here in thy brain-seat until the fingers of Death grasp thy Soul. Then as thou pass through the state of transition, surely the memories of life shall pass, too. Then shalt the past be as one with the present. Then shall the memory of all be retained.

Free shalt thou be from all retrogression. The things of the past shall live in today.

Man, ye have heard the voice of my wisdom. Follow and ye shall live through the ages as I.

31

EMERALD TABLET XIV

Supplementary
List ye, O Man, to the deep hidden wisdom, lost to thc world since the time of the Dwellers, lost and forgotten by men of this age.

Know ye this Earth is but a portal, guarded by powers unknown to man. Yet, the Dark Lords hide the entrance that leads to the Heaven-born land. Know ye, the way to the sphere of Arulu is guarded by barriers opened only to Light-born man.

Upon Earth, I am the holder of the keys to the gates of the Sacred Land. Command I, by the powers beyond me, to leave the keys to the world of man. Before I depart, I give ye the Secrets of how ye may rise from the bondage of darkness, cast off the fetters of flesh that have bound ye, rise from the darkness into the Light. Know ye, the soul must be cleansed of its darkness, ere ye may enter the portals of Light. Thus, I established among ye the Mysteries so that the Secrets may always be found. Aye, though man may fall into darkness, always the Light will shine as a guide. Hidden in darkness, veiled in symbols, always the way to the portal will be found. Man in the future will deny the mysteries but always the way the seeker will find.

Now I command ye to maintain my secrets, giving only to those ye have tested, so that the pure may not be corrupted, so that the power of Truth may prevail. List ye now to the unveiling of Mystery. List to the symbols of Mystery I give. Make of it a religion for only thus will its essence remain.

Regions there are two between this life and the Great One, traveled by the Souls who depart from this Earth; Duat, the home of the powers of illusion; Sekhet Hetspet, the House of the Gods. Osiris, the symbol of the guard of the portal, who turns back the souls of unworthy men. Beyond lies the sphere of the heaven-born powers, Arulu, the land where the Great Ones have passed. There, when my work among men has been finished, will I join the Great Ones of my Ancient home.

Seven are the mansions of the house of the Mighty; Three guards the portal of each house from the darkness; Fifteen the ways that lead to Duat. Twelve are the houses of the Lords of Illusion, facing four ways, each of them different. Forty and Two are the great powers, judging the Dead who seek for the portal. Four are the Sons of Horus, Two are the Guards of East and West-Isis, the mother who pleads for her children, Queen of the moon, reflecting the Sun. Ba is the essence, living forever. Ka is the Shadow that man knows as life. Ba cometh not until Ka is incarnate. These are mysteries to preserve through the ages. Keys are they of life and of Death. Hear ye now the mystery of mysteries: learn of the circle beginningless and endless, the form of He who is One and in all. Listen and hear it, go forth and apply it, thus will ye travel the way that I go. Mystery in Mystery, yet clear to the Light-born, the Secret of all I now will reveal. I will declare a secret to the initiated, but let the door be wholly shut against the profane.

Three is the mystery, come from the great one. Hear, and Light on thee will dawn.

In the primeval, dwell three unities. Other than these, none can exist. These are the equilibrium, source of creation: one God, one Truth, one point of freedom.

Three come forth from the three of the balance: all life, all good, all power.

Three are the qualities of God in his Light-home: Infinite power, Infinite Wisdom, Infinite Love. Three are the powers given to the Masters: To transmute evil, assist good, use discrimination. Three are the things inevitable for God to perform: Manifest power, wisdom and love.

Three are the powers creating all things: Divine Love possessed of perfect knowledge, Divine Wisdom knowing all possible means, Divine Power possessed by the joint will of Divine Love and Wisdom.

Three are the circles (states) of existence: The circle of Light where dwells nothing but God, and only God can traverse it; the circle of Chaos where all things by nature arise from death; the Circle of awareness where all things spring from life.

All things animate are of three states of existence: chaos or death, liberty in humanity and felicity of Heaven. Three necessities control all things: beginning in the Great Deep, the circle of chaos, plenitude in Heaven.

Three are the paths of the Soul: Man, Liberty, Light.

Three are the hindrances: lack of endeavor to obtain knowledge; non-attachment to god; attachment to evil. In man, the three are manifest. Three are the Kings of power within. Three are the chambers of the mysteries, found yet not found in the body of man.

Hear ye now of he who is liberated, freed from the bondage of life into Light. Knowing the source of all worlds shall be open. Aye, even the Gates of Arulu shall not be barred. Yet heed, O man, who wouldst enter heaven. If ye be not worthy, better it be to fall into the fire. Know ye the celestials pass through the pure flame. At every revolution of the heavens, they bathe in the fountains of Light.

List ye, O man, to this mystery: Long in the past before ye were man-born, I dwelled in Ancient Atlantis. There in the Temple, I drank of the Wisdom, poured as a fountain of Light from the Dweller. Give the key to ascend to the Presence of Light in the Great world. Stood I before the Holy One enthroned in the flower of fire. Veiled was he by the lightnings of darkness, else my Soul by the Glory have been shattered.

Forth from the feet of his Throne like the diamond, rolled forth four rivers of flame from his footstool, rolled through the channels of clouds to the Man-world. Filled was the hall with Spirits of Heaven. Wonder of wonders was the Starry palace. Above the sky, like a rainbow of Fire and Sunlight, were formed the spirits. Sang they the glories of the Holy One. Then from the midst of the Fire came a voice: "Behold the Glory of the first Cause." I beheld that Light, high above all darkness, reflected in my own being. I attained, as it were, to the God of all Gods, the Spirit-Sun, the Sovereign of the Sun spheres.

Again came the Voice: "There is one, even the First, who hath no beginning, who hath no end; who hath made all things, who govern all, who is good, who is just, who illumines, who sustains."

Then from the throne, there poured a great radiance, surrounding and lifting my soul by its power. Swiftly I moved through the spaces of Heaven, shown was I the mystery of mysteries, shown the Secret heart of the cosmos. Carried was I to the land of Arulu, stood before the Lords in their Houses. Opened they the Doorway so I might glimpse the primeval chaos. Shuddered my soul to the vision of horror, shrank back my soul from the ocean of darkness. Then saw I the need for the barriers, saw the need for the Lords of Arulu. Only they with their Infinite balance could stand in the way of the inpouring chaos. Only they could guard God's creation.

Then did I pass 'round the circle of eight. Saw all the souls who had conquered the darkness. Saw the splendor of Light where they dwelled.

Longed I to take my place in their circle, but longed I also for the way I had chosen, when I stood in the Halls of Amenti and made my choice to the work I would do.

Passed I from the Halls of Arulu down to the earth space where my body lay. Arose I from the earth where I rested. Stood I before the Dweller. Gave my pledge to renounce my Great right until my work on Earth was completed, until the Age of darkness be past.

List ye, O man, to the words I shall give ye. In them shall ye find the Essence of Life. Before I return to the Halls of Amenti, taught shall ye be the Secrets of Secrets, how ye, too, may arise to the Light. Preserve them and guard them, hide them in symbols, so the profane will laugh and renounce. In every land, form ye the mysteries. Make the way hard for the seeker to tread. Thus will the weak and the wavering be rejected. Thus will the secrets be hidden and guarded, held till the time when the wheel shall be turned. Through the dark ages, waiting and watching, my

Spirit shall remain in the deep hidden land. When one has passed all the trials of the outer, summon ye me by the Key that ye hold. Then will I, the Initiator, answer, come from the Halls of the Gods in Amenti. Then will I receive the initiate, give him the words of power.

Hark ye, remember, these words of warning: bring not to me one lacking in wisdom, impure in heart or weak in his purpose. Else I will withdraw from ye your power to summon me from the place of my sleeping.

Go forth and conquer the element of darkness. Exalt in thy nature thine essence of Light.

Now go ye forth and summon thy brothers so that I may impart the wisdom to light thy path when my presence is gone. Come to the chamber beneath my temple. Eat not food until three days are past. There will I give thee the essence of wisdom so that with power ye may shine amongst men. There will I give unto thee the secrets so that ye, to , may rise to the Heavens-God-men in Truth as in essence ye be. Depart now and leave me while I summon those ye know of but as yet know not.

32

EMERALD TABLET XV

S ecret of Secrets
Now ye assemble, my children, waiting to hear the Secret of Secrets which shall give ye power to unfold the God-man, give ye the way to Eternal life. Plainly shall I speak of the Unveiled Mysteries. No dark sayings shall I give unto thee. Open thine ears now, my children. Hear and obey the words that I give.

First I shall speak of the fetters of darkness which bind ye in chains to the sphere of the Earth.

Darkness and light are both of one nature, different only in seeming, for each arose from the source of all. Darkness is disorder. Light is Order. Darkness transmuted is light of the Light. This, my children, your purpose in being; transmutation of darkness to light.

Hear ye now of the mystery of nature, the relations of life to the Earth where it dwells. Know ye, ye are threefold in nature, physical, astral and mental in one. Three are the qualities of each of the natures; nine in all, as above, so below.

In the physical are these channels, the blood which moves in vortical motion, reacting on the heart to continue its beating. Magnetism which moves through the nerve paths, carrier of energies to all cells and tissues. Akasa which flows through channels, subtle yet physical, completing the channels. Each of the three attuned with each other, each affecting the life of the body. Form they the skeletal framework through which the subtle ether flows. In their mastery lies the Secret of Life in the body.

Relinquished only by will of the adept, when his purpose in living is done.

Three are the natures of the Astral, mediator is between above and below; not of the physical, not of the Spiritual, but able to move above and below.

Three are the natures of Mind, carrier it of the Will of the Great One. Arbitrator of Cause and Effect in thy life. Thus is formed the threefold being, directed from above by the power of four. Above and beyond man's threefold nature lies the realm of the Spiritual Self. Four is it in qualities, shining in each of the planes of existence, but thirteen in one, the mystical number. Based on the qualities of man are the Brothers: each shall direct the unfoldment of being, each shall channels be of the Great One.

On Earth, man is in bondage, bound by space and time to the earth plane. Encircling each planet, a wave of vibration, binds him to his plane of unfoldment. Yet within man is the Key to releasement, within man may freedom be found.

When ye have released the self from the body, rise to the outermost bounds of your earth-plane. Speak ye the word Dor-E-Lil-La. Then for a time your Light will be lifted, free may ye pass the barriers of space. For a time of half of the sun (six hours), free may ye pass the barriers of earth-plane, see and know those who are beyond thee. Yea, to the highest worlds may ye pass. See your own possible heights of unfoldment, know all earthly futures of Soul.

Bound are ye in your body, but by the power ye may be free. This is the Secret whereby bondage shall be replaced by freedom for thee.

Calm let thy mind be. At rest be thy body: Conscious only of freedom from flesh. Center thy being on the goal of thy longing. Think over and over that thou wouldst be free. Think of this word-La-Um-I-L-Gan-over and over in thy mind let it sound. Drift with the sound to the place of thy longing. Free from the bondage of flesh by thy will.

Hear ye while I give the greatest of secrets: how ye may enter the Halls of

Amenti, enter the place of the immortals as I did, stand before the Lords in their places.

Lie ye down in rest of thy body. Calm thy mind so no thought disturbs thee. Pure must ye be in mind and in purpose, else only failure will come unto thee. Vision Amenti as I have told in my Tablets. Long with fullness of heart to be there. Stand before the Lords in thy mind's eye. Pronounce the words of power I give (mentally); Mekut-El-Shab-El Hale-Sur-Ben-El-Zabrut Zin-Efrim-Quar-El. Relax thy mind and thy body. Then be sure your soul will be called.

Now give I the Key to Shamballa, the place where my Brothers live in the darkness: Darkness but filled with Light of the Sun-Darkness of Earth, but Light of the Spirit, guides for ye when my day is done.
Leave thou thy body as I have taught thee. Pass to the barriers of the deep, hidden place. Stand before the gates and their guardians. Command thy entrance by these words: "I am the Light. In me is no darkness. Free am I of the bondage of night. Open thou the way of the Twelve and the One, so I may pass to the realm of wisdom." When they refuse thee, as surely they will, command them to open by these words of power: "I am the Light. For me are no barriers. Open, I command, by the Secret of Secrets-Edom-El-Ahim-Sabbert-Zur Adom." Then if thy words have been "Truth" of the highest, open for thee the barriers will fall.
Now, I leave thee, my children. Down, yet up, to the Halls shall I go. Win ye the way to me, my children. Truly my brothers shall ye become.

Thus finish I my writings. Keys let them be to those who come after. But only to those who seek my wisdom, for only for these am I the Key and the Way.

www.ingramcontent.com/pod-product-compliance
Lightning Source LLC
Chambersburg PA
CBHW061728120626
46550CB00005B/1739